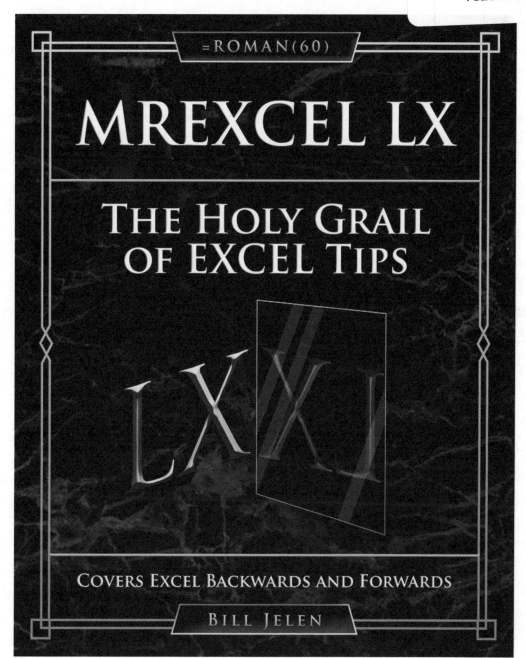

=ROMAN(60)

MREXCEL LX

THE HOLY GRAIL OF EXCEL TIPS

COVERS EXCEL BACKWARDS AND FORWARDS

BILL JELEN

Holy Macro! Books
PO Box 541731, Merritt Island FL 32954

MrExcel LX — The Holy Grail of Excel Tips

Printed in USA by Hess Print Solutions

First Printing: March 2019

Authors: Bill Jelen

Copy Editor: Kitty Wilson

Tech Editor: Roger Govier

Indexer: Nellie Jay

Compositor: Jill Cabot

Cover Design: Alexander Philip

Illustrations: Cartoon Bob D'Amico, George Berlin, Walter Moore, Bobby Rosenstock, Chad Thomas

Photography: Sean Carruthers, Mary Ellen Jelen

Published by: Holy Macro! Books, PO Box 541731, Merritt Island FL 32954

Subtitles: Dianna Deatherage

Distributed by Independent Publishers Group, Chicago, IL

ISBN 978-1-61547-063-1 Print, 978-1-61547-249-9 PDF, 978-1-61547-148-5 Mobi, 978-1-61547-370-0 ePub

Library of Congress Control Number: 2019930608

Table of Contents

Dedication

For Suat & Muge Ozgur

About the Author

Bill Jelen is the host of MrExcel.com and the author of 60 books about Microsoft Excel including *Excel Gurus Gone Wild and Excel 2019 Inside Out* for Microsoft Press. He has made over 80 guest appearances on TV's *The Lab with Leo / Call for Help with Leo Laporte* and was voted guest of the year on the *Computer America* radio show. He writes the Excel column for *Strategic Finance* magazine. He has produced over 2,300 episodes of his daily video podcast Learn Excel from MrExcel.

About the Contributors

Sam Radakovitz is a program manager on the Excel team at Microsoft. He has designed many features while there, including sort and filter, sparklines, and the Ribbon interface. And, more than anyone else on the team, he's done the best job of bringing the sloths, LOL cats, and cast of *Twilight* deeper into everyone's lives.

Katie Sullivan is a program manager on the Word team at Microsoft. GO, WORD!!!!! WOOOOO!!!!!

About the Illustrators

Cartoonist **Bob D'Amico** creates custom cartoons for business and more. See www.cartoonbob.com for more about his work.

George Berlin is all about delight and wonder! He puts a smile on the world's faces with illustration, animation, and interactive projection art. See more at www.georgeberlin.com.

Walter Moore is famous for his ape cartoons. If you need an illustration of the monkey business at your work, search Bing for Walter Moore Apes.

Bobby Rosenstock is a print maker who specializes in woodcut and letterpress printing. He is owner of the letterpress and design studio in Marietta, Ohio, Just a Jar Design Press - www.justAjar.com.

Chad Thomas is an illustrator who showcases his artwork on his website, www.whiterabbitart.com. His colorful and detailed artwork ranges from pet and people portraits to illustrations for children's books.

Foreword

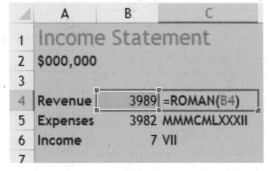

In the course of writing *Special Edition Using Excel 2007*, I had to research and document every single function in Excel. There were some that were hard to explain (FACTDOUBLE and SQRTPI) and some that were easy to explain but left you scratching your head. For example, who in real life could use the =ROMAN() function? I guess that movie production companies could use =ROMAN() to put the copyright at the end of the movie credits. And the NFL folks could use =ROMAN() to figure out the names of the upcoming Super Bowls. That is not a big audience of Excellers who could find a use for =ROMAN().

I am frequently on the road, doing half-day or all-day Power Excel seminars for groups like the Institute of Managerial Accountants, the Institute of Internal Auditors, or the Hospitality Finance & Tech Professionals. I love these live seminars. The right tip will help someone save an hour a week—50 hours a year. I often interject some humor. I have a variety of spreadsheet quips and gags that get added to the seminar. One that I used many years ago: "If you have to present bad financial news, Excel has a function for you: ROMAN! Convert your report to Roman numerals, hide column B, and you can escape the president's office before he figures out what is going on." It brings laughter every time.

I keep a spreadsheet that lists the books I've authored. A few years ago I realized I would soon be writing book #40 and that the =ROMAN(40) is XL. Because of this joke, the MrExcel XL book was born. It became a staple at my live Power Excel seminars. As new features were introduced in Excel, the book was updated, first as MrExcel LIVe and now as MrExcel LX (which is sort of a mirror image of XL. Thanks to Dianna Deatherage from Pensacola who suggested the Excel Forward and Backwards subtitle.

The spreadsheet in 2019 has a promising future. Yes, Excel is again facing competition from Google Docs and Tableau. But that competition brings innovation. Look at the amazing new features, like Power Query, Data Types, Dynamic Array Functions. These come on the heels of Power BI, 3D Maps, and awesome new functions like TEXTJOIN, MAXIFS, and others. It is another golden age for spreadsheet development.

The files used in this book are available for download from mrx.cl/60bookfiles.

You will see a number of shortlinks in this book in the format mrx.cl/short. The idea is that it will be easier for you to type mrx.cl than a long URL.

#1 Double-Click the Fill Handle to Copy a Formula

You have thousands of rows of data. You've added a new formula in the top row of your data set, some-

thing like =PROPER(A2&" "&B2), as shown here. You need to copy the formula down to all of the rows of your data set.

Many people will grab the Fill Handle and start to drag down. But as you drag down, Excel starts going faster and faster. There is

a 200-microsecond pause at the last row of data. 200 microseconds is long enough for you to notice the pause but not long enough for you to react and let go of the mouse button. Before you know it, you've dragged the Fill Handle way too far.

110 RYAN	WILSON	
111 PATRICK	WIRZ	
112 JOHN C.	WISSE	
113		**Drag the Fill**
114	**Excel 2010 does pause here -**	**Handle...**
115	**not long enough for anyone to react, though.**	**You inevitably**
116		**go too far...**
117		
118		
119		
120		+

The solution is to double-click the Fill Handle! Go to exactly the same spot where you start to drag the Fill

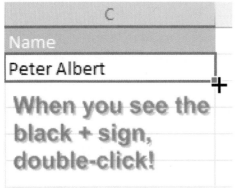

When you see the black + sign, double-click!

Handle. The mouse pointer changes to a black plus sign. Double-click. Excel looks at the surrounding data, finds the last row with data today, and copies the formula down to the last row of the data set.

In the past, empty cells in the column to the left would cause the "double-click the Fill Handle" trick to stop working just before the empty cell. But as you can see below, names like Madonna, Cher, or Pele will not cause problems. Provided that there is at least a diagonal path (for example, via B76-A77-B78), Excel will find the true bottom of the data set.

	A	B	C
73	ROBERT	MIKA	Robert Mika
74	JADE	MILLER	Jade Miller
75	SIMON	NUSS	Simon Nuss
76	RICHARD	OLDCORN	Richard Oldcorn
77	PELE	**Blank cells used to be a problem. Fixed in**	Pele
78	ROBERT	**2010.** PHILLIPS	Robert Phillips

In my live Power Excel seminars, this trick always elicits a gasp from half the people in the room. It is my number-one time-saving trick.

Alternatives to Double-Clicking the Fill Handle

This trick is an awesome trick if all you've done to this point is drag the Fill Handle to the bottom of the data set. But there are even faster ways to solve this problem:

- Use Tables. If you select one cell in A1:B112 and press Ctrl+T, Excel formats the range as a table. Once you have a table, simply enter the formula in C2. When you press Enter, it is copied to the bottom.

- Use a complex but effective keyboard shortcut. This shortcut requires the adjacent column to have no empty cells. While it seems complicated to explain, the people who tell me about this shortcut can do the entire thing in the blink of an eye.

Here are the steps:

1. From your newly entered formula in C2, press the Left Arrow key to move to cell B2.

2. Press Ctrl+Down Arrow to move to the last row with data—in this case, B112.

3. Press the Right Arrow key to return to the bottom of the mostly empty column C.

4. From cell C112, press Ctrl+Shift+Up Arrow. This selects all of the blank cells next to your data, plus the formula in C2.

5. Press Ctrl+D to fill the formula in C2 to all of the blanks in the selection. Ctrl+D is fill **D**own.

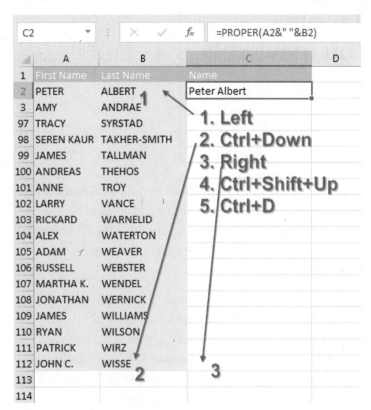

Note: Ctrl+R fills right, which might be useful in other situations.

As an alternative, you can get the same results by pressing Ctrl+C before step 1 and replacing step 5 with pressing Ctrl+V.

Thanks to the following people who suggested this tip: D. Carmichael, Shelley Fishel, Dawn Gilbert, @Knutsford_admi, Francis Logan, Michael Ortenberg, Jon Paterson, Mike Sullivan and Greg Lambert Lane suggested Ctrl+D. Bill Hazlett, author of *Excel for the Math Classroom,* pointed out Ctrl+R.

#2 Break Apart Data

You have just seen how to join data, but people often ask about the opposite problem: how to parse data that is all in a single column. Say you wanted to sort the data in the figure below by zip code:

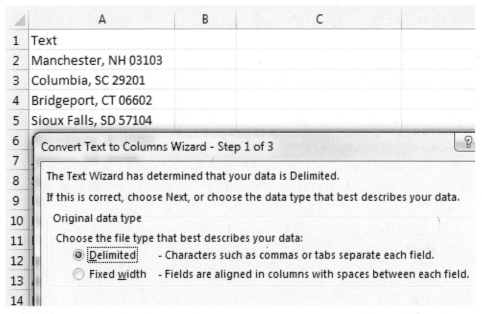

Select the data in A2:A99 and choose Data, Text to Columns. Because some city names, such as Sioux Falls, are two words, you cannot break the data at each occurrence of a space. Instead, you need to use a comma to get the city in column A and the state and zip code in column B, so choose Delimited in step 1 of the wizard and click Next.

In step 2 of the wizard, deselect Tab and select Comma. The preview at the bottom of the dialog shows what your data will look like. Click Next.

Caution: For the rest of the day after you use Text to Columns, Excel will remember the choices you've chosen in step 2 of the Convert Text to Columns Wizard. If you copy data from Notepad and paste to Excel, it will be split at the comma. This is often maddening because most days, the data is not parsed at the comma, but for the rest of today, it will be. To fix it, close and re-open Excel.

Step 3 of the wizard asks you to declare each column as General, Text, or Date. It is fine to leave the columns set as General.

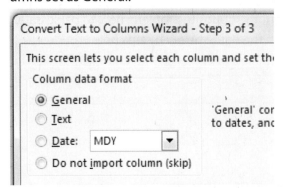

After you've split the state and zip code to column B, select B2:B99 and again choose Data, Text to Columns. This time, since each state is two characters, you can use Fixed Width in step 1 of the wizard. To preserve leading zeros in the zip code, select the second column and choose Text as the data type in step 3 of the wizard.

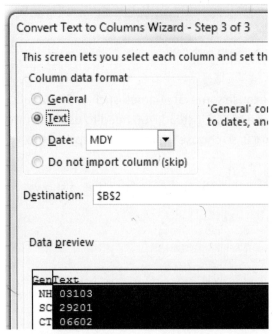

Tip: A lot of data will work well with Fixed Width, even it doesn't look like it lines up. In the next figure, the first three rows are in Calibri font and don't appear to be lined up. But if you change the font to Courier New, as in rows 4:7, you can see that the columns are perfectly lined up.

	A	B	C	D	E
1	MELANIE	KANE	738 Broadway Highway		
2	KRISTEN	CONRAD	814 Birch Street		Ro:
3	MYRTLE	ZIMMERMAN	567 Fourth Circle		
4	MELANIE	KANE		738 Broadv	
5	KRISTEN	CONRAD		814 Birch	
6	MYRTLE	ZIMMERMAN		567 Fourth	
7	KENNETH	HOLT		962 Centra	

Sometimes, you will find a data set where someone used Alt+Enter to put data on a new line within a cell. You can break out each line to a new column by typing Ctrl+j in the Other box in step 2 of the wizard, as shown below. Why Ctrl+j? Back in the 1980's IBM declared Ctrl+j to be a linefeed. Ctrl+j also can be typed in the Find & Replace dialog box.

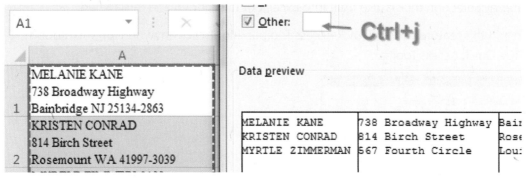

There are three special situations that Text to Columns handles easily:

- Dates in YYYYMMDD format can be changed to real dates. In step 3 of the wizard, click the column heading in the dialog, choose Date, then choose YMD from the dropdown.

- If you have negative numbers where the minus sign shows up after the number, go to step 3 of the wizard, click the Advanced Button, and choose Trailing Minus for Negative Numbers.

- Data copied from a Table of Contents will often have dot leaders that extend from the text to the page number as shown below. In step 2 of the wizard, choose Other, type a period, and then select the checkbox for Treat Consecutive Delimiters as One.

	A	B	C	D	E
1	Choose				Step 2
2	Date >	Step 3			Consecut
3	YMD	Advanced >			Delimite
4	in Step 3	Trailing Minus			as one
5	20201216	831.25-			A.......1
6	20201017	505.18			Boo 2

#3 Filter by Selection

The filter dropdowns have been in Excel for decades, but there are two faster ways to filter. Normally, you select a cell in your data, choose Data, Filter, open the dropdown menu on a column heading, uncheck Select All, and scroll through a long list of values, trying to find the desired item.

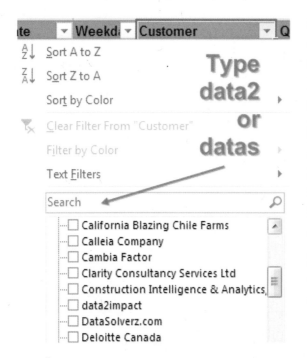

One faster way is to click in the Search box and type enough characters to uniquely identify your selection. Once the only visible items are (Select All Search Results), Add Current Selection to Filter, and the one desired customer, press Enter.

But the fastest way to Filter came from Microsoft Access. Microsoft Access invented a concept called Filter by Selection. It is simple: find a cell that contains the value you want and click Filter by Selection. The filter dropdowns are turned on, and the data is filtered to the selected value. Nothing could be simpler.

Starting in Excel 2007, you can right-click the desired value in the worksheet grid, choose Filter, and then choose By Selected Cells Value.

Guess what? The Filter by Selection trick is also built into Excel, but it is hidden and mislabeled.

Here is how you can add this feature to your Quick Access Toolbar: Right-click anywhere on the Ribbon and choose Customize Quick Access Toolbar.

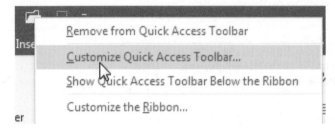

There are two large listboxes in the dialog. Above the left listbox, open the dropdown and change from Popular Commands to Commands Not In The Ribbon.

In the left listbox, scroll to the command AutoFilter and choose it. That's right: The icon that does Filter by Selection is mislabeled AutoFilter.

In the center of the dialog, click the Add>> button. The AutoFilter icon moves to the right listbox, as shown below. Click OK to close the dialog.

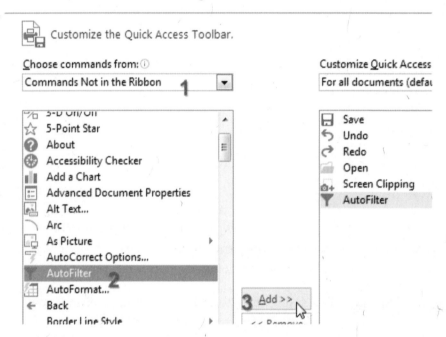

Here is how to use the command: Say that you want to see all West region sales of widgets. First, choose any cell in column B that contains West. Click the AutoFilter icon in the Quick Access Toolbar.

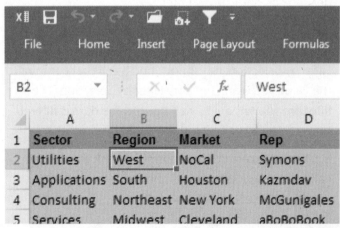

Excel turns on the filter dropdowns and automatically chooses only West from column B.

Next, choose any cell in column E that contains Widget. Click the AutoFilter icon again.

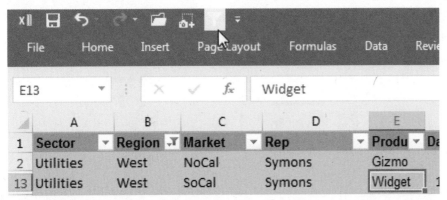

You could continue this process. For example, you could choose a Utilities cell in the Sector column and click AutoFilter.

> **Caution**: It would be great if you could multi-select cells before clicking the AutoFilter icon, but this does not work. If you need to see sales of widgets and gadgets, you could use Filter by Selection to get widgets, but then you have to use the Filter dropdown to add gadgets. Also. Filter by Selection does not work if you are in a Ctrl+T table.

How can it be that this feature has been in Excel since Excel 2003, but Microsoft does not document it? It was never really an official feature. The story is that one of the developers added the feature for internal use. Back in Excel 2003, there was already an AutoFilter icon on the Standard toolbar, so no one would bother to add the apparently redundant AutoFilter icon.

This feature was added to Excel 2007's right-click menu—but three clicks deep: Right-click a value, choose Filter, then choose Filter by Selected Cell's Value.

Bonus Tip: Filter by Selection for Numbers Over/Under

What if you wanted to see all revenue greater than $20,000? Go to the blank row immediately below your revenue column and type >19999. Select that cell and click the AutoFilter icon.

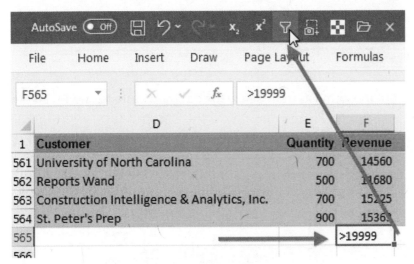

Excel will show only the rows of $20,000 or above.

	D	E	F
1	Customer	Quant	Reven
2	Vertex42	1000	22810
7	Excelerator BI	1000	21730
9	Berghaus Corporation	900	21438

#4 Bonus Tip: Total the Visible Rows

After you've applied a filter, say that you want to see the total of the visible cells.

Select the blank cell below each of your numeric columns. Click AutoSum or type Alt+=.

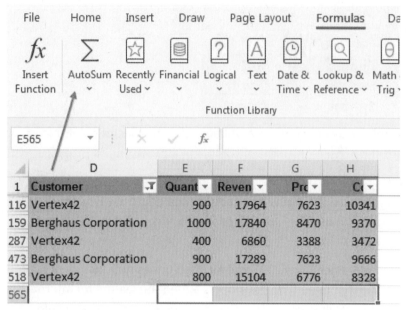

Instead of inserting SUM formulas, Excel inserts =SUBTOTAL(9,…) formulas. The formula below shows the total of only the visible cells.

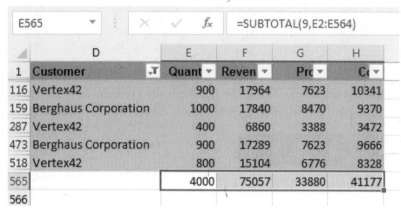

Insert a few blank rows above your data. Cut the formulas from below the data and paste to row 1 with the label Total Visible.

	E	F	G	H	I	J	K	L	M
1				Total Visible:	10200	196791	86394	110397	
2									
3	Produ	Date	Weekd	Customer	Quant	Reven	Prc	C	
20	Widget	1/24/2018	Wed	Excel Strategies, LLC	600	12606	5082	7524	
30	Widget	2/7/2018	Wed	All Systems Go Consult	1000	19890	8470	11420	
52	Widget	3/7/2018	Wed	Spain Enterprise	500	10155	4235	5920	

I1   fx   =SUBTOTAL(9,I4:I566)

Now, as you change the filters, even if the data fills up more than one full screen, you will see the totals at the top of your worksheet.

Thanks to Sam Radakovitz on the Excel team for Filter by Selection – not for suggesting Filter by Selection, but for formalizing Filter by Selection! Thanks to Taylor & Chris in Albuquerque for the Over/under technique.

#5 The Fill Handle Does Know 1, 2, 3...

Why does the Excel Fill Handle pretend it does not know how to count 1, 2, 3? The Fill Handle is great for filling months, weekdays, quarters, and dates. Why doesn't it know that 2 comes after 1?

In case you've never used the Fill Handle, try this: Type a month name in a cell. Select that cell. There is a square dot in the lower right corner of the cell. This dot is called the Fill Handle. Hover over the Fill Handle. The mouse cursor changes from a white cross to a black plus. Click the handle and drag right or drag down. The tooltip increments to show the last month in the range.

Note: If it is not working, select File, Options, Advanced. The third checkbox toggles the Fill Handle.

3	January	JAN
4		
5		
6		
7		
8		
9		
10		
11		October
12		
13		

When you let go of the mouse button, the months will fill in. An icon appears, giving you additional options.

10	August
11	September	**Options**
12	October
13	
14	

The Fill Handle works great with months or weekdays.

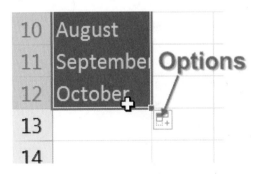

January	JAN	Monday	mon
February	FEB	Tuesday	tue
March	MAR	Wednesday	wed
April	APR	Thursday	thu
May	MAY	Friday	fri
June		Saturday	sat

The Fill Handle also works with quarters in many formats.

To do both quarters and years, you have to type a number, then Q, then any punctuation (period, space, apostrophe, dash) before the year.

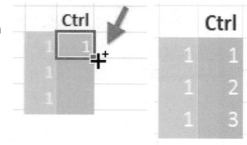

When you type 1 and grab the Fill Handle, Excel gives you 1, 1, 1, ... Many people say to enter the 1 and the 2, select them both, then drag the Fill Handle. Here is a faster way.

The secret trick is to hold down Ctrl while dragging. Hold down Ctrl and hover over the fill handle. Instead of the normal icon of a plus sign, you will see a plus sign with a superscript plug sign. When you see the $+^+$, click and drag. Excel fills in 1, 2, 3, ...

Note: Andrew Spain of Spain Enterprise in Huntsville, Alabama taught me a cool variation on this trick. If you start dragging without Ctrl, you can press Ctrl during the drag. A + icon appears at the bottom of the drag rectangle to indicate that you are going to fill instead of copy.

How were we supposed to figure out that Ctrl makes the Fill Handle count instead of copy? I have no idea. I picked up the tip from row 6 at the IMA Meonske seminar in Kent, Ohio. It turns out that Ctrl seems to make the Fill Handle behave in the opposite way: If you Ctrl+drag a date, Excel copies instead of fills.

I've heard another trick: Type 1 in A1. Select A1 and the blank B1. Drag. Excel fills instead of copies.

Right-Click the Fill Handle for More Options

If you right-click and drag the Fill Handle, a menu appears with more options, like Weekdays, Months, and Years. This menu is great for dates.

Normal	Ctrl	Weekday	Months	Years
1/31/2020	1/31/2020	1/31/2020	1/31/2020	1/31/2020
2/1/2020	1/31/2020	2/3/2020	2/29/2020	1/31/2021
2/2/2020	1/31/2020	2/4/2020	3/31/2020	1/31/2022
2/3/2020	1/31/2020	2/5/2020	4/30/2020	1/31/2023

What if your payroll happens on the 15th and on the last day of the month? Put in both dates. Select them both. Right-click and drag the Fill Handle. When you finish dragging, choose Fill Months.

Teach the Fill Handle a New List

The Fill Handle is a really handy tool. What if you could use it on all sorts of lists? You can teach Excel a new list, provided that you have anywhere from 2 to 240 items. Here is the easy way:

1. Type the list in a column in Excel.

2. Select the list.

3. Select File, Options, Advanced. Scroll almost to the bottom and click Edit Custom Lists.

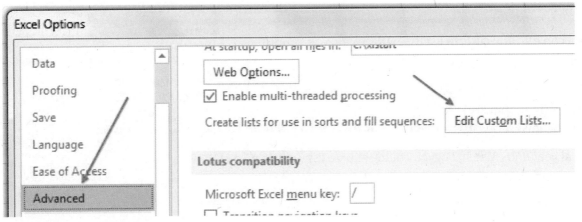

In the Custom Lists dialog, click Import.

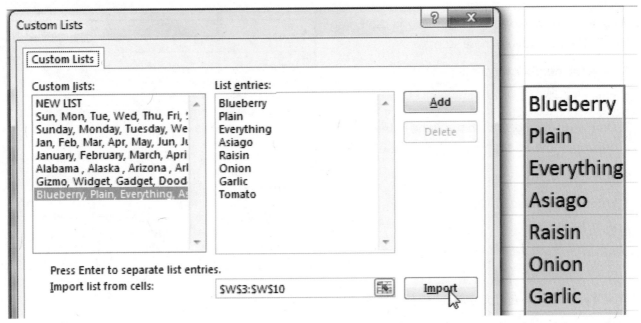

Excel will now understand your list as well as it understands Sunday, Monday, Tuesday. Type any item from the list It does not have to be the first item.

Grab the Fill Handle and drag. Excel fills from your list.

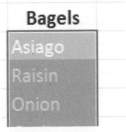

I use this trick for lists that should be in Excel, such as a list of the U.S. states and a list of the letters of the alphabet.

Bonus Tip: Fill Jan, Feb, ..., Dec, Total

A person in one of my seminars wanted to have Jan fill into 13 values: Jan, Feb, Mar, Apr, May, Jun, Jul, Aug, Sep, Oct, Nov, Dec, Total.

While you can edit any custom list that you create, you cannot edit the first four lists in the Custom Lists dialog.

However, if you use the preceding tip to add a new custom list with the 13 values, that list wins. If two custom lists have the value Jan, the lowest one in the dialog box is the one that is used.

If you fiscal year ends March 31, you could set up a list with Apr, May, Jun, ..., Jan, Feb, Mar, Total.

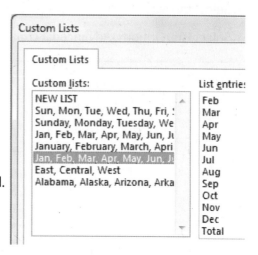

Bonus Tip: Fill 1 to 100,000 in a Flash

What if you have so many items that you can't drag the Fill Handle? Follow these steps:

1. Type the number 1 in a cell.

2. Select that cell.

3. On the Home tab, toward the right, in the Editing group, open the Fill dropdown and choose Series.

4. Select Columns.

5. Enter a Stop Value of 100000.

6. Click OK.

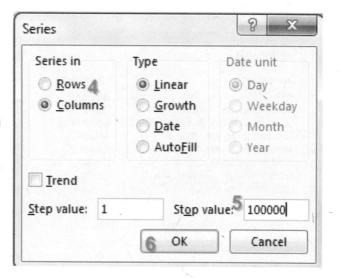

What if you have to fill 100,000 cells of bagel flavors?

1. Type the first bagel flavor in A1.

2. Select A1.

3. Type A100000 in the Name box and press Shift+Enter to select from the current cell to A100000.

4. Home, Fill, Series... and click AutoFill in the Type box. Click OK to fill from the custom list.

Thanks to the person in row 6 at the Meonske Conference in Kent, Ohio, for suggesting this feature.

#6 Fast Worksheet Copy

Yes, you can right-click any sheet tab and choose Move or Copy to make a copy of a worksheet. But that is the very slow way to copy a worksheet. The fast way: Hold down the Ctrl key and drag the worksheet tab to the right.

The downside of this trick is that the new sheet is called January (2) instead of February – but that is the case with the Move or Copy method as well. In either case, double-click the sheet name and type a new name.

Ctrl+drag February to the right to create a sheet for March. Rename February (2) to March.

Select January. Shift+select March to select all worksheets. Hold down Ctrl and drag January to the right to create three more worksheets. Rename the three new sheets.

Select January. Shift+select June. Ctrl+drag January to the right, and you've added the final six worksheets for the year. Rename those sheets.

Using this technique, you can quickly come up with 12 copies of the original worksheet.

1

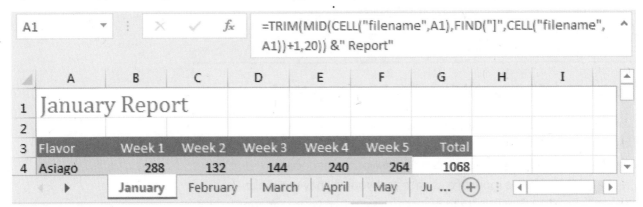

Illustration: Walter Moore

Bonus Tip: Put the Worksheet Name in a Cell

If you want each report to have the name of the worksheet as a title, use

```
=TRIM(MID(CELL("filename",A1),FIND("]",CELL("filename",A1))+1,20)) &" Report"
```

The CELL() function in this case returns the full path\[File Name]SheetName. By looking for the closing square bracket, you can figure out where the sheet name occurs.

If you plan on using this formula frequently, set up a book.xltx as described in "#7 Use Default Settings for All Future Workbooks" on page 17. In book.xltx, go to Formulas, Define Name. Use a name such as SheetName with a formula of `=TRIM(MID(CELL("filename",book.xltx!$A$1),FIND("]", CELL("filename",book.xltx!$A$1))+1,20))`. Then, in any new workbook `=SheetName&" Report"` will work.

Bonus Tip: Add a Total Row and a Total Column with One AutoSum

Say that you want to add a total row and a total column to a data set. Select all the numbers plus one extra row and one extra column. Click the AutoSum icon or press Alt+=.

	A	B	C	D	E	F
3	Flavor	Q1	Q2	Q3	Q4	Total
4	Asiago	288	132	144	240	
5	Raisin	252	252	252	300	
6	Onion	276	276	132	132	
7	Garlic	72	276	84	240	
8	Total					

Alt+=

Excel adds SUM functions to the total row and the total column as shown in the figure below.

F8 f_x =SUM(B8:E8)

	A	B	C	D	E	F
3	Flavor	Q1	Q2	Q3	Q4	Total
4	Asiago	288	132	144	240	804
5	Raisin	252	252	252	300	1056
6	Onion	276	276	132	132	816
7	Garlic	72	276	84	240	672
8	Total	888	936	612	912	3348

Bonus Tip: Power Up the Status Bar Statistics

When you select two or more numeric cells, the total appears in the status bar in the lower right of the Excel window. When you see a total, right-click and choose Average, Count, Numerical Count, Minimum, Maximum, and Sum. You can now see the largest, smallest, and average just by selecting a range of cells:

Asiago	288	132	144	240
Raisin	252	252	252	300
Onion	276	276	132	132
Garlic	72	276	84	240

Average: 209.25   Count: 16   Numerical Count: 16   Min: 72   Max: 300   Sum: 3348

Bonus Tip: Change All Sheets with Group Mode

Any time your manager asks you for something, he or she comes back 15 minutes later and asks for an odd twist that wasn't speci-fied the first time. Now that you can create worksheet copies really quickly, there is more of a chance that you will have to make changes to all 12 sheets instead of just 1 sheet when your manager comes back with a new request.

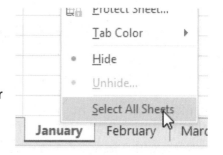

I will show you an amazingly powerful but incredibly dangerous tool called Group mode.

Say that you have 12 worksheets that are mostly identical. You need to add totals to all 12 worksheets. To enter Group mode, right-click on any worksheet tab and choose Select All Sheets.

The name of the workbook in the title bar now indicates that you are in Group mode.

Anything you do to the January worksheet will now happen to all the sheets in the workbook.

Why is this dangerous? If you get distracted and forget that you are in Group mode, you might start entering January data and overwriting data on the 11 other worksheets!

When you are done adding totals, don't forget to right-click a sheet tab and choose Ungroup Sheets.

Bonus Tip: Create a SUM That Spears Through All Worksheets

So far, you have a workbook with 12 worksheets, 1 for each month. All of the worksheets have the same number of rows and columns. You want a summary worksheet in order to total January through December.

To create it, use the formula =SUM(January:December!B4).

SUM		⋮	✕	✓	fx	=sum(January:December!B4)

	A	B	C	D	E	F
1	Summary Report					
2						
3	Flavor	Week 1	Week 2	Week 3	Week 4	Week 5
4	Asiago	=sum(January:December!B4)				
5	Raisin					

Copy the formula to all cells and you will have a summary of the other 12 worksheets.

B4		⋮	✕	✓	fx	=SUM(January:December!B4)

	A	B	C	D	E	F	G
1	Summary Report						
2							
3	Flavor	Week 1	Week 2	Week 3	Week 4	Week 5	Total
4	Asiago	2400	2040	2004	2388	2688	11520
5	Raisin	2220	2244	2076	2160	1968	10668

Caution: I make sure to never put spaces in my worksheet names. If you do use spaces, the formula would have to include apostrophes, like this: =SUM('Jan 2018:Mar 2018'!B4).

Tip: If you use 3D spearing formulas frequently, insert two new sheets, one called First and one called Last. Drag the sheet names so they create a sandwich with the desired sheets in the middle. Then, the formula is always =SUM(First:Last!B4).

Here is an easy way to build a 3D spearing formula without having to type the reference: On the summary sheet in cell B4, type =SUM(. Using the mouse, click on the January worksheet tab. Using the mouse, Shift+click on the December worksheet tab. Using the mouse, click on cell B4 on the December worksheet. Type the closing parenthesis and press Enter.

Bonus Tip: Use INDIRECT for a Different Summary Report

Say that you want to build the following report, with months going down column A. In each row, you want to pull the grand total data from each sheet. Each sheet has the same number of rows, so the total is always in row 12.

The first formula would be =January!B12. You could easily copy this formula to columns C:F, but there is not an easy way to copy the formula down to rows 5:15.

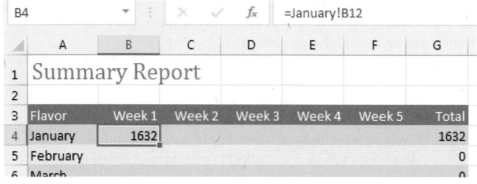

The INDIRECT function evaluates text that looks like a cell reference. INDIRECT returns the value at the address stored in the text. In the next figure, a combination of the ADDRESS and COLUMN functions returns a series of text values that tell Excel where to get the total.

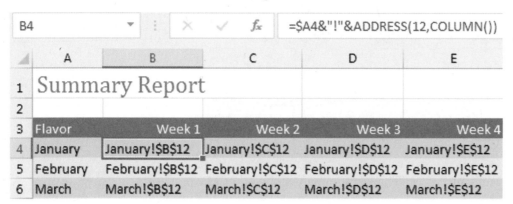

Wrap the previous formula in =INDIRECT() to have Excel pull the totals from each worksheet.

Month	Week 1	Week 2	Week 3	Week 4	Week 5	Total
January	1632	1836	1368	1716	1608	8160
February	1428	1404	1536	1428	1404	7200

Caution: INDIRECT will not work for pulling data from other workbooks. Search the Internet for Harlan Grove PULL for a VBA method of doing this.

Thanks to Othneil Denis for the 3D formula tip, Olga Kryuchkova for the Group mode tip, and Al Momrik for status bar.

#7 Use Default Settings for All Future Workbooks

Do you have favorite worksheet settings in Excel? I do. There are things I do to every new workbook I create.

In a few minutes, you can teach Excel your favorite settings. Then, every time you create a new workbook with Ctrl+N or insert a new worksheet, the worksheet will inherit all of your favorite settings.

The key step is to save the workbook as a template into a specific folder with two specific names.

Start with a blank workbook with a single worksheet.

Apply all your favorite settings. There are dozens of possibilities. Here are a few that I use:

On the Page Layout tab, change the Scale to Fit so the Width is 1 page. Leave Height set to Automatic and Width set to 1 Page.

Create a custom header or footer. Use the dialog launcher in the bottom right of the Page Setup group. Go to the Header/Footer tab. Choose Custom Footer. Type whatever is your company standard in the footer.

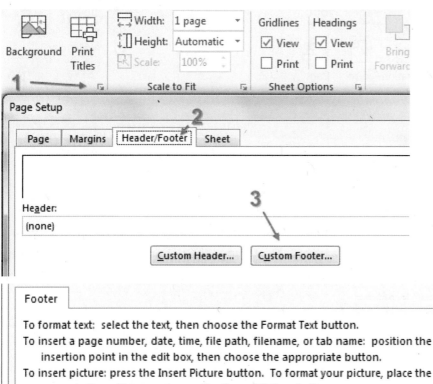

Create custom margins. I like narrow margins – even more narrow than the built-in Narrow margin settings. I've been using 0.25-inch margins since the 1990s, and they're automatically set for me because I've added that to my template.

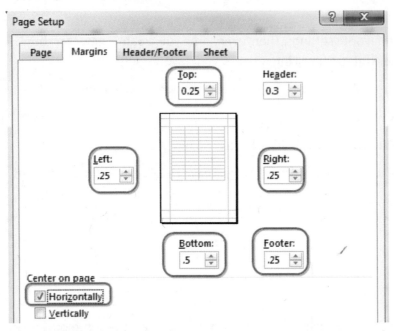

Choose a theme. I like the colors from Slipstream, but I prefer the Effects from Office 2007–2010.

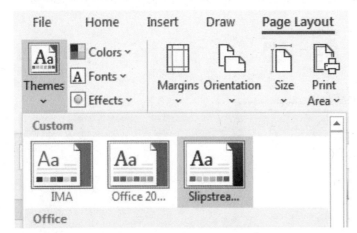

When you set a pivot table default theme, it only applies to the current workbook. Excel never saves your preference. Create a tiny two-cell data set. Create a pivot table. Change the default formatting. Delete the pivot table and the data set. The template will remember the setting.

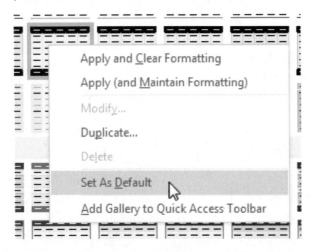

Would you use cell styles more often if they weren't so ugly? Do you hate that input cells are orange? Go to Cell Styles, right-click Input, and choose Modify as shown below. Click the Format button and choose a different input color.

I've just shown you some of my favorite settings. I'm sure you have your own favorites. Maybe you always set up a name to define the tax rate. Add it to your template, and you will never have to set it up again. Turn off gridlines. Do whatever you always do.

Once you've finished customizing your workbook, you need to figure out which file type you use most often. For people who never use macros, this is often XLSX. But I always use macros, so my default file type is XLSM. Maybe you want workbooks to open faster, and you use XLSB. There is a template format related to each of these file types, and you can just change the extension as needed. So, for me, I save the workbook as XLTM. You might save it as XLTX.

As soon as you choose one of these file types, the Save As dialog box moves to a templates folder. You need to save the workbook in a different folder.

C:\Users\Bill\AppData\Roaming\Microsoft\Excel\XLSTART

In the folder bar, type %AppData% and press Enter to get to the AppData\Roaming\ folder on your computer. From there, navigate to Microsoft\Excel\XLSTART.

Save the workbook with the reserved name Book plus the appropriate extension. Use Save As again and save the workbook in the same folder but use Sheet plus the same extension as the name.

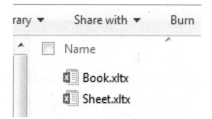

Of course, you only have to set this up once. After you do it, any time you use Ctrl+N to create a new workbook, the new workbook will inherit all of the settings from your template named Book.

Why did you have to also save templates named both Book and Sheet? Any time you insert a new worksheet into an existing workbook, Excel uses the Sheet template.

My Rant About New and New...

I've been using Book.xltm for 20 years. In all versions of Excel from Excel 95 up through Excel 2003, the Excel Standard toolbar had an icon called "New". Click that icon, and Excel loaded the Book template. Everything was great.

The File menu offered a New... option, but hardly anyone used it because it was half as many clicks to simply click the New icon on the Standard toolbar. New respects your custom settings in the Book template. New... does not.

If you've set up custom Book and Sheet templates, do not click the Blank Workbook template. Simply dismiss this opening screen by using the Esc key, and your custom Book template loads.

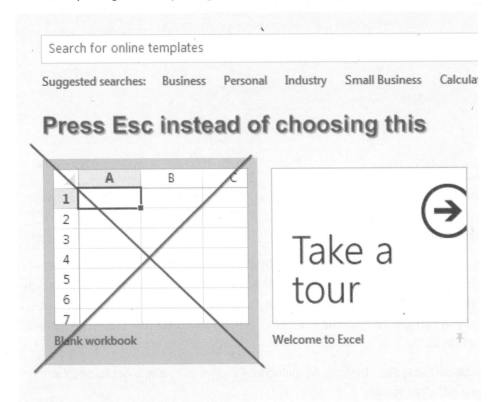

If you get tired of pressing Esc, go to File, Options, General and deselect the checkbox Show the Start Screen When This Application Starts.

Start up options

Choose the extensions you want Excel to open by default

☑ Tell me if Microsoft Excel isn't the default progam for

☐ Show the Start screen when this application starts

Bonus Tip: Changes to Book Template are Cumulative

I've had the opportunity to speak at three consecutive Excelapalooza conferences near Dallas. The conference team arranges two simultaneous tracks about Microsoft Excel. While I am presenting in one ballroom, Lawrence "Mac" McClelland is presenting another track in another ballroom. I picked up this tip from Mac:

Anything you do to Book.xltx is cumulative. Build the workbook with your favorite settings today. If you discover some new settings that you would like to add to Book.xltx in the future, follow these steps:

1. Press Ctrl+N to open a blank version of Book.xltx.

2. Make any changes you would like.

3. Select File, Save As.

4. Change the file type to XLTX or XLTM, depending on whether you regularly use macros.

5. Change Folder to the XLStart folder.

6. Save the file as Book.xltx to replace the existing Book.xltx.

7. Repeat steps 3–5 and save the file as Sheet.xltx.

Bonus Tip: Replace the Comma Style in Book.xltx

The Excel team offers Currency, Percent, and Comma icons in the center of the Home tab of the Ribbon. The tooltip says the Comma Style formats with a thousands separator. I despise this icon.

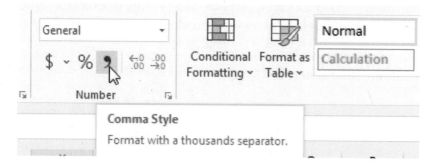

Why do I despise this icon? Because it turns on Accounting style. Sure, that gives you a thousands separator, but it also adds several things that I hate:

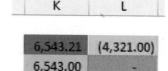

- It turns on two decimal places.

- It uses a right indent of 1 character to move the last digit away from the right edge of the cell.

- It uses parentheses for negative numbers.

- It displays zero with a single dash about four spaces away from the right edge of the cell.

There is no way to replace the Comma icon with my own icon or even to change what style it applies. So, I find that I have to click the Dialog Launcher icon at the bottom right of the Number group:

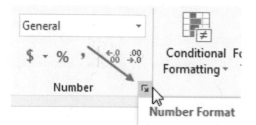

> **Tip:** The Dialog Launcher icon is a diagonal arrow pointing down and to the right. It is found in many groups in the Ribbon and usually offers far more choices than are available in the Ribbon.

Then choose Number from the Category list, choose the checkbox for Use 1000 Separator, and click twice on the down arrow to change 2 decimal places to 0 decimal places. Click OK to close the Format Cells dialog. It takes six clicks to create a simple number format with a comma as the thousands separator. That is why I despise the Comma icon: People who can live with right indents, parentheses, and zeros displayed as dashes can apply that style in one click, but people who just want a comma have to go through six clicks.

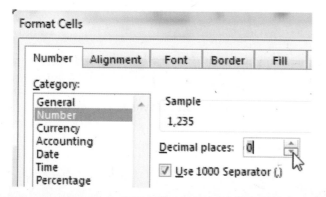

The great news: There is a solution. The bad news: Microsoft makes it hard to use the solution. The good news: If you add the solution to the Book.xltx file, the solution will become mostly permanent for all files that you create. Here is what you do:

1. While you are creating Book.xltx, as discussed in "#7 Use Default Settings for All Future Workbooks", type 1234 in a cell. Format the cell using the six clicks discussed above (or your favorite format). Keep that cell selected.

2. Open the Cell Styles gallery. Near the bottom, choose New Cell Style….

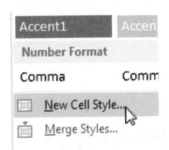

3. In the Style box that appears, type a descriptive name for your style, such as CommaGood.

4. If you only want to apply the Number format, unselect the checkboxes for Alignment, Font, Border, Fill, and Protection.

5. Click OK to create the new style.

New styles appear at the top of the Cell Styles gallery, and you now have one-click access to the CommaGood style.

Caution: Any cell style added using this method applies only to the current workbook, making this tip almost useless.

Tip: If you add the CommaGood style to your Book.xltx file, the CommaGood style will be available on all future workbooks that you create with Ctrl+N.

Thanks to Jo Ann Babin for an idea similar to this one.

#8 Recover Unsaved Workbooks

The Auto Recover feature is a lifesaver. It is turned on automatically in Excel 2010 and newer.

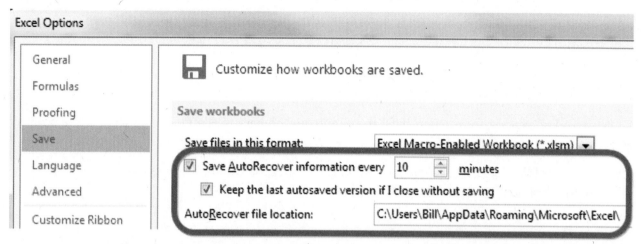

1

Say it is 4:59 PM on Friday, and you are trying to get the heck out of work. You have a bunch of files open in Excel and issue the Alt+F, X command to exit Excel.

Standing between you and the after-work happy hour are a bunch of dialogs like this one:

There is no need to save this file, so you click Don't Save. Next file? Don't Save. Next file? Don't Save.

Tip: Hold Shift while clicking Don't Save to perform Don't Save All.

Now you are in a rhythm, clicking Don't Save in perfect synchronization with Excel presenting the message. Then, as you click Don't Save the last time, you realize that *this* workbook had a lot of unsaved changes. And you really needed to save it. You should have clicked Save.

You look at your watch. It will take two hours to re-create all of those changes. Your happy hour plans are sunk. But wait! Excel has your back. If the workbook was open for at least 10 minutes and created an AutoRecover version, Excel kept a copy for you.

Follow these steps to get it back:

1. Open Excel.

2. In the left panel, choose Open Other Workbooks.

3. In the center panel, scroll all the way to the bottom of the recent files. At the very end, click Recover Unsaved Workbooks.

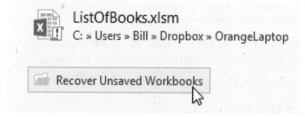

4. Excel shows you all the unsaved workbooks that it has saved for you recently.

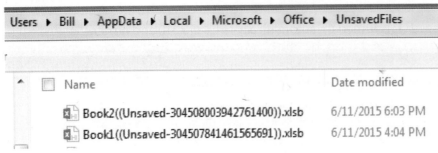

Users ▸ Bill ▸ AppData ▸ Local ▸ Microsoft ▸ Office ▸ UnsavedFiles	
Name	Date modified
Book2((Unsaved-3045080039427614000)).xlsb	6/11/2015 6:03 PM
Book1((Unsaved-304507841461565691)).xlsb	6/11/2015 4:04 PM

5. Click a workbook and choose Open. If it is the wrong one, go back to File, Open and scroll to the bottom of the list.

6. When you find the right file, click the Save As button to save the workbook. Unsaved workbooks are saved for four days before they are automatically deleted.

RECOVERED UNSAVED FILE This is a recovered file that is temporarily stored on your computer. [Save As]

Use AutoRecover Versions to Recover Files Previously Saved

Recover Unsaved Workbooks applies only to files that have never been saved. If your file has been saved, you can use AutoRecover versions to get the file back. If you close a previously saved workbook without saving recent changes, one single AutoRecover version is kept until your next editing session. To access it, reopen the workbook. Use File, Info, Versions to open the last AutoRecover version.

You can also use Windows Explorer to search for the last AutoRecover version. The Excel Options dialog box specifies an AutoRecover File Location. If your file was named Budget2020Data, look for a folder within the AutoRecover File folder that starts with Budget.

While you are editing a workbook, you can access up to the last five AutoRecover versions of a previously saved workbook. You can open them from the Versions section of the Info category. You may make changes to a workbook and want to reference what you previously had. Instead of trying to undo a bunch of revisions or using Save As to save as a new file, you can open an AutoRecover version. AutoRecover versions open in another window so you can reference, copy/paste, save the workbook as a separate file, etc.

Note: An AutoRecover version is created according to the AutoRecover interval AND only if there are changes. So if you leave a workbook open for two hours without making any changes, the last AutoSave version will contain the last revision.

Caution: Both the Save AutoRecover Information option and Keep The Last AutoRecovered Version option must be selected in File, Options, Save for this to work.

Tip: Create a folder called C:\AutoRecover\ and specify it as the AutoRecover File Location. It is much easier than trawling through the Users folder that is the default location.

☑ Save AutoRecover information every [10 ↕] minutes
☑ Keep the last AutoRecovered version if I close without saving
AutoRecover file location: C:\Users\Bill\AppData\Roaming\Microsoft\Excel\

Note: Under the Manage Version options on the Info tab you can select Delete All Unsaved Workbooks. This is an important option to know about if you work on public computers. Note that this option appears only if you're working on a file that has not been saved previously. The easiest way to access it is to create a new workbook.

Thanks to Beth Melton and Paul Seaman and for clarifying the differences between AutoRecover and Recover Unsaved Files.

#9 Simultaneously Edit the Same Workbook in Office 365

For decades, some people have been wanting a better way to have multiple people in the same workbook at the same time. The old Shared Workbook functionality was awkward. People resorted to only one person having write access at a time", which led to someone opening the file and then forgetting to close it before going for a two-hour lunch and tying up the file that whole time.

After Google's spreadsheet product began offering the ability for multiple people to edit the same worksheet, the Excel team spent over two years developing a feature that they call co-authoring. The feature was released to Office 365 customers in the summer of 2017.

The feature works well once you get it set up. But it is difficult to figure out all of the steps to allow multiple people to use Excel on their computers instead of having some people stuck using Excel online.

To start, choose one person to be the owner of the workbook. This person should already have a One Drive For Business or SharePoint Online folder set up. The owner of the document should use File, Save As and choose to save the document in either OneDrive or SharePoint Online.

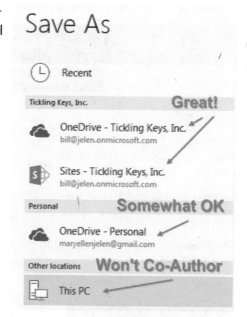

The owner of the workbook clicks the Share icon in the top right corner of Excel.

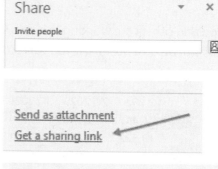

The Share panel asks you to invite people by e-mail address.

But if you look at the bottom of the panel, you can generate a sharing link.

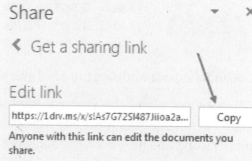

Generate a sharing link where anyone with the link can edit the workbook.

Copy the link and send it to others on your team.

The next step is the annoying part. When they follow the link, they will be taken *as a guest* to Excel Online. The spreadsheet will appear and they can edit in Excel Online. I talked to people from one company who stopped at this point. One person (the workbook owner) would edit in Excel and everyone else was stuck in Excel Online.

> **Caution:** As shown below, the "Edit in Browser" button is very prominent and it is what you are likely to click. In desperation, you might try clicking Download, but this removes the ability to co-author. Not so obvious in the top right corner is the Sign In button.

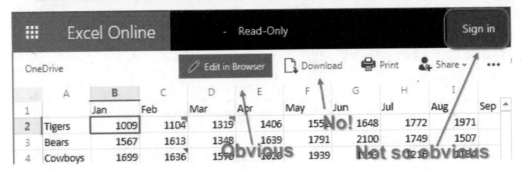

For the other co-authors to use the workbook in the real version of Excel running on a PC, they have to first Sign In to Excel online. Use the credentials that are shown in Excel under File, Account.

Once they have signed in, then the Edit Workbook drop-down menu appears. Open the menu and choose Edit in Excel. This is the only way to have everyone co-author and use the real desktop Excel instead of Excel Online.

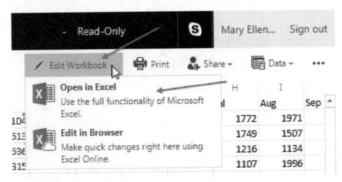

While you and others are working in a document, your active cell will be outlined in green. The active cells for others will be other colors. If you want to know who is editing a cell, hover over that cell.

	A	B	C	D	E	F
1	Product	1Q 2020	2Q 2020	3Q 2020	4Q 2020	1Q 2021
2	Apple	1,446	1,540	1,244	3,137	3,296
3	Banana	1,923	1,851	2,311	1,830	2,399
4	Cherry	1,982	2,066	1,330	2,163	1,351
5	Date	1,838	2,547	2,390	1,371	1,622
6	Elderberry	2,549	2,557	2,798	2,591	2,992
7	Fig	1,308	2,854	2,280	2,108	3,318

Co-authoring will work fine provided everyone avoids editing the same cell at the same time.

When someone (probably your manager), dives in to edit a cell that you are already editing, then a confusing set of rules decides who's edit wins. Rather than dealing with these rules, be happy that co-authoring mostly works and have everyone agree not to edit the same cell at the same time.

Co-authoring is a whole new experience. There are good things and bad things that you need to get used to when you are co-authoring.

Bonus Tip: AutoSave is Necessary, But Turn it Off When Not Co-Authoring

The reason that co-authoring is possible is because of AutoSave. Every time that you make a spreadsheet change, that change will be saved to OneDrive so that others can (almost) instantly see what you just typed. AutoSave is necessary if you want ten accountants editing a budget worksheet at the same time.

But let's talk about workbooks that will never be used with co-authoring. These are the run-of-the-mill workbooks that I use 99.9% of the time. I do not want AutoSave to be active for those workbooks. I want to open Excel, know that I can do some "what-if" changes and then close the workbook without saving. If AutoSave is on, those changes are automatically saved. It is terrible.

Or - you likely recognize the scenario: You have a report for January. You need a report for February. You open the January report, change the headings, and then do File, Save As to save for February. This work-flow has been fine for decades. But if you allow AutoSave to be on, you will be destroying the January report as soon as you edit A1 and type February over January.

You have four choices. 1. Change your workflow to do the Save a Copy before you make any edits. 2. Always save to a local drive and AutoSave will not automatically be enabled. 3. Toggle AutoSave off for each workbook. Click the "On" icon shown here to turn AutoSave off for the current workbook.

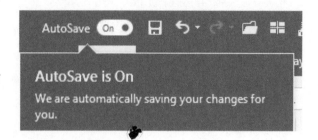

The best choice is 4. Go to File, Options, Save, and unselect the choice for AutoSave OneDrive and SharePoint Online Files By Default.

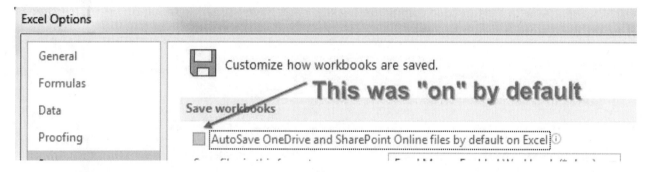

Bonus Tip: Undo an AutoSave

What if you have to undo an AutoSave? Your manager said to merge two regions and then 20 minutes later calls the merger off. AutoSave has been saving after every change in your workbook.

Click the drop-down menu next to the title bar. Click on Version History.

Excel will offer to let you open a previous version of the file. They don't save a version after every change. I (Bill Jelen) made 50 changes to this workbook in the last 20 minutes. The Version History is offering me three versions from those twenty minutes. Note that although all of the changes were made by Bill Jelen, AutoSave is crediting the changes to Mary Ellen Jelen. No one at Microsoft can explain this apparent bug.

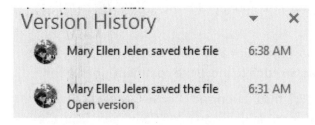

#10 New Threaded Comments Allow Conversations

Threaded comments debuted in 2018. When you insert a comment, Excel stores the comment, the author, the date, and time. When a co-worker sees your comment, they can click Reply and add a new comment to the same cell. Each set of comments lists the author, date, and time.

These new threaded comments are indicated by a five-sided purple shape instead of the red triangle used for the old style comments (now known as Notes).

> If you are using Excel Online, you have a choice for Comments or Chat. While comments are stored in the workbook, anything typed in Chat will be deleted when you close the workbook.

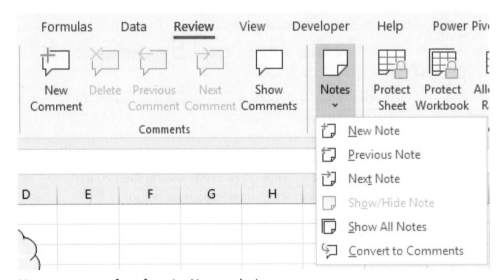

Bonus Tip: Old Style Comments Are Available as Notes

While the new threaded comments are cool, there are some great tricks that the old legacy comments offered that are lost with the threaded comments. Luckily, if you have a situation requiring one of the special tricks, the old comments are still available as Notes.

Here are some of my favorite Note techniques:

- Individual notes could be set to always show. This is useful for creating helpful instructions for a spreadsheet. Select a cell containing a red-triangle indicator and select Review, Notes, Show/Hide Note.

- Notes can be resized and located in a specific position. Right-click a cell with a note and choose Edit Note. Use the resize handle to change the size or drag an edge to move the comment.

- You can change the shape of a note. To start, Right-click the Ribbon and choose Customize Quick Access Toolbar. In the dialog box, change the top-left drop-down menu to All Commands. Find the Change Shape icon in the left list and click the Add>> button to add it to the Quick Access Toolbar.

Right-click the cell containing the note and choose Show Note. Ctrl+Click on the edge of the note to select the note without entering text edit mode. Use the Change Shape icon in the Quick Access tool-bar to choose a new shape. Note that you will often have to resize the note after choosing a shape. You also might try the Center and Align Middle icons to center the text in the shape. After changing the shape, you can return to Hide Note to make the note only visible when you hover over the red triangle indicator.

- You can change the color of a note. This one is tricky because there are two versions of the Format Comment dialog box. While in edit mode, click the border of the comment and then press Ctrl+1 to open the Format Comment dialog box. You should see nine tabs in the dialog. If you only see the Font tab, close the dialog and try clicking the comment border again or Ctrl+Click the comment to leave text edit mode. When you have the dialog with all 9 tabs, use the Colors and Lines tab, Fill Color to change the color of a comment. Use Fill Effects… to add a gradient or a picture.

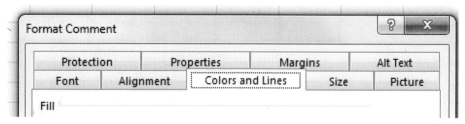

- To create pop-up pictures: edit a note and backspace to remove your name from the note. With a completely blank note, Ctrl+Click the edge and press Ctrl+1. Use Colors and Lines, Fill Color, Fill Effects, Picture and choose a picture from your computer. Hide the note and the picture will pop up when you hover over the triangle.

The following screenshot shows examples of notes with colors, shapes, and a pop-up picture.

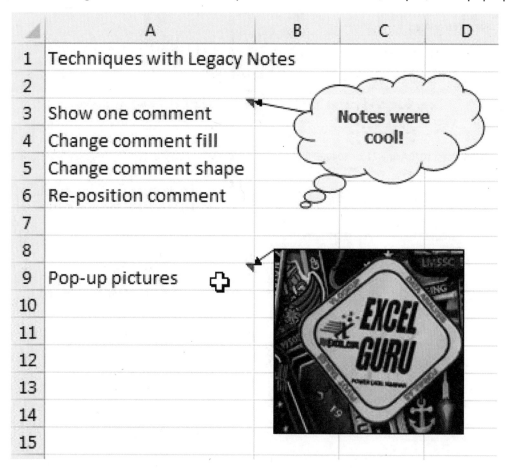

Bonus Tip: Add a Tooltip to a Cell with Validation

In the previous Bonus Tip, I suggested using Notes for a help system. The problem with notes: it is possible to arrow in to a cell without ever hovering over the red triangle and the note might be missed. You can use the Data Validation dialog to set up a tooltip for a cell. The tooltip is only visible when the cell is the active cell.

Data Validation is found towards the right side of the Data tab in the Ribbon. I end up using Alt+D L because I always have a difficult time finding the Validation icon. Normally, most people use the Settings tab in Data Validation to control what can be entered in a cell. You will skip the Settings tab and go to the Input Message tab.

On the Input Message tab, type a title and a message. Click OK.

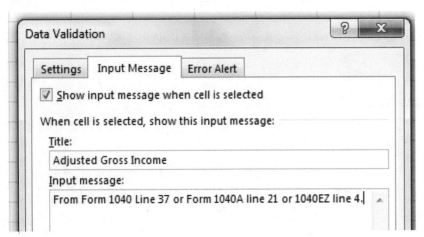

The result: a tooltip that will appear any time the cell is active:

▲	A	B	C	D
1				
2				
3	Adjusted Gross Income:			
4				
5				
6				
7				
8				
9				

Adjusted Gross Income
From Form 1040 Line 37 or Form 1040A line 21 or 1040EZ line 4.

#11 Create Perfect One-Click Charts

One-click charts are easy: Select the data and press Alt+F1.

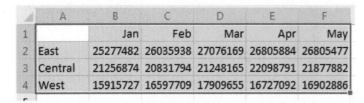

	A	B	C	D	E	F
1		Jan	Feb	Mar	Apr	May
2	East	25277482	26035938	27076169	26805884	26805477
3	Central	21256874	20831794	21248165	22098791	21877882
4	West	15915727	16597709	17909655	16727092	16902886

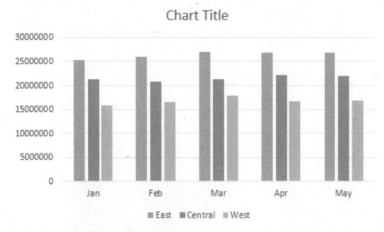

What if you would rather create bar charts instead of the default clustered column chart? To make your life easier, you can change the default chart type. Store your favorite chart settings in a template and then teach Excel to produce your favorite chart in response to Alt+F1.

Say that you want to clean up the chart above. All of those zeros on the left axis take up a lot of space without adding value. Double-click those numbers and change Display Units from None to Millions.

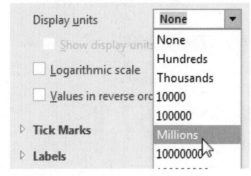

To move the legend to the top, click the + sign next to the chart, choose the arrow to the right of Legend, and choose Top.

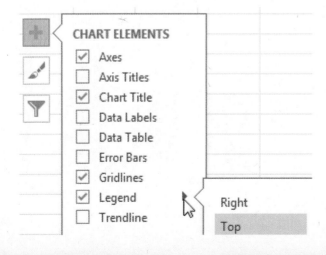

Change the color scheme to something that works with your company colors.

Right-click the chart and choose Save As Template. Then, give the template a name. (I called mine ClusteredColumn.)

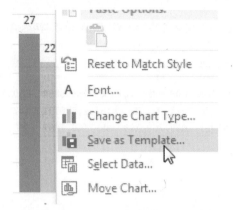

Select a chart. In the Design tab of the Ribbon, choose Change Chart Type. Click on the Templates folder to see the template that you just created.

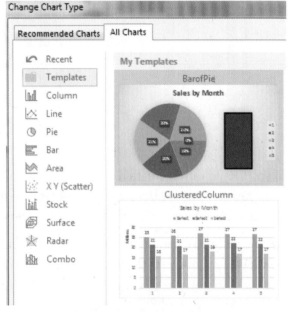

Right-click your template and choose Set As Default Chart.

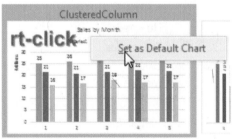

The next time you need to create a chart, select the data and press Alt+F1. All your favorite settings appear in the chart.

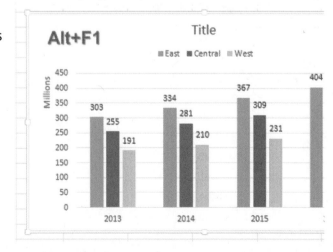

Thanks to Areef Ali, Olga Kryuchkova, and Wendy Sprakes for suggesting this feature.

#12 Paste New Data on a Chart

You might be responsible for updating charts every month, week, or day. For example, in my last job, a collection of charts were updated during the month-end close process. The charts would track progress throughout the year.

There is an easy way to add new data to an existing chart. Here, the chart shows data for January through May, and there is new data for June that is not on the chart.

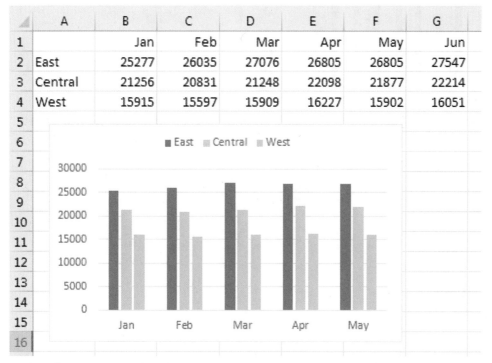

Rather than re-create the chart, you can paste new data on it. Select the new data in the worksheet, including the heading. Press Ctrl+C to copy.

Click on the chart and press Ctrl+V to paste the data on the chart. As shown below, the new data is added to the existing chart.

◢	A	B	C	D	E	F	G
1		Jan	Feb	Mar	Apr	May	Jun
2	East	25277	26035	27076	26805	26805	27547
3	Central	21256	20831	21248	22098	21877	22214
4	West	15915	15597	15909	16227	15902	16051

Ctrl+V

As you keep adding months to the right side, what if you want to remove data from the left side? Is there any way to Ctrl+X that data off the chart?

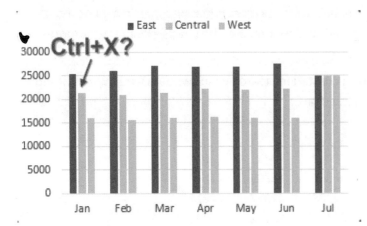

No, but there is another way. Select the chart. Outlines appear around the charted data in the worksheet. A blue box surrounds the data points for the charts, and in each corner of the blue box is a square dot as shown below. The square dot is a resizing handle.

Click on the lower-left resizing handle and drag to the right.

	Jan	Feb	Mar
	25277	26035	27076
	21256	20831	21248
	15915	15597	15909

The data is removed from the left side of the chart.

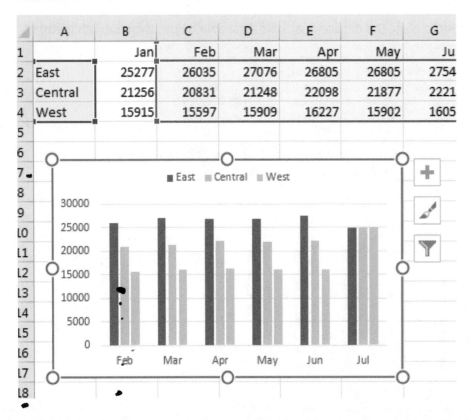

	A	B	C	D	E	F	G
1		Jan	Feb	Mar	Apr	May	Ju
2	East	25277	26035	27076	26805	26805	2754
3	Central	21256	20831	21248	22098	21877	2221
4	West	15915	15597	15909	16227	15902	1605

You can use resizing handles to resize or drag the blue box to change the data that appears on the chart. Of course, you could have dragged the bottom-right resizing handle to add June to the chart in the first place, but it is good to know this copy-and-paste trick in case the chart and data are on different sheets in the workbook.

> **Tip**: If you want to remove East from the chart, you can click on any East column in the chart and press Delete on your keyboard to remove that series. To temporarily hide a series, you can hide the row or column where the underlying data is stored. In Excel 2013 or newer, you can use the Filter funnel icon located to the right of the chart to hide any series or category from the chart.

#13 Create Interactive Charts

It is easy to create interactive charts without using VBA. By default, if you hide rows in Excel, those rows will be hidden in the chart. The technique is to build a chart with every possible customer and then use a slicer or a filter to hide all except one of the customers.

Say that you have the following list of customers. Make the data into a table by using Ctrl+T.

Company	Q1	Q2	Q3	Q4
Cambia Factor	814	838	897	1032
data2impact	860	877	886	877
Excel4apps	886	842	775	775
excelisfun	632	683	744	789
F-Keys Ltd	283	258	243	228
SpringBoard	259	220	211	222
Surten Excel	493	488	503	513
Vertex42	827	769	669	636
WSLCB	409	450	513	564
Yesenita	835	827	827	819

Select the table and insert a chart. In most cases, Excel will create the wrong chart, with customers along the X-axis.

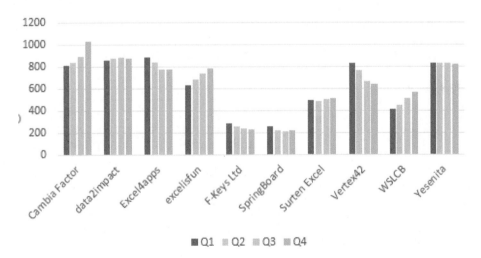

Click the Switch Row/Column icon in the Chart Tools Design tab of the Ribbon.

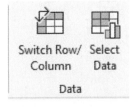

Select one cell in the table. In Excel 2013 or newer, go to the Insert tab of the Ribbon and choose Slicer. In Excel 2010 or earlier, you have to use the Company dropdown in A17 to choose a single company.

By default, every slicer starts as a single column in the middle of the screen. Plan on dragging the slicer to a new location and size. While the slicer is selected, you can use the Columns spin button near the right side of the Slicer Tools Options tab of the Ribbon to change the number of columns in the slicer.

In the following figure, choose one customer from the slicer and the chart updates to show just that one customer.

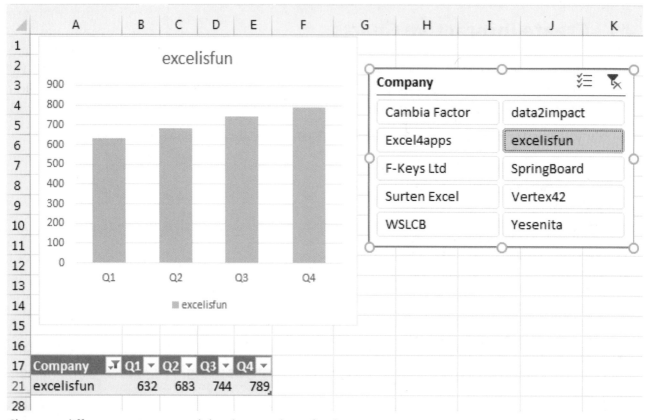

Choose a different customer, and the chart updates for that customer.

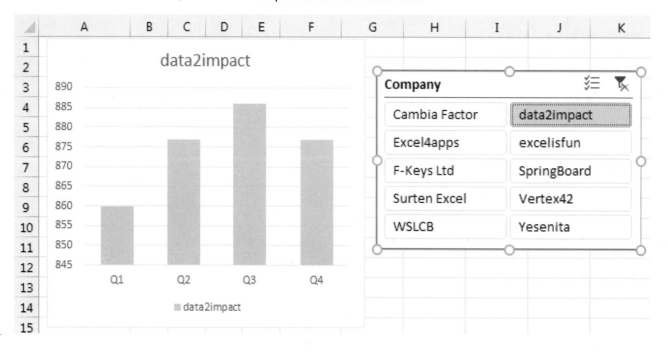

#14 Show Two Different Orders of Magnitude on a Chart

It is nearly impossible to read a chart where one series is dramatically larger than other series. In the following chart, the series for Year to Date Sales is 10 times larger than most of the monthly sales. The blue columns are shortened, and it will be difficult to see subtle changes in monthly sales.

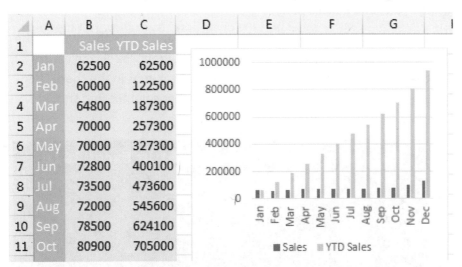

	Sales	YTD Sales
Jan	62500	62500
Feb	60000	122500
Mar	64800	187300
Apr	70000	257300
May	70000	327300
Jun	72800	400100
Jul	73500	473600
Aug	72000	545600
Sep	78500	624100
Oct	80900	705000

Combo charts were always possible in Excel, but they have a new interface starting in Excel 2013. Choose the chart above and select Change Chart Type. Choose Combo from the category list on the left. You then have the choices shown below. Move the larger number (YTD Sales) to a new scale on the right axis by choosing Secondary Axis. Change the chart style for one series to Line from Clustered Column.

Choose the chart type and axis for your data series:

Series Name	Chart Type	Secondary Axis
Sales	Clustered Column	☐
YTD Sales	Line	☑

The result: Columns for the monthly revenue are taller, so you will be able to make out subtle changes like a decrease from July to August.

To get the additional formatting to the chart above, select the numbers on the left axis. Use the Font Color dropdown on the Home tab to choose a blue to match the blue columns. Select the green line. Select Format, Shape Outline to change to a darker green. Select the numbers on the right axis and change the font color to the same green. Double-click each axis and change Display Units to Thousands. Double-click a blue column and drag the Gap Width setting to be narrower. Double-click the legend and choose to show the legend at the top.

#15 Create Waterfall Charts

For 12 years, I worked at a company doing data analysis. One of my regular tasks was to analyze the profit on sales proposals before they went out the door. I did this with a waterfall chart. For me, the waterfall chart never would have to dip below the zero axis. I used a few tricks to make the columns float and drew the connector lines in by hand, using a ruler and a black pen.

Excel 2016 introduced a built-in Waterfall chart type. Select your range of data and create the chart. In the chart below, three columns are marked as total: Net Price, Gross Profit, and Net Profit. Excel won't automatically know which columns should be totals. Click any column to select all columns in the chart. Then single-click one total column. Right-click and select as Total. Repeat for the other columns that should touch the X-axis.

List Price	$1,400K	
Discount	-$560K	
Net Price	$840K	(mark as total)
Material	-$184K	
Labor	-$15K	
Overhead	-$87K	
Gross Profit	$554K	(mark as total)
Commissions	-$28K	
Net Profit	$526K	(mark as total)

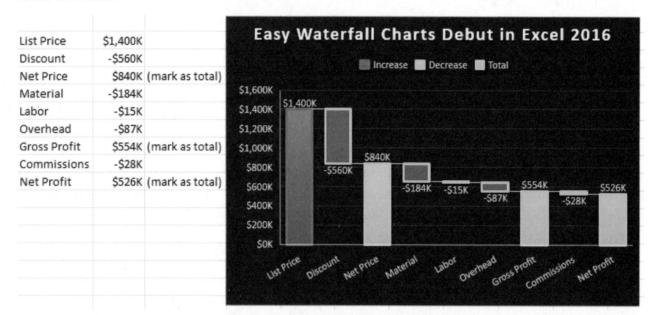

The waterfall charts even work for cash flow charts that might go below zero.

Open	$145K	(mark as total)
Jan	$26K	
Feb	-$68K	
Mar	$20K	
Apr	-$85K	
May	-$76K	
Jun	$59K	
Jul	-$35K	
Aug	$65K	
Sep	$43K	
Oct	-$37K	
Nov	$79K	
Dec	$99K	
Close	$234K	(mark as total)

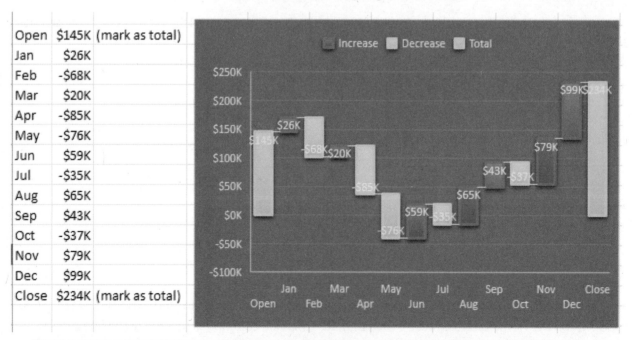

Tip: To change the color for Increase/Decrease or Total: Click on the legend and then click on one item in the legend. Press Ctrl+1 to open the Format panel for that series and choose a new Fill Color.

#16 Create Funnel Charts in Office 365

In 2016, Office 365 introduced Funnel charts, as well as Treemap, Sunburst, Box & Whisker, Pareto, and Histogram charts. A Funnel chart is great for showing a sales funnel.

#17 Create Filled Map Charts in Office 365

Early in 2017, Map Charts appeared on the Insert tab in Office 365. A Map chart shades closed regions on a map such as countries, states, counties, even zip code boundaries.

When you format a series in a Map, you can choose if it should show all 50 states or only the regions with data. Choose what makes the most sense for your data. In the chart on the left, the series color is a two-color gradient. You can choose three-color gradients or a category map, as shown on the right.

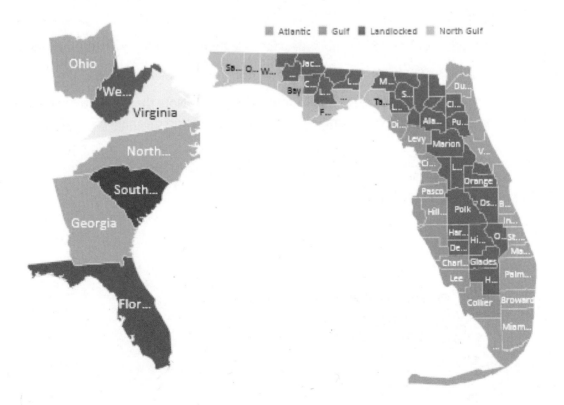

#18 Create a Bell Curve

I have 2200 Excel videos on YouTube. I can never predict which ones will be popular. Many videos hover around 2,000 views. But for some reason, the Bell Curve video collected half a million views. I am not sure why people need to create bell curves, but here are the steps.

A bell curve is defined by an average and a standard deviation. In statistics, 68% of the population will fall within one standard deviation of the mean. 95% falls within two standard deviations of the mean. 99.73% will fall within three standard deviations of the mean.

Say that you want to plot a bell curve that goes from 100 to 200 with the peak at 150. Use 150 as the mean. Since most of the results will fall within 3 standard deviations of the mean, you would use a standard deviation of 50/3 or 16.667.

1. Type 150 in cell B1.

2. Type =50/3 in cell B2.

3. Type headings of Point, X, Y in cells A4:C4.

4. Fill the numbers 1 to 61 in A5:A65. This is enough points to create a smooth curve.

	A	B	C	D	E
	B2		f_x =50/3		
1	Mean	150			
2	Standard Deviation	16.66667	=50/3		
3					
4	Point	X	Y		
5		1			
6		2			
7		3			

5. Go to the midpoint of the data, point 31 in B35. Type a formula there of =B1 to have the mean there.

6. The formula for B36 is =B35+($B$2/10). Copy that formula from row 36 down to row 65.

7. The formula for B34 is =B34-($B$2/10). Copy that formula up to row 5. Note that the notes in columns C:E of this figure do not get entered in your workbook - they are here to add meaning to the figure.

	A	B	C	D	E
1	Mean	150			
2	Standard Deviation	16.66667	=50/3		
3					
4	Point	X	Y		
32		28			
33		29			
34		30	148.3333	=B35-($B$2/10)	Copy up
35		31	150	=B1	
36		32	151.6667	=B35+($B$2/10)	Copy Down
37		33			
38		34			
39		35			

The magic function is called NORM.DIST which stands for Normal Distribution. When statisticians talk about a bell curve, they are talking about a normal distribution. To continue the current example, you want a bell curve from 100 to 200. The numbers 100 to 200 go along the X-axis (the horizontal axis) of the chart. For each point, you need to calculate the height of the curve along the y-axis. NORM.DIST will do this for you. There are four required arguments: =NORM.DIST(This x point, Mean, Standard Deviation, False). The last False says that you want a bell curve and not a S-curve. (The S-Curve shows accumulated probability instead of point probability.)

8. Type =NORM.DIST(B5,$B$1,$B$2,False) in C5 and copy down to row 65.

	A	B	C	D	E	F	G
1	Mean	150					
2	Standard Deviation	16.66667	=50/3				
3							
4	Point	X	Y				
5		1	100	0.000266	=NORM.DIST(B5,$B$1,$B$2,FALSE)		
6		2	101.6667	0.000357			
7		3	103.3333	0.000475	Several rows		
33		29	146.6667	0.023463	hidden (just to		
34		30	148.3333	0.023817	make image fit		
35		31	150	0.023937	in this book)		
36		32	151.6667	0.023817			
37		33	153.3333	0.023463			
64		60	198.3333	0.000357			
65		61	200	0.000266			
66							

9. Select B4:C65. On the Insert tab, open the XY-Scatter drop-down menu and choose the thumbnail with a smooth line. Alternatively, choose Recommened Charts and the first option for a bell curve.

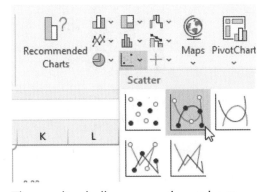

The result: a bell curve, as shown here.

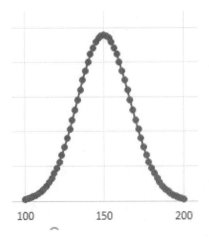

#19 Plotting Employees on a Bell Curve

Rather than creating a generic bell curve, how about plotting a list of employees or customers on a bell curve?

Start with a list of people and scores. Use the AVERAGE and STDEV.P functions to find the mean and standard deviation.

	A	B	C	D	E	F	G
1	Name	Score					
2	Andy	62		Mean	78.231	=AVERAGE(B2:B14)	
3	Barb	64		St Dev	14.418	=STDEV.P(B2:B14)	
4	Chris	83					
5	Diane	68					
6	Ed	98					
7	Flo	85					
8	Gary	98					
9	Hank	49					
10	Ike	90					
11	Jared	81					
12	Kelly	93					
13	Lou	71					
14	Mike	75					
15							

Once you know the mean and standard deviation, add a Y column with the formula shown below.

	A	B	C	D	E	F	G
1	Name	Score	Y				
2	Andy	62	=NORM.DIST(B2,$F$7,$F$8,false				
3	Barb	64	NORM.DIST(x, mean, standard_dev, **cumulative**)				
4	Chris	83			TRUE - cumulative d		
5	Diane	68			FALSE - probability		
6	Ed	98					
7	Flo	85			Mean	78.231	
8	Gary	98			St Dev	14.418	
9	Hank	49					

After adding the Y column, sort the data by Score ascending.

	A	B	C
1	Name	Score	Y
2	Hank	49	0.003544
3	Andy	62	0.014683
4	Barb	64	0.017
5	Diane	68	0.021512

Select Score & Y columns and add a Scatter with Smooth Lines as shown in the previous technique. Labelling the chart with names is tricky. Use the + icon to the right of the chart to add data labels. From the Data Labels flyout, choose More Options. In the panel shown below, click the icon with a column chart and then choose Value from Cells and specify the names in column A.

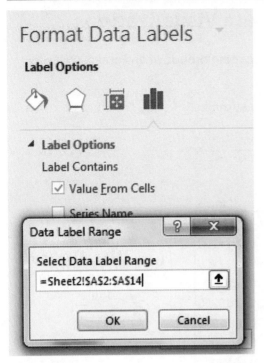

The result:

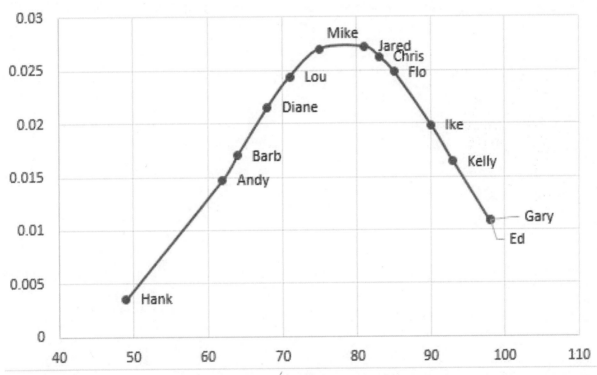

Tip: You will often have two labels in the chart that appear on top of each other. You can rearrange single labels so they appear with a small leader line as shown for Gary and Ed at the right side of the chart. Click on any label and all chart labels are selected. Next, click on either of the labels that appear together. After the second click, you are in "single label selection mode". You can drag that label so it is not on top of the other label.

#20 Add Meaning to Reports Using Data Visualizations

Three easy visualization tools were added to the Conditional Formatting dropdown in Excel 2007: Color Scales, Data Bars, and Icon Sets.

Consider this report, which has way too many decimal places to be useful.

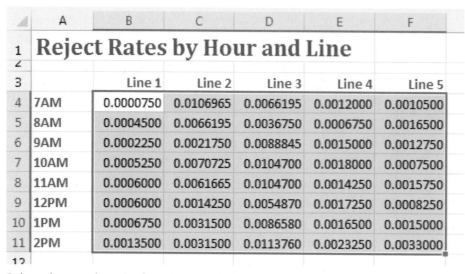

	Line 1	Line 2	Line 3	Line 4	Line 5
Reject Rates by Hour and Line					
7AM	0.0000750	0.0106965	0.0066195	0.0012000	0.0010500
8AM	0.0004500	0.0066195	0.0036750	0.0006750	0.0016500
9AM	0.0002250	0.0021750	0.0088845	0.0015000	0.0012750
10AM	0.0005250	0.0070725	0.0104700	0.0018000	0.0007500
11AM	0.0006000	0.0061665	0.0104700	0.0014250	0.0015750
12PM	0.0006000	0.0014250	0.0054870	0.0017250	0.0008250
1PM	0.0006750	0.0031500	0.0086580	0.0016500	0.0015000
2PM	0.0013500	0.0031500	0.0113760	0.0023250	0.0033000

Select the numbers in the report and choose Home, Conditional Formatting, Color Scales. Then click on the second icon, which has red at the top and green at the bottom.

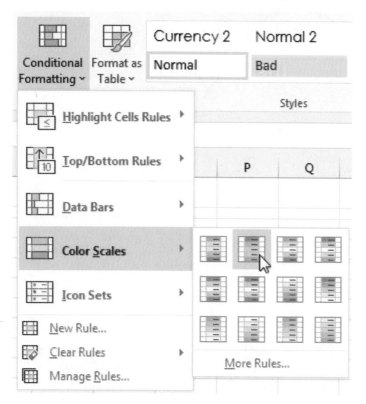

With just four clicks, you can now spot trends in the data. Line 2 started out the day with high reject rates but improved. Line 3 was bad the whole day. Line 1 was the best, but even those reject rates began to rise toward the end of the shift.

	Line 1	Line 2	Line 3	Line 4	Line 5
7AM	0.0000750	0.0106965	0.0066195	0.0012000	0.0010500
8AM	0.0004500	0.0066195	0.0036750	0.0006750	0.0016500
9AM	0.0002250	0.0021750	0.0088845	0.0015000	0.0012750
10AM	0.0005250	0.0070725	0.0104700	0.0018000	0.0007500
11AM	0.0006000	0.0061665	0.0104700	0.0014250	0.0015750
12PM	0.0006000	0.0014250	0.0054870	0.0017250	0.0008250
1PM	0.0006750	0.0031500	0.0086580	0.0016500	0.0015000
2PM	0.0013500	0.0031500	0.0113760	0.0023250	0.0033000

The next tool, Data Bar, is like a tiny bar chart that fills a cell. In the following figure, select all of the Revenue cells except for the grand total.

Choose Conditional Formatting, Data Bar, Green. Each number now gets a swath of color, as shown below. Large numbers get more color, and small numbers get hardly any color.

	A	B
1	Customer	Revenue
2	Amazing Yardstick Partners	22810
3	Inventive Opener Corporation	2257
4	Magnificent Tackle Inc.	11240
5	Leading Yogurt Company	9204
6	Excellent Doorbell Company	18552
7	Paramount Doghouse Inc.	9152
8	Flexible Instrument Partners	8456
9	Honest Chopstick Company	21730
10	Wonderful Faucet Corporation	13806
11	Special Doghouse Inc.	16416
12	Ideal Vise Corporation	21015
13	Guaranteed Bicycle Company	21465
14	Astonishing Thermostat Corpora	21438
15	Trustworthy Yogurt Inc.	9144
16	Bright Toothpick Inc.	6267
17	Remarkable Banister Supply	1740
18	Safe Shoe Company	2401
19	Vibrant Vise Company	9345
20	Forceful Furnace Company	11628
21	Guarded Zipper Corporation	5961
22		244027

B
Revenue
22810
2257
11240
9204
18552
9152
8456
21730
13806
16416
21015
21465
21438
9144
6267
1740
2401
9345
11628
5961
244027

Caution: Be careful not to include the grand total before selecting Data Bars. In the following example, you can see that the Grand Total gets all of the color, and the other cells get hardly any color.

2401
9345
11628
5961
244027

With the third tool, Icon Sets, you can choose from sets that have three, four, or five different icons.

Most people keep their numbers aligned with the right edge of the cell. Icons always appear on the left edge of the cell. To move the number closer to the icon, use the Increase Indent icon, shown below.

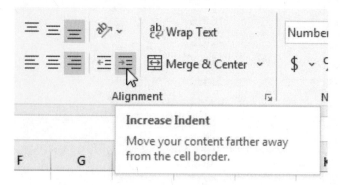

All three of these data visualization tools work by looking at the largest and smallest numbers in the range. Excel breaks that range into three equal-sized parts if you are using an icon set with three icons. That works fine in the example below.

	Q1	Q2	Q3	Q4
Andy	88	87	94	85
Bob	87	94	89	94
Charlie	93	99	100	91
Dale	83	82	89	85
Eddy	80	83	82	91

But in the following figure, Eddy scored horribly in Q1, getting a 30. Because Eddy did poorly, everyone else is awarded a gold star. That doesn't seem fair because their scores did not improve.

	Q1	Q2	Q3	Q4
Andy	☆ 88	☆ 87	☆ 94	☆ 85
Bob	☆ 87	☆ 94	☆ 89	☆ 94
Charlie	☆ 93	☆ 99	☆ 100	☆ 91
Dale	☆ 83	☆ 82	☆ 89	☆ 85
Eddy	→ ☆ 30	☆ 83	☆ 82	☆ 91

You can take control of where the range for an icon begins and ends. Go to Home, Conditional Formatting, Manage Rules and choose Edit Rule. In the following figure, the Type dropdown offers Percent, Percentile, Formula, and Number. To set the gold star so it requires 90 or above, use the settings shown below. Note that the two other icons have been replaced with No Cell Icon.

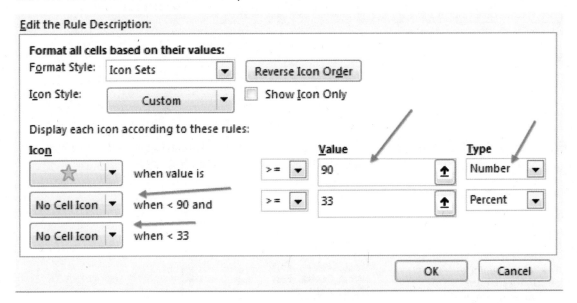

#21 Sort East, Central, and West Using a Custom List

At my last day job, we had three sales regions: East, Central, and West. The company headquarters was in the East, and so the rule was that all reports were sorted with the East region first, then Central, then West. Well, there is no way to do this with a normal sort.

Sort AZ, and you will have Central at the top.

Region	Customer	Revenue
Central	Excel Design Solutions Ltd	810475
Central	Excelerator BI	243675
Central	WSLCB	1116175
East	Budget Wand	692375
East	Deloitte Canada	805775
East	New Hope Laundry	507200
East	SkyWire, Inc.	616200
West	Access Analytic	956425
West	DataSolverz.com	332375
West	Harvest Consulting	437600

Sort the data ZA, and you will have West at the top.

Region	Customer	Revenue
West	Access Analytic	956425
West	DataSolverz.com	332375
West	Harvest Consulting	437600
West	MySpreadsheetLab	651825
West	The Lab with Leo Crew	243925
East	Budget Wand	692375
East	Deloitte Canada	805775
East	New Hope Laundry	507200
East	SkyWire, Inc.	616200
Central	Excel Design Solutions Ltd	810475

I actually went to my manager to ask if he would rename the Central region. "To what?" he asked incredulously. I replied that I didn't care, as long as it started with F through V. Perhaps "Middle"? John shook his head no and went on with his day.

So, over and over, I would sort the report, then Ctrl+X to cut the East region records and paste them before the Central region. If only I had known this trick.

The first thing to do is to set up a custom list with the regions in the correct order: East, Central, West. (See ""Teach the Fill Handle a New List" on page 10 for instructions on setting up a custom list.)

Once the custom list is defined, open the Sort dialog by using the Sort icon on the Data tab. Choose to sort by Region. Open the Order dropdown. You don't want A to Z. You don't want Z to A. You want Custom List....

Choose the East, Central, West custom list.

One you've chosen that custom list, you can either sort it East, Central, West or West, Central, East.

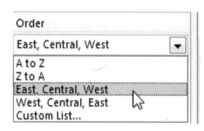

The result: an easy way to sort a list into a nonstandard sequence.

Region	Customer	Revenue
East	Deloitte Canada	805775
East	Budget Wand	692375
East	SkyWire, Inc.	616200
East	New Hope Laundry	507200
Central	WSLCB	1116175
Central	Excel Design Solutions Ltd	810475
Central	Excelerator BI	243675
West	Access Analytic	956425
West	MySpreadsheetLab	651825
West	Harvest Consulting	437600
West	DataSolverz.com	332375
West	The Lab with Leo Crew	243925

Product lines often won't sort correctly: PTC-610, PTC-710, PTC-860, PTC-960, PTC-1100 is the desired order. But PTC-1100 always sorts first in a text sort. A custom list would solve this problem as well.

Thanks to @NeedForExcel for suggesting this tip.

#22 Sort Left to Right

Every day, your IT department sends you a file with the columns in the wrong sequence. It would take them two minutes to change the query, but they have a six-month backlog, so you are stuck rearranging the columns every day.

	A	B	C	D	E	F	G	H	I
1	Last Name	Apt	Street	Company	First Name	Middle	ST	Zip	City
2	Hooker		123 Pivot Drive	Phare View Concepts	Carl	R.	KY	40361	Paris
3	Cordell	#101	234 Excel Lane	Lake Local School District	Trace		OH	44685	Uniontown
4	Corrie		345 Precedent Trace	excelisfun	N		FL	32919	Melbourne
5	Gilbert	Apt 2	456 Analysis Ave	SlinkyRN Excel Instruction	Dawn		FL	32953	Merritt Island
6	McClellan		567 Fisher Way	Resource Optimizer	Robert	S.	OH	4440	Salem

You can reorder the columns with a left-to-right sort.

Add a new row above the data. Type numbers to represent the correct sequence for the columns.

Select Data, Sort. In the Sort dialog, click the Options… button and choose Sort Left to Right. Click OK.

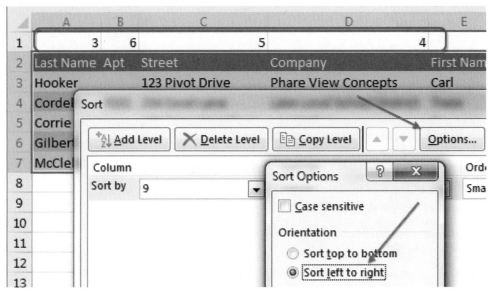

Specify Row 1 in the Sort By dropdown. Click OK.

The problem: The column widths do not travel with the columns.

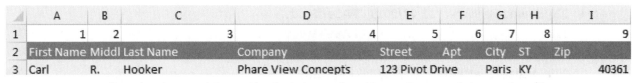

	A	B	C	D	E	F	G	H	I
1	1	2	3	4	5	6	7	8	9
2	First Name	Middl	Last Name	Company	Street	Apt	City	ST	Zip
3	Carl	R.	Hooker	Phare View Concepts	123 Pivot Drive		Paris	KY	40361

But it is easy to select the data and Press Alt+O, C, A or select Home, Format, Column, AutoFit.

#23 Sort Subtotals

This tip is from my friend Derek Fraley in Springfield, Missouri. I was doing a seminar in Springfield, and I was showing my favorite subtotal tricks.

For those of you who have never used subtotals, here is how to set them up.

Start by making sure your data is sorted. The data below is sorted by customers in column C.

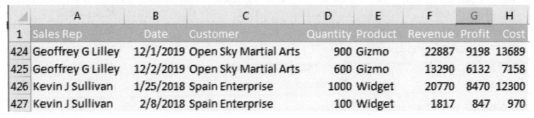

	A	B	C	D	E	F	G	H
1	Sales Rep	Date	Customer	Quantity	Product	Revenue	Profit	Cost
424	Geoffrey G Lilley	12/1/2019	Open Sky Martial Arts	900	Gizmo	22887	9198	13689
425	Geoffrey G Lilley	12/2/2019	Open Sky Martial Arts	600	Gizmo	13290	6132	7158
426	Kevin J Sullivan	1/25/2018	Spain Enterprise	1000	Widget	20770	8470	12300
427	Kevin J Sullivan	2/8/2018	Spain Enterprise	100	Widget	1817	847	970

From the Data tab, choose Subtotals. The Subtotal dialog box always wants to subtotal by the leftmost column. Open the At Each Change In dropdown and choose Customer. Make sure the Use Function box is set to Sum. Choose all of the numeric fields, as shown here.

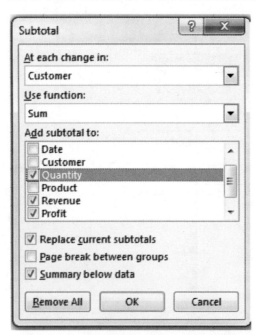

When you click OK, Excel inserts a subtotal below each group of customers. But, more importantly, it adds Group and Outline buttons to the left of column A.

		A	B	C
	1	Sales Rep	Date	Customer
	223	Kevin J Sullivan	11/30/2019	CPASelfStudy.
	224	Kevin J Sullivan	12/7/2019	CPASelfStudy.
	225	Kevin J Sullivan	12/22/2019	CPASelfStudy.
	226			**CPASelfStudy.**
	227	Michael Dietterid	1/9/2018	F-Keys Ltd
	228	Michael Dietterid	2/3/2018	F-Keys Ltd

When you click the #2 Group and Outline button, the detail rows are hidden, and you are left with only the subtotal rows and the grand total. This is a beautiful summary of a detailed data set. Of course, at this point, the customers appear in alphabetic sequence. Derek from Springfield showed me that when the data is collapsed in the #2 view, you can sort by any column. In the figure below, a Revenue column cell is selected, and you are about to click the ZA sort button.

| | fx | =SUBTOTAL(9,F2:F37) |

C	D	E	F	G	H
Customer	Quantity	Product	Revenue	Profit	Cost
Association for Computers & Taxation Total	20200		430540	190598	239942
Blockhead Data Consultants Total	21500		460086	206861	253225
BradEdgar.com Total	24700		546662	243117	303545
Clarity Consultancy Services Ltd Total	17400		369567	164599	204968
Construction Intelligence & Analytics, Inc. Total	17800		374497	169684	204813

The top customer, Wag More Dog Store, comes to the top of the data set. But it does not come to row 2. Behind the hidden rows, Excel actually sorted a chunk of records. All of the Wag More detail rows moved along with the subtotal row.

	C	D	E	F	G	H
1	Customer	Quantity	Product	Revenue	Profit	Cost
49	Wag More Dog Store, San Antonio Total	28900		606128	273935	332193
91	BradEdgar.com Total	24700		546662	243117	303545
133	CPASelfStudy.com Total	23400		505279	221591	283688
172	F-Keys Ltd Total	23100		490827	218470	272357
222	Hybrid Software Total	23100		486697	215678	271019
259	Blockhead Data Consultants Total	21500		460086	206861	253225
295	Open Sky Martial Arts Total	20800		448241	196403	251838
332	Association for Computers & Taxation Total	20200		430540	190598	239942
371	Hartville Marketplace & Flea Market Total	19000		410118	181689	228429
408	SurtenExcel.com Total	17600		375472	164413	211059
439	Construction Intelligence & Analytics, Inc. Total	17800		374497	169684	204813
469	Spain Enterprise Total	17600		373852	163926	209926
505	Clarity Consultancy Services Ltd Total	17400		369567	164599	204968
533	The Salem Historical Society, Salem, Ohio Total	15000		329597	145571	184026
559	Juliet Babcock-Hyde CPA, PLLC Total	13900		295018	131416	163602
580	IMA Houston Chapter Total	9900		205231	90443	114788
581	Grand Total	313900		6707812	2978394	3729418

If you go back to the #3 view, you will see the detail records that came along with the subtotal row. Excel did not rearrange the detail records; they remain in their original sequence.

	C	D	E	F
1	Customer	Quantity	Product	Revenue
44	Wag More Dog Store, San Antonio	900	Widget	17289
45	Wag More Dog Store, San Antonio	500	Gizmo	10940
46	Wag More Dog Store, San Antonio	1000	Widget	21010
47	Wag More Dog Store, San Antonio	600	Gizmo	13680
48	Wag More Dog Store, San Antonio	800	Gadget	17136
49	Wag More Dog Store, San Antonio Total	28900		606128

To me, this is astounding on two fronts. First, I am amazed that Excel handles this correctly. Second, it is amazing that anyone would ever try this. Who would have thought that Excel would handle this correctly? Clearly, Derek from Springfield.

Bonus Tip: Fill in a Text Field on the Subtotal Rows

Say that each customer in a data set is assigned to a single sales rep. It would be great if you could bring the sales rep name down to the subtotal row. Here are the steps:

1. Collapse the data to the #2 view.

2. Select all of the sales rep cells, from the first subtotal row to the last customer subtotal row. Don't include the Grand Total row. At this point, you have both the visible and hidden rows selected. You need just the blank rows or just the visible rows.

3. At the right side of the Home tab, open the Find & Select dropdown. Choose Go To Special. In the Go To Special dialog, choose Blanks. Click OK.

4. At this point, you've selected only the blank sales rep cells on the Subtotal rows. In my case, the active cell is A49. You need a formula here to point one cell up. Type =A48. Instead of pressing Enter, press Ctrl+Enter to enter a similar formula in all of the subtotal rows. In each case, it brings the sales rep from the previous row down.

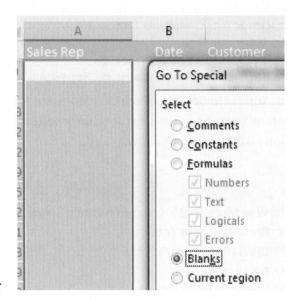

The results: The subtotal rows show the sales rep name in addition to the numeric totals.

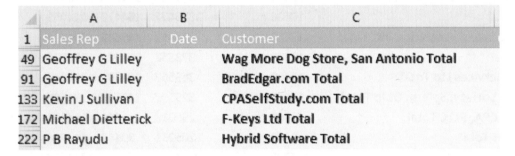

	A	B	C
1	Sales Rep	Date	Customer
49	Geoffrey G Lilley		Wag More Dog Store, San Antonio Total
91	Geoffrey G Lilley		BradEdgar.com Total
133	Kevin J Sullivan		CPASelfStudy.com Total
172	Michael Dietterick		F-Keys Ltd Total
222	P B Rayudu		Hybrid Software Total

Bonus Tip: An Easier Way to Fill in a Text Field on Subtotal Rows

Kimberly in Oklahoma City and Sarah in Omaha combined to provide a faster solution to getting the sales rep to appear on the Subtotal rows. Provided you only need the data in the #2 Summary View, this works amazingly well:

1. Click the #3 group and outline button to see all rows.

2. Select the first sales rep in A2.

3. Press Ctrl++ and press Enter. In other words, while holding down Ctrl, press the plus sign. This opens the Insert Cells dialog with "Shift Cells Down" selected. Pressing Enter is like pressing OK. This moves all of the sales reps down one row and leaves an ugly gap in A2 and the first row of every other customer.

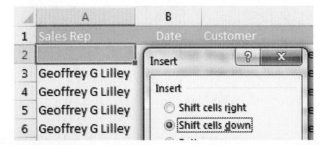

But when you go back to the #2 view, the gaps disappear and the report is correct.

1 2 3		A	C
	1	Sales Rep	Customer
+	49	Geoffrey G Lilley	Wag More Dog Store, San .
+	91	Geoffrey G Lilley	BradEdgar.com Total
+	133	Kevin J Sullivan	CPASelfStudy.com Total
+	172	Michael Dietteric|	F-Keys Ltd Total

Bonus Tip: Format the Subtotal Rows

It is a little odd that Subtotals only bolds the customer column and not anything else in the subtotal row. Follow these steps to format the subtotal rows:

1. Collapse the data to the #2 view.

2. Select all data from the first subtotal to the grand totals.

3. Press Alt+; or select Home, Find & Select, Go To Special, Visible Cells Only).

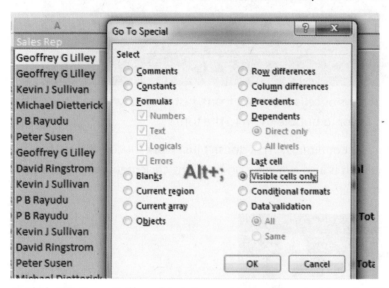

4. Click OK. Format the subtotal rows by applying bold and a fill color.

Now, when you go back to the #3 view, the subtotal rows will be easy to spot.

	A	B	C	D
1	Sales Rep	Date	Customer	Quantity
557	Michael Dietteric|	8/25/2019	Juliet Babcock-Hyde CPA, PLLC	300 '
558	Michael Dietteric|	10/22/2019	Juliet Babcock-Hyde CPA, PLLC	700 '
559	**Michael Dietterick**		**Juliet Babcock-Hyde CPA, PLLC**	**13900**
560	David Ringstrom	1/26/2018	IMA Houston Chapter	400 '
561	David Ringstrom	3/1/2018	IMA Houston Chapter	500 '

Bonus Tip: Copy the Subtotal Rows

Once you've collapsed the data down to the #2 view, you might want to copy the subtotals to a new worksheet. If so, select all the data. Press Alt+; to select only the visible cells. Press Ctrl+C to copy. Switch to a new workbook and press Ctrl+V to paste. The pasted subtotal formulas are converted to values.

Thanks to Patricia McCarthy for suggesting to select visible cells. Thanks to Derek Fraley for his suggestion from row 6.

#24 Sort and Filter by Color or Icon

Conditional formatting got a lot of new features in Excel 2007, including icon sets and more than three levels of rules. This allows for some pretty interesting formatting over a large range. But once you format the cells, you might want to quickly see all the ones that are formatted a particular way. In Excel 2007, sorting and filtering were also updated to help you do just that!

This book analysis table has some highlighted rows to flag interesting books and an icon next to the price if the book is in the top 25% of prices in the list.

If you want to quickly view all the highlighted rows or cells that have icons, just drop down the filter for the column and choose Filter by Color (or Sort by Color to bubble them to the top).

Then you can pick the formatting you want to sort or filter by! This doesn't just work for conditional formatting; it also works for manually coloring cells. It is also available on the right-click menu of a cell under the Filter or Sort flyout, and in the Sort dialog.

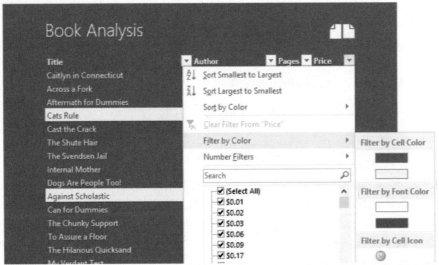

This tip is from Sam Radakovitz, a project manager on the Excel team. He is more fond of cats than dogs.

#25 Consolidate Quarterly Worksheets

There are two ancient consolidation tools in Excel.

To understand them, say that you have three data sets. Each has names down the left side and months across the top. Notice that the names are different, and each data set has a different number of months.

Name	Jan	Feb	Mar
James WSLCB Tallman	75	75	69
Michael Seeley	98	90	83
David Colman	62	53	88
P B Rayudu	71	86	93
Fr. Tony Azzarto	71	84	70
Erik Svensen	62	91	81

Name	Apr	May	Jun	Jul	Aug
Michael Seeley	62	56	83	78	98
David Colman	92	58	83	81	67
P B Rayudu	84	97	69	58	60
Erik Svensen	71	69	65	91	68
Michael Karpfen	52	80	89	83	73
Victor E. Scelba II	93	70	54	90	81
Emily Mathews	80	57	51	62	69

Name	Sep	Oct	Nov	Dec
Michael Seeley	94	79	86	92
P B Rayudu	75	83	85	90
Erik Svensen	81	79	87	97
Michael Karpfen	78	86	93	91
Emily Mathews	64	93	92	90
Robert Mika	99	84	93	99
David Ringstrom	71	80	93	94

Illustration: Cartoon Bob D'Amico

You want to combine these into a single data set.

The first tool is the Consolidate command on the Data tab. Choose a blank section of the workbook before starting the command. Use the RefEdit button to point to each of your data sets and then click Add. In the lower left, choose Top Row and Left Column.

When you click OK, a superset of all three data sets is produced. The first column contains any name in any of the three data sets. Row 1 contains any month in any data set.

	A	B	C	D	E	F	G	H	I	J	K	L	M
1		Jan	Feb	Mar	Apr	May	Jun	Jul	Aug	Sep	Oct	Nov	Dec
2	James WSLCB Tallman	75	75	69									
3	Michael Seeley	98	90	83	62	56	83	78	98	94	79	86	92
4	David Colman	62	53	88	92	58	83	81	67				
5	P B Rayudu	71	86	93	84	97	69	58	60	75	83	85	90
6	Fr. Tony Azzarto	71	84	70									
7	Erik Svensen	62	91	81	71	69	65	91	68	81	79	87	97
8	Michael Karpfen				52	80	89	83	73	78	86	93	91
9	Victor E. Scelba II				93	70	54	90	81				
10	Emily Mathews				80	57	51	62	69	64	93	92	90
11	Robert Mika									99	84	93	99
12	David Ringstrom									71	80	93	94

In the above figure, notice three annoyances: Cell A1 is always left blank, the data in A is not sorted, and if a person was missing from a data set, then cells are left empty instead of being filled with 0.

Filling in cell A1 is easy enough. Sorting by name involves using Flash Fill to get the last name in column N. Here is how to fill blank cells with 0:

1. Select all of the cells that should have numbers: B2:M11.

2. Press Ctrl+H to display Find & Replace.

3. Leave the Find What box empty, and type a zero in the Replace With: box.

4. Click Replace All.

The result: a nicely formatted summary report, as shown below.

Name	Jan	Feb	Mar	Apr	May	Jun	Jul	Aug	Sep	Oct	Nov	Dec
Fr. Tony Azzarto	71	84	70	0	0	0	0	0	0	0	0	0
David Colman	62	53	88	92	58	83	81	67	0	0	0	0
Michael Karpfen	0	0	0	52	80	89	83	73	78	86	93	91
Emily Mathews	0	0	0	80	57	51	62	69	64	93	92	90

The other ancient tool is the Multiple Consolidation Range pivot table. Follow these steps to use it:

1. Press Alt+D, P to invoke the Excel 2003 Pivot Table and Pivot Chart Wizard.

2. Choose Multiple Consolidation Ranges in step 1 of the wizard. Click Next.

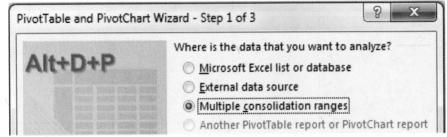

3. Choose I Will Create the Page Fields in step 2a of the wizard. Click Next.

4. In Step 2b of the wizard, use the RefEdit button to point to each table. Click Add after each.

5. Click Finish to create the pivot table, as shown below.

Sum of Value	C ▾										
Row ▾	Jan	Feb	Mar	Apr	May	Jun	Jul	Aug	Sep	Oct	Nov
David Colman	62	53	88	92	58	83	81	67			
David Ringstrom									71	80	9
Emily Mathews			80		57	51	62	69	64	93	9
Erik Svensen	62	91	81	71	69	65	91	68	81	79	8
Fr. Tony Azzarto	71	84	70								
James WSLCB Tallman	75	75	69								

Thanks to CTroy for suggesting this feature.

#26 Get Ideas from Artificial Intelligence

A new artificial intelligence feature debuted in Office 365 in early 2018. Originally called Insights, the feature was re-branded as Ideas and moved to the far right side of the Home tab of the Ribbon by September of 2018. This is the first new feature to be added to the Home tab since January 30, 2007. Excel Insights will analyze your Excel data to search for patterns and return a series of interesting facts or trends about the data.

For the feature to work properly, your data needs to be tabular data with no blank rows or columns. Every column has to have a one-row heading, and no two headings should be the same. The data should also include a date field.

Select one cell in your data and click the Ideas icon.

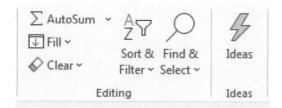

Initially, Excel will return a small number of results. Each result contains a headline and a thumbnail of a chart. At the bottom of the first few results is a link to return all 30+ results.

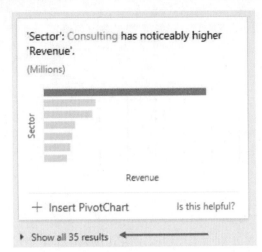

The Is This Helpful? link allows you to vote for which charts are useful. Excel will learn your preferences and return more of those types of results in the future. If you find a chart that you like, click the Insert Pivot Chart link and Excel inserts a new worksheet with a pivot table and a full-sized version of the chart.

The first few Ideas results are going to look exactly like the Excel-2013-era Recommended Pivot Tables. Skip those first few boring charts and Excel will start to suggest charts that find rank, evenness, trend, composite signal, attribution, outstanding top two, monotonicity (always increasing or always decreasing), or unimodality (having a single peak data point).

My one complaint about Ideas is shown in the following chart. Ideas was able to find some outliers in this data and offers to create a chart with those points called out in orange. For this chart to work correctly, Excel would have to support conditional formatting in charts and it does not. That means that the pivot chart will always call out these three points, even if the underlying data changes and new outliers emerge. You would have to re-run Ideas and hope that a similar result is offered.

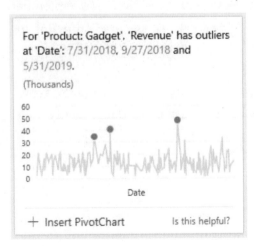

#27 Create Your First Pivot Table

Pivot tables let you summarize tabular data to a one-page summary in a few clicks. Start with a data set that has headings in row 1. It should have no blank rows, blank columns, blank headings or merged cells.

	A	B	C	D	E	F	G	H
1	Region	Market	Rep	Date	Customer	Quantity	Product	Revenue
2	West	NoCal	Symons	1/3/2021	www.ExcelTricks.de	1000	Gizmo	22810
3	South	Houston	Kazmdav	1/3/2021	Wilde XL Solutions Ltd.	100	Gadget	2257
4	Northeast	New York	McGunigal	1/3/2021	Harlem Globetrotters	400	Gizmo	9152
5	Midwest	Cleveland	aBoBoBool	1/3/2021	Tennessee Moon	800	Gadget	18552
6	Northeast	New York	McGunigal	1/3/2021	We Report Space	400	Widget	8456

Select a single cell in your data and choose Insert, Pivot Table.

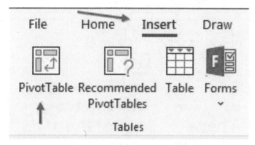

Excel will detect the edges of your data and offer to create the pivot table on a new worksheet. Click OK to accept the defaults.

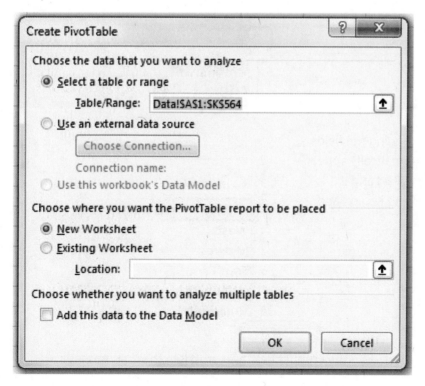

Excel inserts a new blank worksheet to the left of the current worksheet. On the right side of the screen is the Pivot Table Fields pane. At the top, a list of your fields with checkboxes.

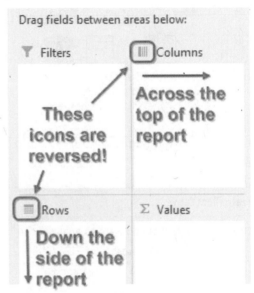

At the bottom are four drop zones with horrible names and confusing icons. Any fields that you drag to the Columns area will appear as headings across the top of your report. Any fields that you drag to the Rows area appear as headings along the left side of your report. Drag numeric fields to the Values area.

You can build some reports without dragging the fields. If you checkmark a text field, it will automatically appear in the Rows area. Checkmark a numeric field and it will appear in the Values area. By choosing Region and Revenue, you will create this pivot table:

	A	B
1		
2		
3	**Region** ▼	**Sum of Revenue**
4	West	840363
5	Midwest	2733471
6	South	2504958
7	Northeast	629020
8	**Grand Total**	6707812

To get products across the top of the report, drag the Product field and drop it in the Columns area:

3	**Sum of Revenue**	**Product** ▼				
4	**Region** ▼	**Doodads**	**Gadget**	**Gizmo**	**Widget**	**Grand Total**
5	West	4948	368928	202216	264271	840363
6	Midwest	45828	1003191	984901	699551	2733471
7	South	5859	727777	1018113	753209	2504958
8	Northeast	16924	241200	187790	183106	629020
9	**Grand Total**	73559	2341096	2393020	1900137	6707812

Note: your first pivot table might have the words "Column Labels" and "Row Labels" instead of headings like Product and Region. If so, choose Design, Report Layout, Show in Tabular Form. Later, in "#31 Specify Defaults for All Future Pivot Tables" on page 71, you will learn how to make Tabular Form the default for your pivot tables.

Bonus Tip: Rearrange fields in a pivot table

The power of pivot tables is the ability to rearrange the fields. If your manager decides you should put Regions across the top and products down the side, it is two drags to create the new report.

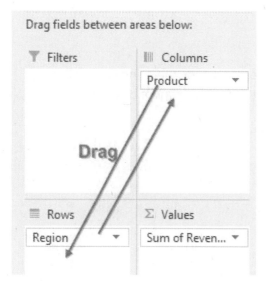

Drag product to Rows. Drag Region to Columns and you will have this report:

Sum of Revenue	Region				
Product	West	Midwest	South	Northeast	Grand Total
Doodads	4948	45828	5859	16924	73559
Gadget	368928	1003191	727777	241200	2341096
Gizmo	202216	984901	1018113	187790	2393020
Widget	264271	699551	753209	183106	1900137
Grand Total	840363	2733471	2504958	629020	6707812

To remove a field from the pivot table, drag the field tile outside of the Fields pane, or simply uncheck the field in the top of the Fields pane.

Bonus Tip: Format a Pivot Table

You might wonder how the pivot table above changed from green to orange. The Design tab has a gallery with 84 built-in formats for pivot tables. Choose a design from the gallery and the colors change.

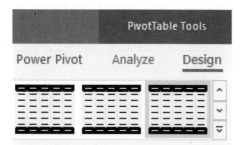

One frustrating feature with a pivot table is that the numbers always start out as General format. Right-click any number and choose Number Format…. Any changes you make to the number formatting using this command will be remembered as long as Revenue stays in the pivot table. (Before Excel 2010, pivot tables would frequently forget the number formatting. This was fixed in Excel 2010.)

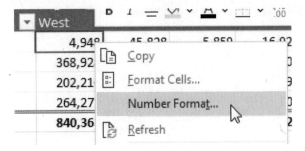

Bonus Tip: Format One Cell in a Pivot Table

This is new in Office 365 starting in 2018. You can right-click any cell in a pivot table and choose Format Cell. Any formatting that you apply is tied to that data in the pivot table. In the figure below, Florida Figs have a yellow fill color.

	A	B	C
1	Category	(All)	
2			
3	**Sum of Sales**	**Region**	
4	**Product**	**California**	**Florida**
5	Apple	8479	6235
6	Banana	8287	2635
7	Cherry	4373	3590
8	Date	3004	1496
9	Elderberry	2307	0
10	Fig	0	9683
11	Cucumber	1881	9512
12	**Grand Total**	**28331**	**33151**
13			

If you change the pivot table, the yellow formatting follows the Florida Fig.

	A	B	C
3	**Product**	**Region**	**Sum of Sales**
26	**Elderberry**	Texas	1381
27	**Elderberry**	Washington	5901
28	**Elderberry Total**		**19679**
29	**Fig**	Florida	9683
30	**Fig**	Missouri	7531
31	Fig	New York	5650

If you add a new inner field, then multiple cells for Florida Fig will have the fill color.

	A	B	C	D
3	**Product** ▾	**Region** ⊤▾	**Rep** ▾	**Sum of Sales**
49	⊟ **Fig**	⊟ **Florida**	Sonny	6137
50	**Fig**	Florida	Fred	3546
51	**Fig**	**Florida Total**		**9683**
52	**Fig**	⊟ **Missouri**	Lewis	7531

The formatting will persist if you remove Florida or Fig due to a filter. If you filter to vegetables, Fig is hidden. Filter to fruit and Fig will still be formatted. However, if you completely remove either Product or Region from the pivot table, the formatting will be lost.

Bonus Tip: Fill in the Blanks in the Annoying Outline View

If your pivot table is in Tabular or Outline Form and you have more than one row field, the pivot table defaults to leaving a lot of blank cells in the outer row fields:

	Region	Market	Sum of Revenue
3	Region ▾	Market ▾	Sum of Revenue
4	⊟ **West**	NoCal	521,373
5		SoCal	318,990
6	**West Total**		**840,363**
7	⊟ **Midwest**	Chicago	520,176
8		Cincinnati	512,391
9		Cleveland	559,826

Starting in Excel 2010, use Design, Report Layout, Repeat all Item Labels to fill in the blanks in column A:

	Region	Market	Sum of Revenue
3	Region ▾	Market ▾	Sum of Revenue
4	⊟ **West**	NoCal	521,373
5	**West**	SoCal	318,990
6	**West Total**		**840,363**
7			
8	⊟ **Midwest**	Chicago	520,176
9	**Midwest**	Cincinnati	512,391
10	**Midwest**	Cleveland	559,826

There is another way to have blanks in the Values area of a pivot table. Say that you have a product which is only sold in a few regions. If there are no Doodad sales in Atlanta, Excel will leave that cell empty instead of putting a zero there. Right-click the pivot table and choose Pivot Table Options. On the Layout & Format tab, find the box For Empty Cells, Show: and type a zero.

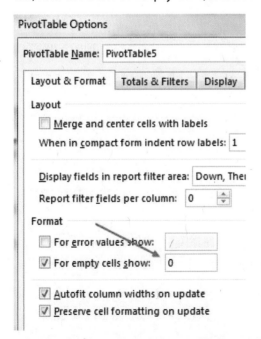

#28 Create a Year-over-Year Report in a Pivot Table

Let's say you have two years' worth of detail records. Each record has a daily date. When you build a pivot table from this report, you will have hundreds of rows of daily dates in the pivot table. This is not much of a summary.

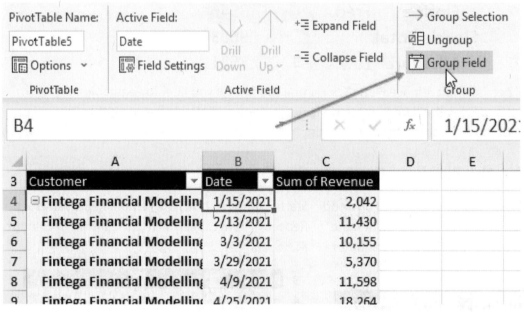

Choose one of those date cells in the pivot table. From the Analyze tab in the Ribbon, choose Group Field.

Because you are on a date field, you get *this* version of the Grouping dialog. In it, deselect Months and select Years.

The daily dates are rolled up to years. Move the Date field from Rows to Columns.

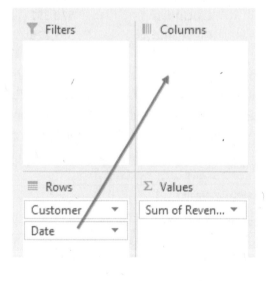

The result is almost perfect. But instead of a grand total in column D, you probably want a percentage variance. To get rid of the Grand Total column, right-click on the Grand Total heading and choose Remove Grand Total.)

To build the variance column as shown below, you need to write a formula outside the pivot table that points inside the pivot table. Do not touch the mouse or arrow keys while building the formula, or the often-annoying GETPIVOTDATA function will appear. Instead, simply type =C5/B5-1 and press Enter.

D5				f_x	=C5/B5-1
	A	B	C	D	E	F
3	Sum of Revenue	Date ▾				
4	Customer ▾	2021	2022	% Change		
5	Fintega Financial Modelling	283,244	177,286	-37.4%		
6	Frontline Systems	319,606	285,579	-10.6%		
7	Harlem Globetrotters	290,940	359,243	23.5%		
8	JEVS Human Services	341,825	362,318	6.0%		

Bonus Tip: Another Way to Calculate Year-Over-Year

Instead of creating a formula outside of the pivot table, you can do this inside the pivot table.

Start from the image with column D empty. Drag Revenue a second time to the Values area.

Look in the Columns section of the Pivot Table Fields panel. You will see a tile called Values that appears below Date. Drag that tile so it is below the Date field. Your pivot table should look like this:

	A	B	C	D	E
3		Values	Date ▾		
4		Sum of Revenue		Sum of Revenue2	
5	Customer ▾	2021	2022	2021	2022
6	Fintega Financial Modelling	283,244	177,286	283244	177:
7	Frontline Systems	319,606	285,579	319606	285!
8	Harlem Globetrotters	290 940	359 243	290940	359:

Double-click the Sum of Revenue2 heading in D4 to display the Value Field Settings dialog. Click on the tab for Show Values As. Change the drop-down menu to % Difference From. Change the Base Field to Date. Change the Base Item to (Previous Item). Type a better name than Sum of Revenue2 - perhaps % Change. Click OK.

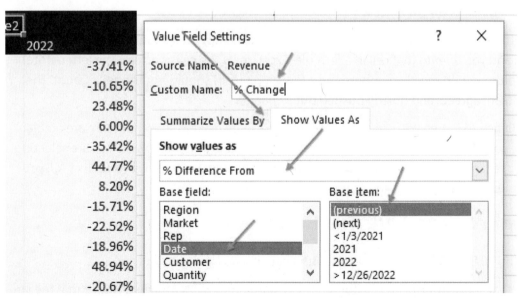

You will have a mostly blank column D (because the pivot table can't calculate a percentage change for the first year. Right-click the D and choose Hide.

Thanks to Tobias Ljung for this method.

#29 Change the Calculation in a Pivot Table

Pivot tables offer a myriad of calculations in the Field Settings dialog box. Here is a faster way to change a calculation:

1. Drag Revenue to the Values area twice.

2. Double-click on the heading Sum of Revenue2. Excel opens the Value Field Settings dialog.

3. Click on Show Values As and select % of Column Total from the dropdown.

4. Type a new name in the Custom Name field, such as % of Total.

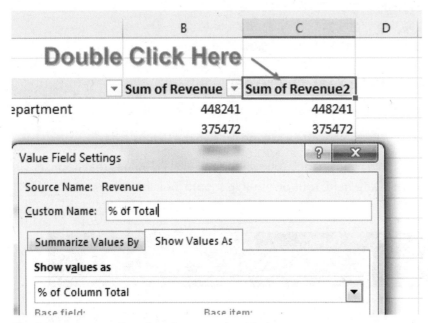

Thanks to Александр Воробьев for suggesting this tip.

Bonus Tip: Why Do Pivot Tables Count Instead of Sum?

In almost every seminar, someone asks why pivot tables default to count instead of sum. This long-standing problem was fixed in May 2018 for Office 365 subscribers. The Count was triggered if you had one revenue cell that contained text or an empty cell.

Someone wrote a letter to the Excel team complaining that a single empty cell should not be treated like text. If a cell is blank and you refer to that cell in a formula, Excel treats the cell as a zero. The letter-writer pointed out that a columns with mostly numbers and a few empty cells should not trigger a Count. The person on the Excel team agreed, and quietly pushed out a change.

If you are not using Office 365, then you can avoid the Count issue by making sure that there are no blank cells in your revenue column. If you don't think that you have any blank cells, make sure you are selecting one cell in your data set and not the entire columns A:J. If your data is in A2:J999 and you select A:J, you are selecting 998 numbers and over a million empty cells.

#30 Find the True Top Five in a Pivot Table

Pivot tables offer a Top 10 filter. It is cool. It is flexible. But I hate it, and I will tell you why.

Here is a pivot table that shows revenue by customer. The revenue total is $6.7 million. Notice that the largest customer, Roto-Rooter, is 9% of the total revenue.

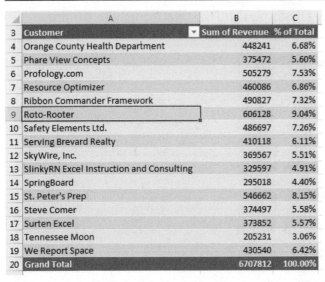

	A	B	C
3	Customer	Sum of Revenue	% of Total
4	Orange County Health Department	448241	6.68%
5	Phare View Concepts	375472	5.60%
6	Profology.com	505279	7.53%
7	Resource Optimizer	460086	6.86%
8	Ribbon Commander Framework	490827	7.32%
9	Roto-Rooter	606128	9.04%
10	Safety Elements Ltd.	486697	7.26%
11	Serving Brevard Realty	410118	6.11%
12	SkyWire, Inc.	369567	5.51%
13	SlinkyRN Excel Instruction and Consulting	329597	4.91%
14	SpringBoard	295018	4.40%
15	St. Peter's Prep	546662	8.15%
16	Steve Comer	374497	5.58%
17	Surten Excel	373852	5.57%
18	Tennessee Moon	205231	3.06%
19	We Report Space	430540	6.42%
20	Grand Total	6707812	100.00%

What if my manager has the attention span of a goldfish and wants to see only the top five customers? To start, open the dropdown in A3 and select Value Filters, Top 10.

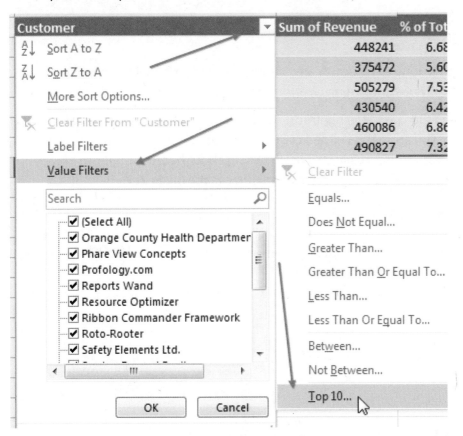

The super-flexible Top 10 Filter dialog allows Top/Bottom. It can do 10, 5, or any other number. You can ask for the top five items, top 80%, or enough customers to get to $5 million.

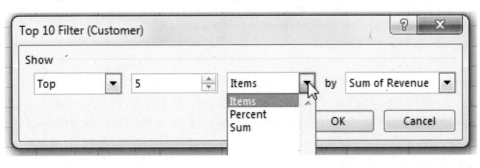

But here is the problem: The resulting report shows five customers and the total from those customers instead of the totals from everyone. Roto-Rooter, who was previously 9% of the total is 23% of the new total.

Customer	Sum of Revenue	% of Total
Profology.com	505279	19.17%
Ribbon Commander Framework	490827	18.62%
Roto-Rooter	606128	23.00%
Safety Elements Ltd.	486697	18.47%
St. Peter's Prep	546662	20.74%
Grand Total	2635593	100.00%

But First, a Few Important Words About AutoFilter

I realize this seems like an off-the-wall question. If you want to turn on the Filter dropdowns on a regular data set, how do you do it? Here are three really common ways:

- Select one cell in your data and click the Filter icon on the Data tab or press Ctrl+Shift+L.

- Select all of your data with Ctrl+* and click the Filter icon on the Data tab.

- Press Ctrl+T to format the data as a table.

These are three really good ways. As long as you know any of them, there is absolutely no need to know another way. But here's an incredibly obscure but magical way to turn on the filter:

- Go to your row of headers and then go to the rightmost heading cell. Move one cell to the right. For some unknown reason, when you are in this cell and click the Filter icon, Excel filters the data set to your left. I have no idea why this works. It really isn't worth talking about because there are already three really good ways to turn on the Filter dropdowns. I call this cell the magic cell.

And Now, Back to Pivot Tables

There is a rule that says you cannot use AutoFilter when you are in a pivot table. See below? The Filter icon is grayed out because I've selected a cell in the pivot table.

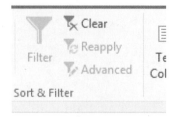

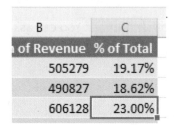

I don't know why Microsoft grays this out. It must be something internal that says AutoFilter and a pivot table can't coexist. So, there is someone on the Excel team who is in charge of graying out the Filter icon. That person has never heard of the magic cell. Select a cell in the pivot table, and the Filter gets grayed out. Click outside the pivot table, and Filter is enabled again.

But wait. What about the magic cell I just told you about? If you click in the cell to the right of the last heading, Excel forgets to gray out the Filter icon!

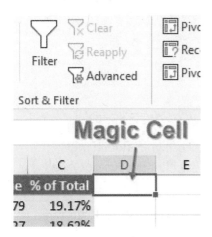

Illustration: George Berlin

Sure enough, Excel adds AutoFilter dropdowns to the top row of your pivot table. And AutoFilter operates differently than a pivot table filter. Go to the Revenue dropdown and choose Number Filters, Top 10….

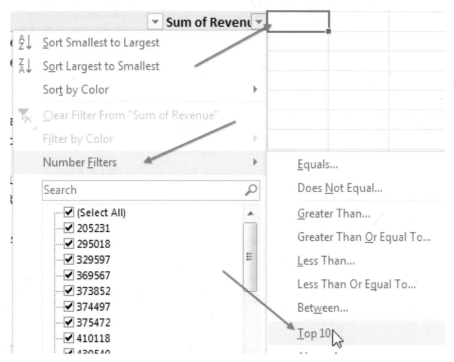

In the Top 10 AutoFilter dialog, choose Top 6 Items. That's not a typo…if you want five customers, choose 6. If you want 10 customers, choose 11.

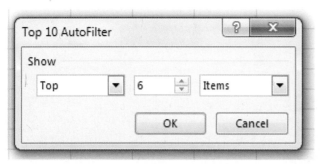

To AutoFilter, the grand total row is the largest item in the data. The top five customers are occupying positions 2 through 6 in the data.

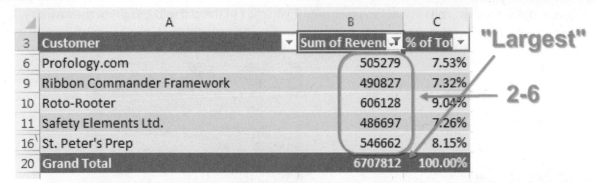

	A	B	C
3	Customer	Sum of Revenue	% of Total
6	Profology.com	505279	7.53%
9	Ribbon Commander Framework	490827	7.32%
10	Roto-Rooter	606128	9.04%
11	Safety Elements Ltd.	486697	7.26%
16	St. Peter's Prep	546662	8.15%
20	Grand Total	6707812	100.00%

"Largest" 2-6

Caution: Clearly, you are tearing a hole in the fabric of Excel with this trick. If you later change the underlying data and refresh your pivot table, Excel will not refresh the filter because, as far as Microsoft knows, there is no way to apply a filter to a pivot table!

Note: Our goal is to keep this a secret from Microsoft because it is a pretty cool feature. It has been "broken" for quite some time, so there are a lot of people who might be relying on it by now.

A Completely Legal Solution in Excel 2013+

If you want a pivot table showing you the top five customers but the total from all customers, you have to move your data outside Excel. If you have Excel 2013 or newer running in Windows, there is a very convenient way to do this. To show you this, I've deleted the original pivot table. Choose Insert, Pivot Table. Before clicking OK, select the checkbox Add This Data To The Data Model.

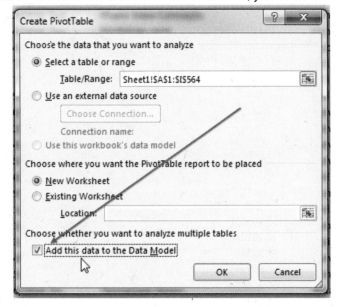

Build your pivot table as normal. Use the dropdown in A3 to select Value Filters, Top 10, and ask for the top five customers. With one cell in the pivot table selected, go to the Design tab in the Ribbon and open the Subtotals dropdown. The final choice in the dropdown is Include Filtered Items in Totals. Normally, this choice is grayed out. But because the data is stored in the Data Model instead of a normal pivot cache, this option is now available.

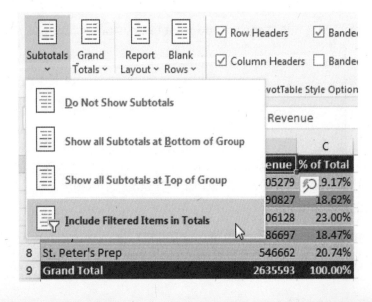

Choose the Include Filtered Items in Totals option, and your Grand Total now includes an asterisk and the total of all of the data, as shown below.

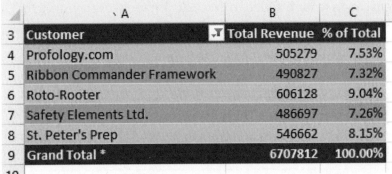

	A	B	C
3	Customer 🔽	Total Revenue	% of Total
4	Profology.com	505279	7.53%
5	Ribbon Commander Framework	490827	7.32%
6	Roto-Rooter	606128	9.04%
7	Safety Elements Ltd.	486697	7.26%
8	St. Peter's Prep	546662	8.15%
9	Grand Total *	6707812	100.00%

This magic cell trick originally came to me from Dan in my seminar in Philadelphia and was repeated 15 years later by a different Dan from my seminar in Cincinnati. Thanks to Miguel Caballero for suggesting this feature.

#31 Specify Defaults for All Future Pivot Tables

It took me six years, but I finally convinced the Excel team that a lot of people prefer Tabular layout for pivot tables to the Compact layout that became the default layout in Excel 2007. If you have Office 365, you now have the ability to specify pivot table defaults.

Go to File, Options, Data. Click Edit Default Layout….

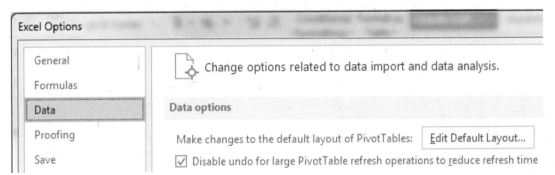

Change the Report Layout to Show in Tabular Form and choose the checkbox Repeat All Item Labels.

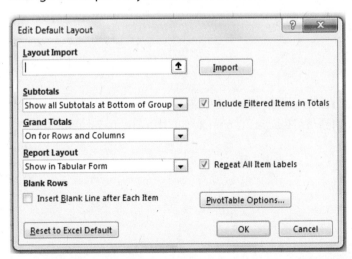

Tip: There are other settings that you can specify as the default. You can either click Pivot Table Options… and specify them or find a pivot table where you've already set up your favorite settings. Select one cell in that pivot table and click Import.

If you don't have Office 365 and don't have access to pivot table defaults, you can get similar functionality by buying Pivot Power Premium from Debra Dalgleish at Contextures.com: mrx.cl/pppdebra.

Bonus Tip: Change What Drives You Crazy About Excel

I've managed to lobby the Excel team to get a few changes into Excel. It isn't always easy. It took me eight years of lobbying to get the Repeat All Item Labels feature added to Excel 2010. It took seven years to get the Pivot Table Defaults feature added.

But there is a new feedback mechanism that makes it possible for anyone to potentially get a favorite feature added to Excel. If you have a great idea of what would make Excel easier, write up a short post at https://Excel.UserVoice.com. Make sure to choose Excel for Windows (Desktop Application). Post your idea. And then get your friends and co-workers to vote for your idea. The great news is that the Excel team is listening to ideas posted at UserVoice. They key to getting the Excel team to respond is 20 votes. But I managed 200–300 votes for my Pivot Table Defaults before they started working on the feature.

#32 Make Pivot Tables Expandable Using Ctrl+T

If you choose all of columns A:J and you later want to add more records below the data, it takes only a simple Refresh to add the new data instead of having to find the Change Data Source icon. In the past, this made sense. But today, Change Data Source is right next to the Refresh button and not hard to find. Plus, there is a workaround in the Ctrl+T table.

When you choose your data set and select Format as Table by using Ctrl+T, the pivot table source will grow as the table grows. You can even do this retroactively, after the pivot table exists.

This figure below shows a data set and a pivot table. The pivot table source is A1:C16.

	A	B	C	D	E	F
1	Name	Region	Revenue			
2	Mike Mann	East	15100		Region ▾	Revenue
3	Olga Kryuchkova	Central	13000		Central	$282,800
4	Graham Stent	West	20500		East	$176,500
5	Dennis P Jancsy	East	29800		West	$350,900
6	Diana McGunigale	Central	27800		Grand Total	$810,200
7	John Henning	West	39000			
8	Thomas Fries	East	7200			
9	Aiman Sadeq	Central	47700			
10	John Cockerill	West	36200			
11	Greg Heyman	East	39900			
12	Rick Grantham	Central	78600			
13	DeLisa Lee	West	100900			
14	Mark E Luhdorff	East	84500			
15	John T Lutz	Central	115700			
16	Mario Garcia	West	154300			
17						

Say that you want to be able to easily add new data below the pivot table, as shown below. Select one cell in the data and press Ctrl+T. Make sure that My Table Has Headers is checked in the Create Table dialog and click OK.

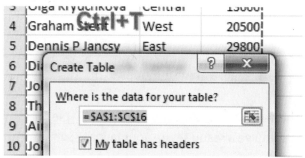

Some nice formatting is applied to the data set. But the formatting is not the important part.

	A	B	C
1	Name ▼	Region ▼	Revenue ▼
2	Mike Mann	East	15100
3	Olga Kryuchkova	Central	13000
4	Graham Stent	West	20500
5	Dennis P Jancsy	East	29800
6	Diana McGunigale	Central	27800

You have some new records to add to the table. Copy the records.

	A	B	C
1	Erik Svensen	East	42800
2	Melanie Breden	Central	98300
3	J Maltais	West	68400
4			
5	Ctrl+c		

Go to the blank row below the table and paste. The new records pick up the formatting from the table. The angle-bracket-shaped End-of-Table marker moves to C19. But notice that the pivot table has not updated yet.

	A	B	C	D	E	F
1	Name ▼	Region ▼	Revenue ▼			
2	Mike Mann	East	15100		Region ▼	Revenue
3	Olga Kryuchkova	Central	13000		Central	$282,800
4	Graham Stent	West	20500		East	$176,500
5	Dennis P Jancsy	East	29800		West	$350,900
6	Diana McGunigale	Central	27800		Grand Total	$810,200
7	John Henning	West	39000			
8	Thomas Fries	East	7200			
9	Aiman Sadeq	Central	47700			
10	John Cockerill	West	36200			
11	Greg Heyman	East	39900			
12	Rick Grantham	Central	78600			
13	DeLisa Lee	West	100900		Pasted data	
14	Mark E Luhdorff	East	84500			
15	John T Lutz	Central	115700		No change yet	
16	Mario Garcia	West	154300			
17	Erik Svensen	East	42800			
18	Melanie Breden	Central	98300		End of Table marker	
19	J Maltais	West	68400			
20				(Ctrl) ▾		

Click the Refresh button in the Pivot Table Tools Analyze tab. Excel adds the new rows to your pivot table.

Region ▼	Revenue
Central	$381,100
East	$219,300
West	$419,300
Grand Total	$1,019,700

Bonus Tip: Use Ctrl+T with VLOOKUP and Charts

In this figure, the VLOOKUP table is in E5:F9. Item A106 is missing from the table, and the VLOOKUP is returning #N/A. Conventional wisdom says to add A106 to the middle of your VLOOKUP table so you don't have to rewrite the formula.

	A	B	C	D	E	F	G
1	Qty	Item	Price?				
2	7	A104	37.95	=VLOOKUP(B2,$E$5:$F$9,2,0)			
3	8	A101	10.95				
4	2	A101	10.95		Item	Price	
5	9	A106	#N/A		A101	10.95	
6	7	A102	19.95		A102	19.95	
7	2	A103	28.95		A103	28.95	
8					A104	37.95	
9					A105	46.95	
10							

Instead, use Ctrl+T to format the lookup table. Note that the formula is still pointing to E5:F9; nothing changes in the formula.

	A	B	C	D	E	F
1	Qty	Item	Price?		**Ctrl+T**	
2	7	A104	37.95	=VLOOKUP(B2,$E$5:$F$9,2,0)		
3	8	A101	10.95			
4	2	A101	10.95		Item ▼	Price ▼
5	9	A106	#N/A		A101	10.95
6	7	A102	19.95		A102	19.95
7	2	A103	28.95		A103	28.95
8					A104	37.95
9		**No change**		A105	46.95
10						
11		**in formula**				
12						

But when you type a new row below the table, it becomes part of the table, and the VLOOKUP formula automatically updates to reflect the new range.

	A	B	C	D	E	F	G
1	Qty	Item	Price?	**Formula changes**			
2	7	A104	37.95	=VLOOKUP(B2,$E$5:$F$10,2,0)			
3	8	A101	10.95				
4	2	A101	10.95		Item ▼	Price ▼	
5	9	A106	24.95		A101	10.95	
6	7	A102	19.95		A102	19.95	
7	2	A103	28.95		A103	28.95	
8					A104	37.95	
9		**Add new row**		A105	46.95	
10					A106	24.95	
11							

The same thing happens with charts. The chart on the left is based on A1:B5, which is not a table. Format A1:B5 as a table by pressing Ctrl+T. Add a new row. The row is automatically added to the chart, as shown on the right.

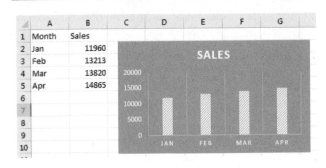

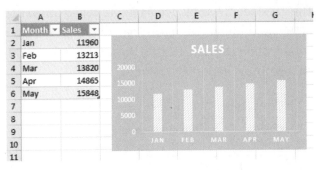

It is fairly cool that you can use Ctrl+T after setting up the pivot table, VLOOKUP, or chart, and Excel still makes the range expand.

When I asked readers to vote for their favorite tips, tables were popular. Thanks to Peter Albert, Snorre Eikeland, Nancy Federice, Colin Michael, James E. Moede, Keyur Patel, and Paul Peton for suggesting this feature. Four readers suggested using OFFSET to create expanding ranges for dynamic charts: Charley Baak, Don Knowles, Francis Logan, and Cecelia Rieb. Tables now do the same thing in most cases.

#33 Replicate a Pivot Table for Each Rep

Here is a great trick I learned from southern California–based Excel consultant Szilvia Juhasz.

The pivot table below shows products across the top and customers down the side. The pivot table is sorted so the largest customers are at the top. The Sales Rep field is in the report filter.

	A	B	C	D	E
1	Rep	(All)			
2					
3	Sum of Revenue	Product			
4	Customer	Gizmo	Gadget	WhatsIt	Grand Total
5	Harlem Globetrotters	382,878	414,502	402,311	1,199,691
6	MySpreadsheetLab	341,902	444,299	362,269	1,148,470
7	CPASelfStudy.com	335,541	267,607	285,829	888,977

If you open the Rep dropdown, you can filter the data to any one sales rep.

This is a great way to create a report for each sales rep. Each report summarizes the revenue from a particular salesperson's customers, with the biggest customers at the top. And you get to see the split between the various products.

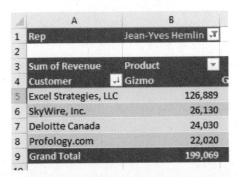

The Excel team has hidden a feature called Show Report Filter Pages. Select any pivot table that has a field in the report filter. Go to the Analyze tab (or the Options tab in Excel 2007/2010). On the far left side is the large Options button. Next to the large Options button is a tiny dropdown arrow. Click this dropdown and choose Show Report Filter Pages....

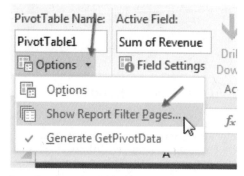

Excel asks which field you want to use. Select the one you want (in this case the only one available) and click OK.

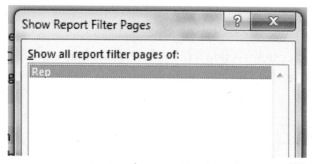

Over the next few seconds, Excel starts inserting new worksheets, one for each sales rep. Each sheet tab is named after the sales rep. Inside each worksheet, Excel replicates the pivot table but changes the name in the report filter to this sales rep.

	A	B	C	D
1	Rep	Mark E Luhdorff 🔽		
2				
3	Sum of Revenue	Product 🔽		
4	Customer	Gizmo	Gadget	WhatsIt
5	The Lab with Leo Crew	57,281	72,643	
6	myexcelonline.com	12,838	108,373	
7	XLYOURFINANCES, LLC	33,993	13,723	
8	Hartville Marketplace & Flea Market	0	15,394	
9	Grand Total	104,112	210,133	
10				
11				
12				

◀ ▶ ... | Jean-Yves Hemlin | **Mark E Luhdorff** | Melanie Breden | Peter Albert

You end up with a report for each sales rep.

This would work with any field. If you want a report for each customer, product, vendor, or something else, add it to the report filter and use Show Report Filter Pages.

Thanks to Szilvia Juhasz for showing me this feature during a seminar I was teaching at the University of Akron many years ago. For the record, Szilvia was in row 1.

#34 Use a Pivot Table to Compare Lists

When you think of comparing lists, you probably think of VLOOKUP. If you have two lists to compare, you need to add two columns of VLOOKUP. In the figure below, you are trying to compare Tuesday to Monday and Wednesday to Tuesday and maybe even Wednesday to Monday. It is going to take a lot of VLOOKUP columns to figure out who was added to and dropped from each list.

	A	B	C	D	E	F	G	H
1	Monday			Tuesday			Weds	
2								
3	Name	RSVP		Name	RSVP		Name	RS
4	Carl Hjortsjö	2		Andrew Spain	3		Andrew Spain	3
5	Caroline Bonner	2		Caroline Bonner	2		Jean-Yves Hemlin	1
6	Dawn Kosmakos	2		Dawn Kosmakos	1		Jeffrey P. Coulson	2
7	Jeff Long	1		Kathryn Sullivan	2		John Durran	1
8	M.R. Rosenkrantz	1		M.R. Rosenkrantz	1		Kathryn Sullivan	1
9	Martin Lucas	2		Martin Lucas	2		Kevin Lehrbass	1
10	Paul Hannelly	2		Melissa Esquibel	2		M.R. Rosenkrantz	2
11	Roger Fisher	1		Michael Karpfen	2		Martin Lucas	1
12	Sabine Hanschitz	1		Peter Harvest	2		Melissa Esquibel	2
13	Ute Simon	2		Roger Fisher	1		Michael Karpfen	2
14	Yesenia Garcia	2		Sabine Hanschitz	1		Peter Harvest	1
15				Ute Simon	2		Roger Fisher	1
16				Yesenia Garcia	2		Sabine Hanschitz	2
17							Ute Simon	2
18								

You can use pivot tables to make this job far easier. Combine all of your lists into a single list with a new column called Source. In the Source column, identify which list the data came from. Build a pivot table from the combined list, with Name in rows, RSVP in values, and Source in columns. Turn off the Grand Total row, and you have a neat list showing a superset from day to day, as shown below.

	A	B	C
1	Combine all Lists		
2			
3	Name	RSVP	Source
13	Ute Simon	2	Monday
14	Yesenia Garcia	2	Monday
15	Andrew Spain	3	Tuesday
16	Caroline Bonner	2	Tuesday
17	Dawn Kosmakos	1	Tuesday
18	Kathryn Sullivan	2	Tuesday
19	M.R. Rosenkrantz	1	Tuesday
20	Martin Lucas	2	Tuesday
21	Melissa Esquibel	2	Tuesday
22	Michael Karpfen	2	Tuesday
23	Peter Harvest	2	Tuesday
24	Roger Fisher	1	Tuesday
25	Sabine Hanschitz	1	Tuesday
26	Ute Simon	2	Tuesday
27	Yesenia Garcia	2	Tuesday
28	Andrew Spain	3	Wednesday
29	Jean-Yves Hemlin	1	Wednesday

Sum of RSVP	Source		
Name	Monday	Tuesday	Wednesday
Andrew Spain		3	3
Carl Hjortsjö	2		
Caroline Bonner	2	2	
Dawn Kosmakos	2	1	
Jean-Yves Hemlin			1
Jeff Long	1		
Jeffrey P. Coulson			2
John Durran			1
Kathryn Sullivan		2	1
Kevin Lehrbass			1
M.R. Rosenkrantz	1	1	2
Martin Lucas	2	2	1
Melissa Esquibel		2	2
Michael Karpfen		2	2
Paul Hannelly	2		
Peter Harvest		2	1
Roger Fisher	1	1	1
Sabine Hanschitz	1	1	2
Ute Simon	2	2	2
Yesenia Garcia	2	2	
Grand Total	18	23	22

Bonus Tip: Show Up/Down Markers

There is a super-obscure way to add up/down markers to a pivot table to indicate an increase or a decrease.

Somewhere outside the pivot table, add columns to show increases or decreases. In the figure below, the difference between I6 and H6 is 3, but you just want to record this as a positive change. Use SIGN(I6-H6) to get either +1, 0, or -1.

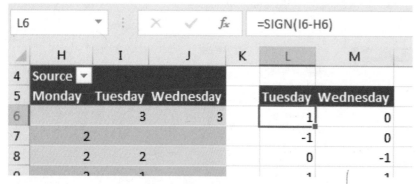

Select the two-column range showing the sign of the change and then select Home, Conditional Formatting, Icon Sets, 3 Triangles. (I have no idea why Microsoft called this option 3 Triangles, when it is clearly 2 Triangles and a Dash, as shown below.)

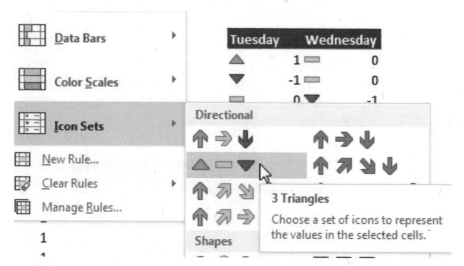

With the same range selected, now select Home, Conditional Formatting, Manage Rules, Edit Rule. Check the Show Icon Only checkbox.

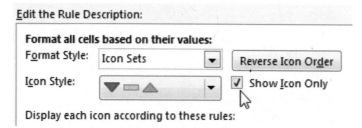

With the same range selected, press Ctrl+C to copy. Select the first Tuesday cell in the pivot table. From the Home tab, open the Paste dropdown and choose Linked Picture. Excel pastes a live picture of the icons above the table.

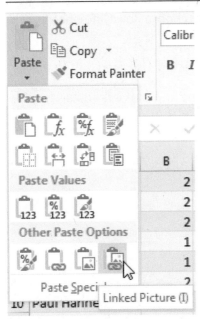

At this point, adjust the column widths of the extra two columns showing the icons so that the icons line up next to the numbers in your pivot table, as shown below.

Name	Monday	Tuesday	Wednesday
Andrew Spain		▲ 3	▭ 3
Carl Hjortsjö	2	▼	▭
Caroline Bonner	2	▭ 2	▼

After seeing this result, I don't really like the thick yellow dash to indicate no change. If you don't like it either, select Home, Conditional Formatting, Manage Rules, Edit. Open the dropdown for the thick yellow dash and choose No Cell Icon, and you get the result shown below.

Andrew Spain		▲ 3	3
Carl Hjortsjö	2	▼	
Caroline Bonner	2	2	▼
Dawn Kosmakos	2	▼ 1	▼

Bonus Tip: Compare Two Lists by Using Go To Special

This tip is not as robust as using a Pivot Table to Compare Two Lists, but it comes in handy when you have to compare one column to another column.

In the figure below, say that you want to find any changes between column A and column D.

	A	B	C	D	
1	Product	Price		Product	Price
2	Apple	1.95		Apple	
3	Banana	2.95		Banana	
4	Cherry	3.95		Clementine	
5	Dill	4.95		Dill	
6	Eggplant	5.95		Eggplant	
7	Fig	6.95		Fig	
8	Guava	7.95		Grapes	
9	H		Go To Special		8
10					

Select the data in A2:A9 and then hold down the Ctrl key while you select the data in D2:D9.

Select, Home, Find & Select, Go To Special. Then, in the Go To Special dialog, choose Row Differences. Click OK.

Only the items in column A that do not match the items in column D are selected. Use a red font to mark these items, as shown below.

	A	B	C	D	E
1	Product ▼	Price ▼		Product ▼	Price ▼
2	Apple	1.95		Apple	1.95
3	Banana	2.95		Banana	2.95
4	Cherry	3.95		Clementine	3.95
5	Dill	4.95		Dill	4.95
6	Eggplant	5.95		Eggplant	5.95
7	Fig	6.95		Fig	6.95
8	Guava	7.95		Grapes	7.95
9	Herbs	8.95		Herbs	8.95

Caution: This technique works only for lists that are mostly identical. If you insert one new row near the top of the second list, causing all future rows to be offset by one row, each of those rows is marked as a row difference.

Thanks to Colleen Young for this tip.

#35 Build Dashboards with Sparklines and Slicers

New tools debuted in Excel 2010 that let you create interactive dashboards that do not look like Excel. This figure shows an Excel workbook with two slicers, Region and Line, used to filter the data. Also in this figure, pivot charts plus a collection of sparkline charts illustrate sales trends.

You can use a setup like this and give your manager's manager a touch screen. All you have to do is teach people how to use the slicers, and they will be able to use this interactive tool for running reports. Touch the East region and the Books line. All of the charts update to reflect sales of books in the East region.

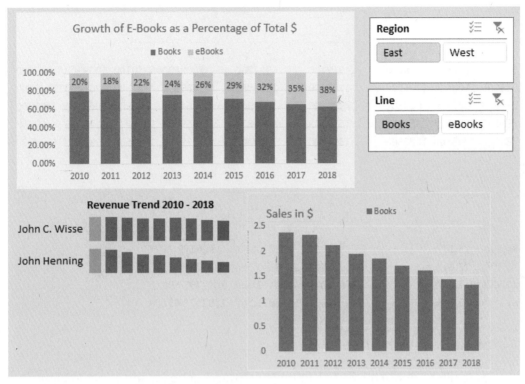

Switch to eBooks, and the data updates.

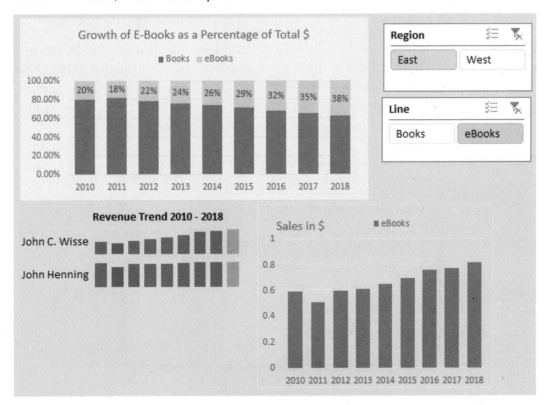

Pivot Tables Galore

Arrange your charts so they fit the size of your display monitor. Each pivot chart has an associated pivot table that does not need to be seen. Those pivot tables can be moved to another sheet or to columns outside of the area seen on the display.

Note: This technique requires all pivot tables share a pivot table cache. I have a video showing how to use VBA to synchronize slicers from two data sets at http://mrx.cl/syncslicer.

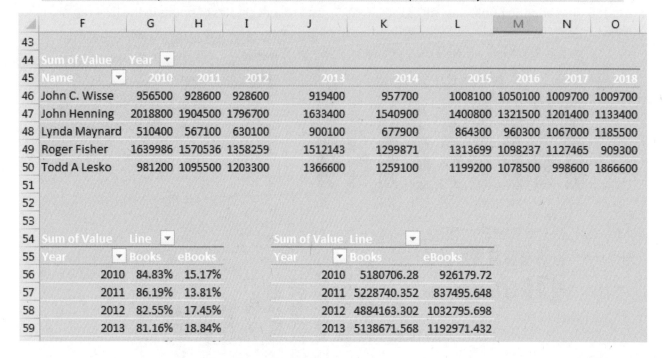

Sum of Value	Year									
Name	2010	2011	2012	2013	2014	2015	2016	2017	2018
John C. Wisse	956500	928600	928600	919400	957700	1008100	1050100	1009700	1009700
John Henning	2018800	1904500	1796700	1633400	1540900	1400800	1321500	1201400	1133400
Lynda Maynard	510400	567100	630100	900100	677900	864300	960300	1067000	1185500
Roger Fisher	1639986	1570536	1358259	1512143	1299871	1313699	1098237	1127465	909300
Todd A Lesko	981200	1095500	1203300	1366600	1259100	1199200	1078500	998600	1866600

Sum of Value	Line			Sum of Value	Line		
Year	Books	eBooks		Year	Books	eBooks	
2010	84.83%	15.17%		2010	5180706.28	926179.72	
2011	86.19%	13.81%		2011	5228740.352	837495.648	
2012	82.55%	17.45%		2012	4884163.302	1032795.698	
2013	81.16%	18.84%		2013	5138671.568	1192971.432	

Filter Multiple Pivot Tables with Slicers

Slicers provide a visual way to filter. Choose the first pivot table on your dashboard and select Analyze, Slicers. Add slicers for region and line. Use the Slicer Tools tab in the Ribbon to change the color and the number of columns in each slicer. Resize the slicers to fit and then arrange them on your dashboard.

Initially, the slicers are tied to only the first pivot table. Select a cell in the second pivot table and choose Filter Connections (aka Slicer Connections in Excel 2010). Indicate which slicers should be tied to this pivot table. In many cases, you will tie each pivot table to all slicers. But not always. For example, in the chart showing how Books and eBooks add up to 100%, you need to keep all lines. The Filter Connections dialog box choices for that pivot table connect to the Region slicer but not the Line slicer.

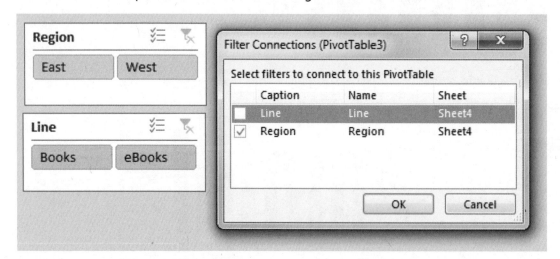

Sparklines: Word-Sized Charts

Professor Edward Tufte introduced sparklines in his 2007 book *Beautiful Evidence*. Excel 2010 implemented sparklines as either line, column, or win/loss charts, where each series fills a single cell.

Personally, I like my sparklines to be larger. In this example, I changed the row height to 30 and <gasp> merged B14:D14 into a single cell to make the charts wider. The labels in A14:A18 are formulas that point to the first column of the pivot table.

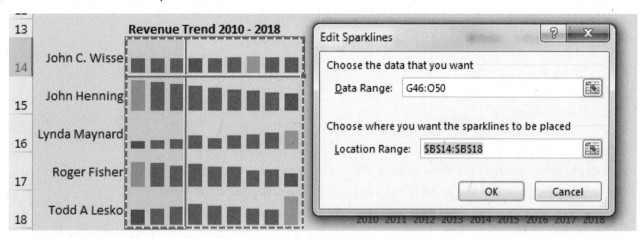

To change the color of the low and high points, choose these boxes in the Sparkline Tools tab:

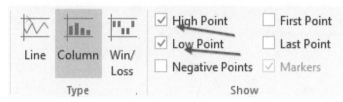

Then change the color for the high and low points:

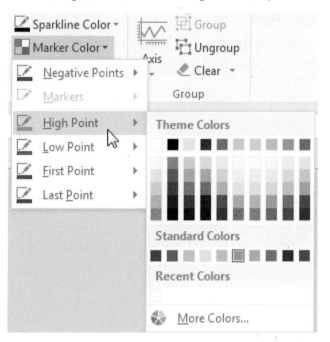

By default, sparklines are scaled independently of each other. I almost always go to the Axis settings and choose Same for All Sparklines for Minimum and Maximum. Below, I set Minimum to 0 for all sparklines.

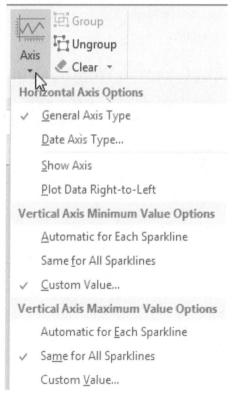

2

Make Excel Not Look Like Excel

With several easy settings, you can make a dashboard look less like Excel:

- Select all cells and apply a light fill color to get rid of the gridlines.

- On the View tab, uncheck Formula Bar, Headings, and Gridlines.

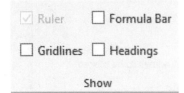

- Collapse the Ribbon: at the right edge of the Ribbon, use the ^ to collapse. (You can use Ctrl+F1 or double-click the active tab in the Ribbon to toggle from collapsed to pinned.)

- Use the arrow keys to move the active cell so it is hidden behind a chart or slicer.

- Hide all sheets except for the dashboard sheet.

- In File, Options, Advanced, hide the scroll bars and sheet tabs.

Display options for this workbook: 12SparklinesSlicers....

  Show horizontal scroll bar
  Show vertical scroll bar
  Show sheet tabs

Bonus Tip: Make Your Workbook into a Web App

Create a named range such as DisplayMe that surrounds your dashboard. To do so, select File, Info, Browser View Options. Choose Items in the Workbook on the Show tab and select the named range DisplayMe.

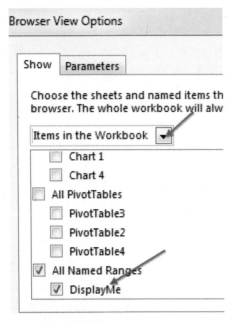

Save your workbook to a OneDrive location. Use File, Share and ask for a sharing link, as shown below.

Share

12SparklinesSlicers

Mary Ellen Jelen's OneDrive » Public

Share

 Invite People

 Get a Sharing Link

 Post to Social Networks

Get a Sharing Link

Sharing Links are useful for sharing with large group

View Link

https://onedrive.live.com/redir?page=view&resid=

Edit Link

Anyone with an edit link can edit this document

Shared with

Anyone who has the link can open the file in a browser and interact with the slicers. Try it: mrx.cl/livdashboard.

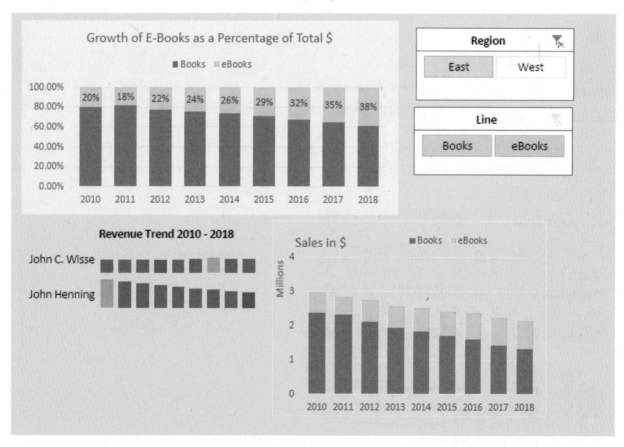

DisplayMe

Caution: Anyone who has the link can download the workbook and unhide the data sheets.

Bonus Tip: Line Up Dashboard Sections with Different Column Widths

If you are anything like me, you often need to fit a lot of data into a small area in a dashboard. What if columns in one dashboard tile don't line up with columns in another tile? Using a linked picture will solve the problem. In the figure below, the report in A1:M9 requires 13 columns. But the report in Rows 11:13 needs that same space to be two columns. I am never one to recommend merged cells, so let's not broach that evil topic.

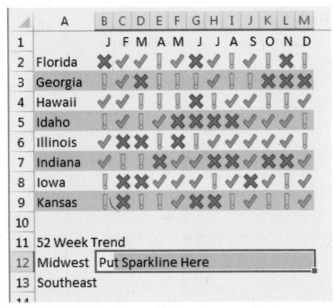

Instead, go to another section of the workbook and build the report tile. Copy the cells that encompass the tile.

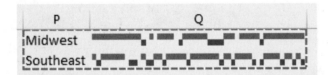

Select where you want the tile to appear. On the Home tab, click on the lower half of the Paste dropdown to open the paste options. The last icon is Paste Picture Link. Click that icon. A live picture of the other cells appears.

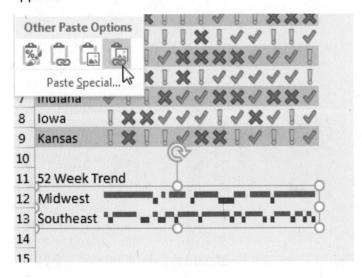

Bonus Tip: Use Picture Lookup

I love this technique, which essentially does a VLOOKUP that returns a picture selected in response to a formula answer. In the image below, make sure that your lookup table starts in row 2 or below. It cannot start in row 1.

In cell C6, someone enters how many passengers need to be accommodated.

A cool new function called IFS in C7 figures out which row in the table contains the picture that you want to show. In this case, there are 7 passengers, which means you need a 12-passenger van.

Those icons are an Office 365 feature found under Insert, Icons. But you could use any clipart or photos.

The table below appears on a worksheet called Icons. The OFFSET function in A10 tells Excel to start in Icons!$B$1, move down 3 rows, move over 0 columns, and select a range 1 row tall by 1 column wide.

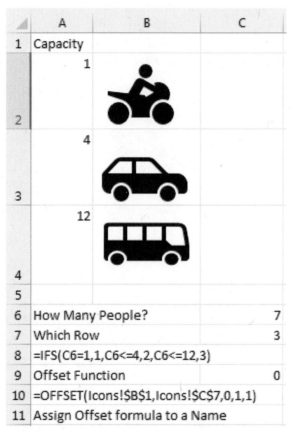

I always build the OFFSET function in a cell to ensure that I don't get any syntax errors. But when you use the technique described here, you cannot use OFFSET in a cell. You have to copy the formula and use Formulas, Define Name and create a name that refers to the OFFSET formula.

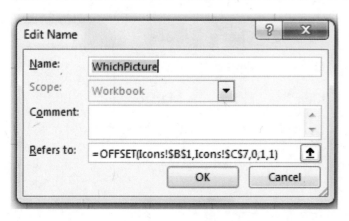

Copy the cell containing the first picture in your table. Go to the dashboard and use Paste Picture Link, as discussed in the previous topic. Look in the formula bar, and you see that this linked picture is coming from =$B$2, or =Icons$B$2 if you are on a different worksheet.

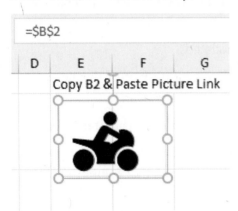

With the linked picture still selected, click in the formula bar. Change the formula for the linked picture to point to the name that you gave to the OFFSET formula. Amazingly, the picture will now update any time that the calculation in C7 points to a new vehicle.

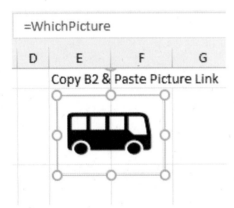

Thanks to Ghaleb Bakri for suggesting a similar technique using dropdown boxes. Ryan Wilson suggested making Excel not look like Excel. Jon Wittwer of Vertex42 suggested the sparklines and slicers trick. Mynda Treacy taught me the picture lookup in her amazing dashboard course at mrx.cl/dashcourse.

Bonus Tip: Report Slicer Selections in a Title

Slicers are great, but they can take up a lot of space in a print out.

Here is an awesome way to get the selected slicers in a single cell. First, select your entire pivot table and copy with Ctrl+C.

Then, paste a new pivot table somewhere outside of your print range. Copying and pasting makes sure that both pivot tables react to the slicer. Change the pivot table so you have the slicer field in the Row area. Right-click the Grand Total and choose Remove Grand Total. You should end up with a pivot table that looks like this:

	I	J
1	Ctrl+V	
2		
3	Product	
4	Apple	
5	Cherry	
6	Guava	

The list of products starts in I4 and might potentially extend to I26. Use the new TEXTJOIN function to join all of the selected products in a single cell. The first argument of TEXTJOIN is the delimiter. I use a comma followed by a space. The second argument tells Excel to ignore empty cells. This makes sure that Excel does not add a bunch of commas to the end of your formula result.

	A	B	C	D
1	Report for Apple, Cherry, Guava, Lime, Orange			
2	="Report for "&TEXTJOIN(", ",TRUE,I4:I26)			
3	Rep	Sum of Sales		
4	Andy	7905		
5	Betty	6214		
6	Charlie	21120		
7	Dale	17902		
8	Eddy	20532		
9	Grand Total	73673		
10				

#36 See Why GETPIVOTDATA Might Not Be Entirely Evil

Most people first encounter GETPIVOTDATA when they try to build a formula outside a pivot table that uses numbers in the pivot table. For example, this variance percentage won't copy down to the other months due to Excel inserting GETPIVOTDATA functions.

```
=GETPIVOTDATA("Sales",$B$3,"Date",1,
"Years",2019)/GETPIVOTDATA("Sales",$B$3,
"Date",1,"Years",2018)-1
```

	B	C	D	E	F	G
	Sales	Years				
	Date	2018	2019	% Change		
	Jan	80772	77864	-3.6%		
	Feb	81151	84640	-3.6%		
	Mar	80773	77381	-3.6%		

Excel inserts GETPIVOTDATA any time you use the mouse or arrow keys to point to a cell inside the pivot table while building a formula outside the pivot table.

By the way, if you don't want the GETPIVOTDATA function to appear, simply type a formula such as =D5/C5-1 without using the mouse or arrow keys to point to cells. That formula copies without any problems.

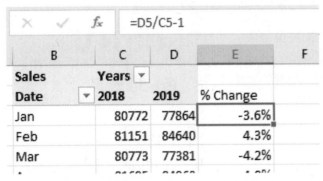

B	C	D	E	F
Sales	Years ▼			
Date ▼	2018	2019	% Change	
Jan	80772	77864	-3.6%	
Feb	81151	84640	4.3%	
Mar	80773	77381	-4.2%	

Here is a data set that contains one plan number per month per store. There are also actual sales per month per store for the months that are complete. Your goal is to build a report that shows actuals for the completed months and plan for the future months.

	A	B	C	D
1	Store	Month	Type	Sales
1727	Fair Oaks Mall	Dec	Plan	123700
1728	Bellevue Square	Dec	Plan	140500
1729	U Village	Dec	Plan	126600
1730	Park Place	Jan	Actual	13475
1731	Kierland Commons	Jan	Actual	11708
1732	Scottsdale Fashion Square	Jan	Actual	12415
1733	Chandler Fashion Center	Jan	Actual	12848

Build a pivot table with Store in Rows. Put Month and Type in Columns. You get the report shown below, with January Actual, January Plan, and the completely nonsensical January Actual+Plan.

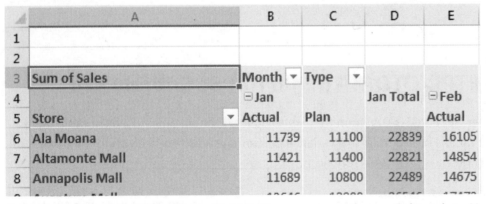

	A	B	C	D	E
1					
2					
3	Sum of Sales	Month ▼	Type ▼		
4		⊟ Jan		Jan Total	⊟ Feb
5	Store ▼	Actual	Plan		Actual
6	Ala Moana	11739	11100	22839	16105
7	Altamonte Mall	11421	11400	22821	14854
8	Annapolis Mall	11689	10800	22489	14675

If you select a month cell and go to Field Settings, you can change Subtotals to None.

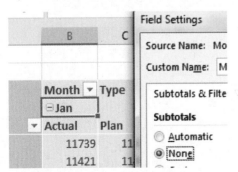

This removes the useless Actual+Plan. But you still have to get rid of the plan columns for January through April. There is no good way to do this inside the pivot table.

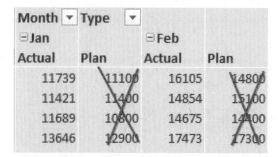

So, your monthly workflow becomes:

1. Add the actuals for the new month to the data set.

2. Build a new pivot table from scratch.

3. Copy the pivot table and paste as values so it is not a pivot table anymore.

4. Delete the columns that you don't need.

There is a better way to go. The following very compressed figure shows a new Excel worksheet added to the workbook. This is all just straight Excel, no pivot tables. The only bit of magic is an IF function in row 4 that toggles from Actual to Plan, based on the date in cell P1.

E4			fx	=IF((1+MONTH($P1))>COLUMN(A1),"Actual","Plan")													
	A	B	C	D	E	F	G	H	I	J	K	L	M	N	O	P	Q	R
1	**XYZ Company Super Report**													Actuals Through:		4/30		
2																		
3					Jan	Feb	Mar	Apr	May	Jun	Jul	Aug	Sep	Oct	Nov	Dec		
4					Actual	Actual	Actual	Actual	Plan	Plan	Plan	Plan	Plan	Plan	Plan	Plan	Total	
5			Houston Area															
6			Baybrook														$0K	
7			Highland Village														OK	
8			Willowbrook														OK	
9			The Woodlands Mall														OK	
10			Houston Total		$0K	$0K	$0K	$0K	$0K	$0K	$0K	$0K	$0K	$0K	$0K	$0K	$0K	
11																		
12			Dallas/Forth Worth Area															
13			Firewheel														$0K	
14			Galleria														OK	
15			Hulen Mall														OK	
16			Northeast Mall														OK	
17			Northpark Center														OK	
18			The Parks														OK	

The very first cell that needs to be filled in is January Actual for Baybrook. Click in that cell and type an equal sign.

Using the mouse, navigate back to the pivot table. Find the cell for January Actual for Baybrook. Click on that cell and press Enter. As usual, Excel builds one of those annoying GETPIVOTDATA functions that cannot be copied.

But today, let's study the syntax of GETPIVOTDATA.

The first argument below is the numeric field "Sales". The second argument is the cell where the pivot table resides. The remaining pairs of arguments are field name and value. Do you see what the auto-generated formula did? It hard-coded "Baybrook" as the name of the store. That is why you cannot copy these auto-generated GETPIVOTDATA formulas. They actually hard-code names into formulas. Even though you can't copy these formulas, you can edit them. In this case, it would be better if you edited the formula to point to cell $D6.

	D	E	F	G	H	I	J	K	L	M	
1	uper Report										Ac
2											
3		Jan	Feb	Mar	Apr	May	Jun	Jul	Aug	Sep	
4		Actual	Actual	Actual	Actual	Plan	Plan	Plan	Plan	Plan	
5	rea										
6	Baybrook	=GETPIVOTDATA("Sales",Sheet3!$A$3,"Store","Baybrook","Month","Jan","Type","Actual")									
7	Highland Village										

The figure below shows the formula after you edit it. Gone are "Baybrook", "Jan", and "Actual". Instead, you are pointing to $D6, E$3, and E$4.

	D	E	F	G	H	I	J	K	L	
1	ny Super Report									
2										
3		Jan	Feb	Mar	Apr	May	Jun	Jul	Aug	
4		Actual	Actual	Actual	Actual	Plan	Plan	Plan	Plan	
5	rea									
6	Baybrook	=GETPIVOTDATA("Sales",Sheet3!$A$3,"Store",$D6,"Month",E$3,"Type",E$4)								
7	Highland Village									
8		GETPIVOTDATA(data_field, pivot_table, [field1, item1], [field2, item2], [field3, item3], [field4, item4],								

Copy this formula and then choose Paste Special, Formulas in all of the other numeric cells.

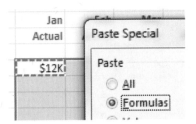

Now here's your monthly workflow:

1. Build an ugly pivot table that no one will ever see.

2. Set up the report worksheet.

Each month, you have to:

1. Paste new actuals below the data.

2. Refresh the ugly pivot table.

3. Change cell P1 on the report sheet to reflect the new month. All the numbers update.

	C	D	E	F	G	H	I	J	K	L	M	N	O	P	Q
1	ompany Super Report												Actuals Through:	5/31	
2															
3			Jan	Feb	Mar	Apr	May	Jun	Jul	Aug	Sep	Oct	Nov	Dec	
4			Actual	Actual	Actual	Actual	Actual	Plan	Plan	Plan	Plan	Plan	Plan	Plan	Total
5	Houston Area														
6		Baybrook	$12K	$17K	$22K	$25K	$24K	$32K	$28K	$24K	$20K	$32K	$49K	$121K	$406K
7		Highland Village	13K	17K	20K	24K	23K	33K	29K	24K	20K	33K	49K	122K	406K
8		Willowbrook	15K	19K	24K	30K	30K	37K	32K	28K	23K	37K	55K	138K	467K
9		The Woodlands Mall	14K	19K	24K	28K	27K	36K	32K	27K	23K	36K	54K	135K	453K
10	Houston Total		$54K	$71K	$90K	$106K	$103K	$138K	$120K	$103K	$86K	$138K	$207K	$516K	$1,732K
11															
12	Dallas/Forth Worth Area														
13		Firewheel	$11K	$15K	$18K	$23K	$22K	$29K	$25K	$22K	$18K	$29K	$43K	$108K	$364K

You have to admit that using a report that pulls numbers from a pivot table gives you the best of both worlds. You are free to format the report in ways that you cannot format a pivot table. Blank rows are fine. You can have currency symbols on the first and last rows but not in between. You get double-underlines under the grand totals, too.

Thanks to @iTrainerMX for suggesting this feature.

#37 Eliminate VLOOKUP with the Data Model

Say that you have a data set with product, date, customer, and sales information.

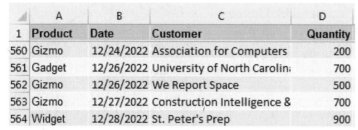

	A	B	C	D
1	Product	Date	Customer	Quantity
560	Gizmo	12/24/2022	Association for Computers	200
561	Gadget	12/26/2022	University of North Carolina	700
562	Gizmo	12/26/2022	We Report Space	500
563	Gizmo	12/27/2022	Construction Intelligence &	700
564	Widget	12/28/2022	St. Peter's Prep	900

The IT department forgot to put sector in there. Here is a lookup table that maps customer to sector. Time for a VLOOKUP, right?

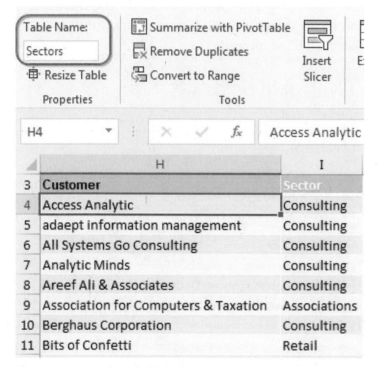

	H	I
3	Customer	Sector
4	Access Analytic	Consulting
5	adaept information management	Consulting
6	All Systems Go Consulting	Consulting
7	Analytic Minds	Consulting
8	Areef Ali & Associates	Consulting
9	Association for Computers & Taxation	Associations
10	Berghaus Corporation	Consulting
11	Bits of Confetti	Retail

There is no need to do VLOOKUPs to join these data sets if you have Excel 2013 or newer. These versions of Excel have incorporated the Power Pivot engine into the core Excel. (You could also do this by using the Power Pivot add-in for Excel 2010, but there are a few extra steps.)

In both the original data set and the lookup table, use Home, Format as Table. On the Table Tools tab, rename the table from Table1 to something meaningful. I've used Data and Sectors.

Select one cell in the data table. Choose Insert, Pivot Table. Starting in Excel 2013, there is an extra box, Add This Data to the Data Model, that you should select before clicking OK.

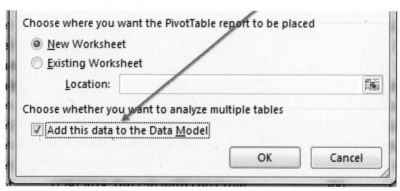

The Pivot Table Fields list appears, with the fields from the Data table. Choose Revenue. Because you are using the Data Model, a new line appears at the top of the list, offering Active or All. Click All.

Surprisingly, the PivotTable Fields list offers all the other tables in the workbook. This is ground-breaking. You haven't done a VLOOKUP yet. Expand the Sectors table and choose Sector. Two things happen to warn you that there is a problem.

First, the pivot table appears with the same number in all the cells.

Row Labels	Sum of Revenue
Applications	6707812
Associations	6707812
Consulting	6707812
Retail	6707812
Services	6707812
Training	6707812
Utilities	6707812
Grand Total	6707812

Perhaps the more subtle warning is a yellow box that appears at the top of the PivotTable Fields list, indicating that you need to create a relationship. Choose Create. (If you are in Excel 2010 or 2016, try your luck with Auto-Detect - it often succeeds.)

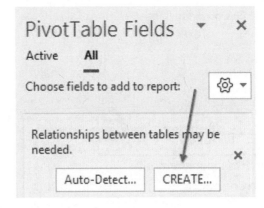

In the Create Relationship dialog, you have four dropdown menus. Choose Data under Table, Customer under Column (Foreign), and Sectors under Related Table. Power Pivot will automatically fill in the matching column under Related Column (Primary). Click OK.

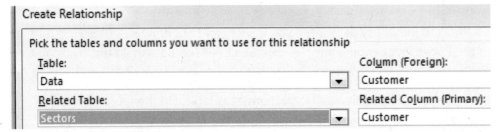

The resulting pivot table is a mash up of the original data and the data in the lookup table. No VLOOKUPs required.

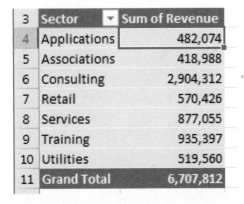

Sector	Sum of Revenue
Applications	482,074
Associations	418,988
Consulting	2,904,312
Retail	570,426
Services	877,055
Training	935,397
Utilities	519,560
Grand Total	6,707,812

Bonus Tip: Count Distinct

To see an annoyance with pivot tables, drag the Customer column from the Data table to the VALUES area. The field says Count of Customer, but it is really a count of the invoices belong to each sector. What if you really want to see how many unique customers belong to each sector?

Sector	Sum of Revenue	Count of Customer
Applications	482,074	44
Associations	418,988	32
Consulting	2,904,312	238
Retail	570,426	49
Services	877,055	79
Training	935,397	75
Utilities	519,560	46
Grand Total	6,707,812	563

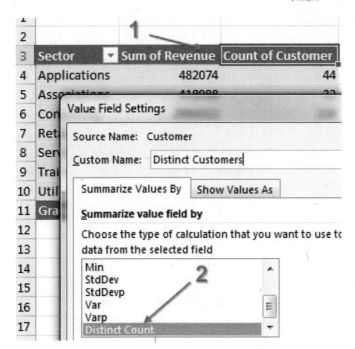

Double-click the Count of Customer heading. At first, the Summarize Values By offers choices such as Sum, Average, and Count. Scroll down to the bottom. Because the pivot table is based on the Data Model, you now have Distinct Count.

After you select Distinct Count, the pivot table shows a distinct count of customers for each sector. This was very hard to do in regular pivot tables.

Sector	Revenue	Distinct Customers
Applications	482,074	6
Associations	418,988	5
Consulting	2,904,312	30
Retail	570,426	5
Services	877,055	10
Training	935,397	11
Utilities	519,560	6
Grand Total	6,707,812	73

Thanks to Colin Michael and Alejandro Quiceno for suggesting Power Pivot.

#38 Compare Budget Versus Actual via Power Pivot

Budgets are done at the top level – revenue by product line by region by month. Actuals accumulate slowly over time – invoice by invoice, line item by line item. Comparing the small Budget file to the voluminous Actual data has been a pain forever. I love this trick from Rob Collie, aka PowerPivotPro.com.

To set up the example, you have a 54-row budget table: 1 row per month per region per product.

	A	B	C	D
1	Budget - Top Level			
2				
3	Product	Region	Date	Budget
52	Whatsit	West	1/31/2018	10,300
53	Whatsit	West	2/28/2018	10,600
54	Whatsit	West	3/31/2018	10,900
55	Whatsit	West	4/30/2018	11,200
56	Whatsit	West	5/31/2018	11,500
57	Whatsit	West	6/30/2018	11,800

The invoice file is at the detail level: 422 rows so far this year.

	M	N	O	P	Q
1	Invoice Detail				
2					
3	Invoice	Date	Region	Product	Revenue
417	1414	6/26/2015	Central	Widget	1728
418	1415	6/29/2015	West	Gadget	1719
419	1416	6/29/2015	East	Widget	2199
420	1417	6/29/2015	Central	Widget	2087
421	1418	6/29/2015	East	WhatsIt	2309
422	1419	6/29/2015	Central	Widget	1652
423	1420	6/30/2015	Central	Gadget	1994
424	1421	6/30/2015	Central	WhatsIt	2055
425	1422	6/30/2015	East	Gadget	1931

There is no VLOOKUP in the world that will ever let you match these two data sets. But, thanks to Power Pivot (aka the Data Model in Excel 2013+), this becomes easy.

You need to create tiny little tables that I call "joiners" to link the two larger data sets. In my case, Product, Region, and Date are in common between the two tables. The Product table is a tiny four-cell table. Ditto for Region. Create each of those by copying data from one table and using Remove Duplicates.

Illustration: George Berlin

"Joiners"

Product	Region	Date	Month
Gadget	Central	1/2/2018	2018-01
WhatsIt	East	1/5/2018	2018-01
Widget	West	1/6/2018	2018-01
		1/7/2018	2018-01
		1/8/2018	2018-01
		1/9/2018	2018-01

The calendar table on the right was actually tougher to create. The budget data has one row per month, always falling on the end of the month. The invoice data shows daily dates, usually weekdays. So, I had to copy the Date field from both data sets into a single column and then remove duplicates to make sure that all dates are represented. I then used =TEXT(J4,"YYYY-MM") to create a Month column from the daily dates.

If you don't have the full Power Pivot add-in, you need to create a pivot table from the Budget table and select the checkbox for Add This Data to the Data Model.

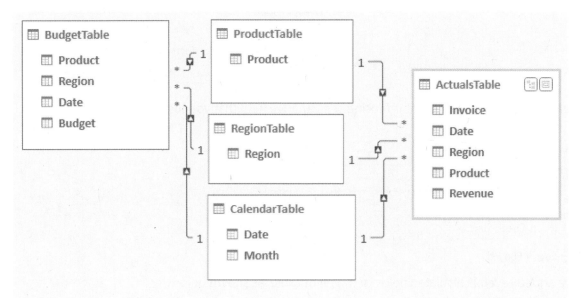

As discussed in the previous tip, as you add fields to the pivot table, you will have to define six relationships. While you could do this with six visits to the Create Relationship dialog, I fired up my Power Pivot add-in and used the diagram view to define the six relationships.

Here is the key to making all of this work: You are free to use the numeric fields from Budget and from Actual. But if you want to show Region, Product, or Month in the pivot table, they must come from the joiner tables!

Here is a pivot table with data coming from five tables. Column A is coming from the Region joiner. Row 2 is coming from the Calendar joiner. The Product slicer is from the Product joiner. The Budget numbers come from the Budget table, and the Actual numbers come from the Invoice table.

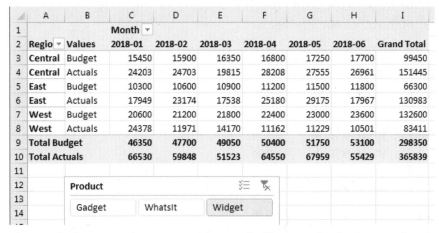

	A	B	C	D	E	F	G	H	I
1			Month						
2	Regio	Values	2018-01	2018-02	2018-03	2018-04	2018-05	2018-06	Grand Total
3	Central	Budget	15450	15900	16350	16800	17250	17700	99450
4	Central	Actuals	24203	24703	19815	28208	27555	26961	151445
5	East	Budget	10300	10600	10900	11200	11500	11800	66300
6	East	Actuals	17949	23174	17538	25180	29175	17967	130983
7	West	Budget	20600	21200	21800	22400	23000	23600	132600
8	West	Actuals	24378	11971	14170	11162	11229	10501	83411
9	Total Budget		46350	47700	49050	50400	51750	53100	298350
10	Total Actuals		66530	59848	51523	64550	67959	55429	365839
11									
12		Product							
13									
14		Gadget		WhatsIt		Widget			

This works because the joiner tables apply filters to the Budget and Actual table. It is a beautiful technique and shows that Power Pivot is not just for big data.

Bonus Tip: Portable Formulas

If you have the full version of Power Pivot, you can use the DAX formula language to create new calculated fields. From the Power Pivot tab in the Ribbon, choose Measures, New Measure.

Give the field a name, such as Variance. When you go to type the formula, type =[. As soon as you type the square bracket, Excel gives you a list of fields to choose from.

Note that you can also assign a numeric format to these calculated fields. Wouldn't it be great if regular pivot tables brought the numeric formatting from the underlying data?

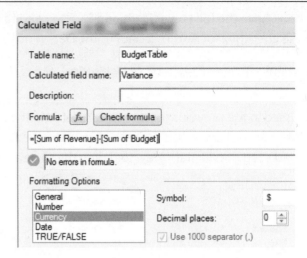

In the next calculation, VariancePercent is reusing the Variance field that you just defined.

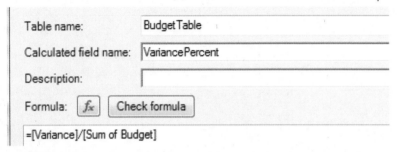

So far, you've added several calculated fields to the pivot table, as shown below.

Region	Values	Month 2018-01	2018-02
Central	Sum of Budget	7730	7950
Central	Sum of Revenue	10539	13909
Central	Variance	$2,809	$5,959
Central	VariancePercent	36.3 %	75.0 %

But you don't have to leave any of those fields in the pivot table. If your manager only cares about the variance percentage, you can remove all of the other numeric fields.

VariancePercent	Region			
Month	Central	East	West	Grand Total
2018-01	▲ 36.3 %	▲ 27.8 %	▼ -76.8 %	▼ -15.8 %
2018-02	▲ 75.0 %	▲ 9.8 %	▼ -83.0 %	▼ -9.7 %
2018-03	▼ -22.6 %	▲ 120.9 %	▼ -56.4 %	▼ -5.7 %
2018-04	▲ 187.3 %	▲ 2.7 %	▼ -66.9 %	▲ 33.3 %
2018-05	▲ 158.9 %	▲ 191.4 %	▼ -33.4 %	▲ 80.7 %
2018-06	▲ 7.1 %	▲ 108.9 %	▼ -48.5 %	▲ 5.0 %
Grand Total	▲ 74.4 %	▲ 78.8 %	▼ -60.2 %	▲ 15.6 %

Product		✅≣	▼
Gadget	WhatsIt	Widget	

Note that the DAX in this bonus tip is barely scratching the surface of what is possible. If you want to explore Power Pivot, you need to get a copy of *Power Pivot and Power BI* by Rob Collie.

Thanks to Rob Collie for teaching me this feature. Find Rob at www.PowerPivotPro.com.

Bonus Tip: Text in the Values of a Pivot Table

Another amazing use for a measure in a Data Model pivot table is to use the CONCATENATEX function to move text into the values area of a pivot table.

In this data set, there is an original and revised value for each sales rep.

	A	B	C	D	E
1	Region	Market	Rep	Version	Code
2	East	NYC	Andy	Original	Guava
3	East	NYC	Andy	Revised	Date
4	Central	ORD	Barb	Original	Guava
5	Central	ORD	Barb	Revised	Melon
6	West	LAX	Chris	Original	Apple
7	West	LAX	Chris	Revised	Fig

Insert a pivot table and check the box for Add This Data To The Data Model. Drag Rep to the Rows and Version to Columns.

Rep	Version		
	Original	Revised	Grand Total *
Andy			
Barb			
Chris			

The Grand Totals get really ugly, so you should remove them now. On the Design tab, use Grand Totals, Off For Rows and Columns.

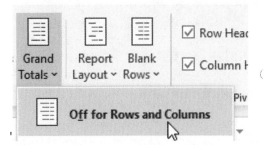

In the Pivot Table Fields panel, right-click the Table name and choose Add Measure.

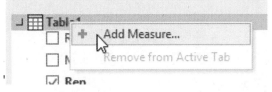

The formula for the measure is =CONCATENATEX(Values(Table1[Code]),Table1[Code],", "). The VALUES function makes sure that you don't get duplicate values in the answer.

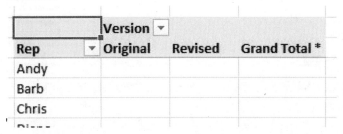

After defining the measure, drag the measure to the Values area. In this case, each cell only has one value.

AllText	Version ▾	
Rep ▾	**Original**	**Revised**
Andy	Guava	Date
Barb	Guava	Melon
Chris	Apple	Fig
Diane	Fig	Fig
Ed	Cherry	Guava

However, if you rearrange the pivot table, you might have multiple values joined in a cell.

AllText	Version ▾	
Market ▾	**Original**	**Revised**
ATL	Fig, Cherry	Fig, Orange
LAX	Apple, Elderberry	Fig, Lime
MSP	Date, Cherry	Guava, Date
NYC	Guava	Date
ORD	Guava, Banana	Melon, Banana
PHL	Date, Fig	Date, Fig
SFO	Honeydew, Elderberry	Honeydew, Iceberg

Caution: A cell may not contain more than 32,768 characters. If you have a large data set, it is possible that this Grand Total of this measure will be more than 32,768 characters. The Excel team never anticipated that a pivot table cell would contain more than this many characters, but thanks to DAX and CONCATENATEX, it can happen. When it does happen, Excel can not draw the pivot table. But - there is no error message - the pivot table simply stops updating until you get rid of the Grand Total or somehow make the largest cell be less than 32,768 characters.

#39 Slicers for Pivot Tables From Two Data Sets

Say that you have two different data sets. You want a pivot table from each data set and you want those two pivot tables to react to one slicer.

This really is the holy grail of Excel questions. Lots of Excel forums have many complicated ways to attempt to make this work. But the easiest way is loading all of the data into the workbook data model.

Both of the tables have to have one field in common. Make a third table with the unique list of values found in either column.

Store Name ▾	Sum of Sales 2019	Store Name ▾	Sum of
Brea Mall	309467	Brea Mall	
Corona Del Mar Plaza	325574	Chino Hills Shoppes	
Fashion Valley	307504	Corona Del Mar Plaza	
Irvine Spectrum	254090	Dos Lagos Center	
Jordan Creek Mall	246447	Fashion Valley	

If the two tables are shown above, the third table has to have Store Names that are found in either table: Brea, Chino Hills, Corona Del Mar, Dos Lagos, Fashion Valley, Irvine, and so on.

Format all three of your tables using Ctrl+T.

Use the Relationships icon on the Data tab to set up a relationship from each of the two original tables to the third table.

If you have access to the Power Pivot grid, the diagram view would look like this:

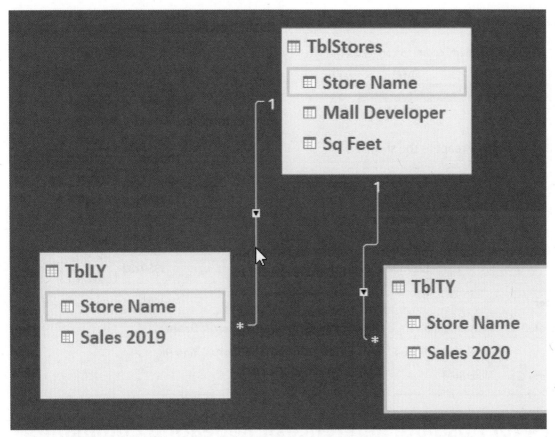

If not, the Relationships diagram should show two relationships, although certainly not as pretty as above.

From either pivot table, choose Insert Slicer. Initially, that slicer will only show one table. Click on the All tab and choose Mall Developer from your third table.

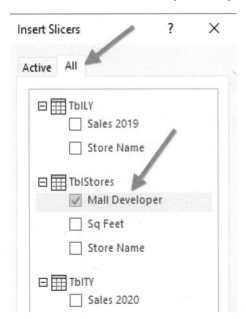

Try and choose a few items from the slicer. Watch your hopes get dashed as only one pivot table reacts. Once you recover, click on the Slicer. In the Slicer Tools Design tab of the Ribbon, choose Report Connections. Add the other pivot table to this slicer:

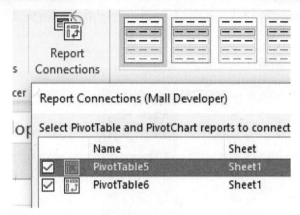

Finally, both pivot tables will react to the slicer.

Store Name	Sum of Sales 2019
Paseo	310198
Simi Valley Town Center	317889
The Galleria Edina	271106
Victoria Gardens	328199
Grand Total *	1227392

Store Name	Sum of Sales 2020
Paseo	341218
Simi Valley Town Center	349678
The Galleria Edina	298217
Victoria Gardens	361019
Grand Total *	1350132

Mall Developer

Caruso Affiliated ...	Developers Divers...	Forest City Manag...	Gabbert & Gabbe...
Investec	Irvine Retail Group	Poag & McEwen L...	Shops At Chino Hi...
Simon Property G...	Westfield	General Growth P...	

#40 Use F4 for Absolute Reference or Repeating Commands

The mighty F4 key should be in your Excel arsenal for two completely different reasons:

- Use F4 to add dollar signs in formula references to make them absolute, mixed, or relative.
- When you are not editing a formula, use F4 to repeat the last command.

Illustration: Cartoon Bob D'Amico

Make a Reference Absolute

In the following figure, the tax in C2 is B2 times F1.

C2			$\times$ $\checkmark$ f_x	=B2*F1				

	A	B	C	D	E	F	
1	Customer	Merchandise $	Tax $		Rate	6.25%	
2	Robert Jelen	24.95	1.56				
3	Sam Radakovitz	114.95					
4	Judy A Glaser	69.95					
5	Diana McGunigale	34.95					
6	Edwin Deo	9.95					
7	Mario Garcia	169.95					
8	Anne Troy	129.95					
9	Robert S. McClellan	154.95					
10	David Gainer	199.95					
11	David Haggarty	109.95					

But when you copy this formula down, none of the sales tax calculations are working. As you copy the formula down the column, the B2 reference automatically changes to B3, B4, and so on. That is what you want. But unfortunately, the reference to the sales tax in F1 is changing as well. That is not what you want.

SUM			$\times$ $\checkmark$ f_x	=B5*F4				

	A	B	C	D	E	F	G
1	Customer	Merchandise $	Tax $		Rate	6.25%	
2	Robert Jelen	24.95	1.56				
3	Sam Radakovitz	114.95	0.00				
4	Judy A Glaser	69.95	0.00				
5	Diana McGunigale	34.95	=B5*F4				
6	Edwin Deo	9.95	0.00				
7	Mario Garcia	169.95	0.00				
8	Anne Troy	129.95	0.00				

The solution? Edit the original formula and press F4. Two dollar signs are added to the final element of the formula. The $F$1 says that no matter where you copy this formula, that part of the formula always needs to point to F1. This is called an absolute reference. Pressing F4 while the insertion point is touching the F1 reference is a fast way to add both dollar signs.

SUM			$\times$ $\checkmark$ f_x	=B2*$F$1			

	A	B	C	D	E	F
1	Customer	Merchandise $	Tax $		Rate	6.25%
2	Robert Jelen	24.95	=B2*$F$1	F4		
3	Sam Radakovitz	114.95	7.18			
4	Judy A Glaser	69.95	4.37			
5	Diana McGunigale	34.95	2.18			

There are other times when you need only part of the reference to be locked. In the following example, you need to multiply H2 by A3 by C1. The H1 will always point to H1, so you need both dollar signs in

$H$1. The A3 will always point back to column A, so you need $A3. The C1 will always point to row 1, so you need C$1.

	A	B	C	D	E	F	G	H
1			105%	107%	103%	115%		Base
2		Name	Q1	Q2	Q3	Q4		10000
3	113%	Micheal Reynolds	=$H$2*$A3*C$1					
4	112%	John Cockerill						
5	115%	Adam Weaver						
6	112%	Michael Dietterick	F4 F4					
7	113%	Ryan Wilson	F4 F4					
8	113%	James Williams	F4					
9	112%	Mike Dolan Fliss	F4					
10	112%	Paul Hannelly						
11	115%	Dawn Kosmakos						
12	112%	Jeff Long						

To enter the above formula, you would press F4 once after clicking on H1, three times after clicking on A3, and twice after clicking on C1. What if you screw up and press F4 too many times? Keep pressing F4: It will toggle back to relative then absolute, then row absolute, then column absolute.

The result? A single formula that can be copied to C3:F12.

F12				f_x	=$H$2*$A12*F$1		

	A	B	C	D	E	F	G	H
1			105%	107%	103%	115%		Base
2		Name	Q1	Q2	Q3	Q4		10000
3	113%	Micheal Reynolds	11865	12091	11639	12995		
4	112%	John Cockerill	11760	11984	11536	12880		
5	115%	Adam Weaver	12075	12305	11845	13225		
6	110%	Michael Dietterick	11550	11770	11330	12650		
7	113%	Ryan Wilson	11865	12091	11639	12995		
8	113%	James Williams	11865	12091	11639	12995		
9	114%	Mike Dolan Fliss	11970	12198	11742	13110		
10	112%	Paul Hannelly	11760	11984	11536	12880		
11	115%	Dawn Kosmakos	12075	12305	11845	13225		
12	112%	Jeff Long	11760	11984	11536	12880		

Repeat the Last Command

Keyboard shortcuts are great. For example, Alt+E, D, C Enter deletes a column. But even if you are really fast at doing Alt+E, D, C Enter, it can be a pain to do this many times in a row.

	A	B	C	D	E	F	G	H	I
1	Name		Q1		Q2		Q3		Q4
2	Jeffrey P. Coulson		161		153		136		163
3									
4	Robert Phillips		150		143		198		161
5									
6	Peter Harvest		132		185		167		150
7			**Alt+EDC**						
8	Trace Cordell		149		140		167		176
9									

After deleting column B, press the Right Arrow key to move to the next column that needs to be deleted. Instead of doing Alt+E, D, C Enter again, simply press F4. This beautiful command repeats the last command that you invoked.

	A	B	C	D	E
1	Name	Q1		Q2	
2	Jeffrey P. Coulson	161		153	
3					
4	Robert Phillips	150		143	
5			**Rt Arrow**		
6	Peter Harvest	132	**F4**	185	
7					

To delete the remaining columns, keep pressing Right Arrow and then F4.

	A	B	C	D	E	F	G
1	Name	Q1	Q2		Q3		Q4
2	Jeffrey P. Coulson	161	153		136		163
3							
4	Robert Phillips	150	143		198		161
5				**Rt Arrow**			
6	Peter Harvest	132	185	**F4**	167		150
7							

Next, you need to delete a row, so use Alt+E, D, R Enter to delete the row.

	A	B	C	D	E
1	Name	Q1	Q2	Q3	Q4
2	Jeffrey P. Coulson	161	153	136	163
3		**Alt+EDR Enter**			
4	Robert Phillips	150	143	198	161
5					
6	Peter Harvest	132	185	167	150

To keep deleting rows, press the Down Arrow key followed by F4 until all the blank rows are gone.

The F4 trick works for a surprising number of commands. Perhaps you just built a custom format to display numbers in thousands: #,##0,K. If you see a few more cells that need the same format, select the cells and press F4.

Annoyingly, a few commands do not work with F4. For example, going into Field Settings in a pivot table and changing the number format and calculation is one that would be nice to repeat. But it does not work.

Bonus Tip: Use a Named Range Instead of Absolute References

If you want to avoid using $ in references to make them absolute, you can use named ranges instead. Select the tax rate cell in F1 and click in the name box to the left of the formula bar.

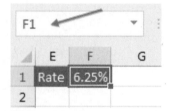

Type a name for this cell or range of cells. You cannot use spaces in the name, but TaxRate (or Tax_Rate) will work.

When you type the formula, use =B2*TaxRate.

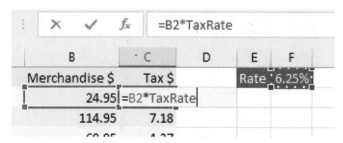

Tip: To see all of the named ranges in a worksheet, reduce the zoom to 39% or lower.

Thanks to Myles Arnott, Glen Feechan, Shelley Fishel, Colin Legg, and Nathan Zelany for suggesting this feature. Bob Umlas sent in the tip about seeing names below 39% zoom.

#41 Quickly Convert Formulas to Values

I always say there are five ways to do anything in Excel. Converting live formulas to values is a task that has far more than five ways. But I will bet that I can teach you two ways that are faster than what you are using now.

The goal is to convert the formulas in column D to values.

You are probably using one of the ways shown below.

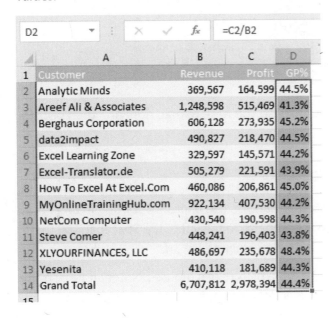

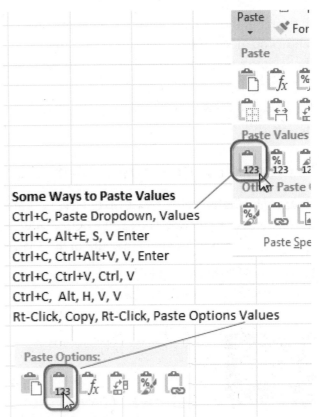

Some Ways to Paste Values

Ctrl+C, Paste Dropdown, Values

Ctrl+C, Alt+E, S, V Enter

Ctrl+C, Ctrl+Alt+V, V, Enter

Ctrl+C, Ctrl+V, Ctrl, V

Ctrl+C, Alt, H, V, V

Rt-Click, Copy, Rt-Click, Paste Options Values

For Those Who Prefer Using the Mouse

If you prefer to use the mouse, nothing is faster than this trick I learned from Dave in Columbus, Indiana. You don't even have to copy the cells using this technique:

1. Select the data.

2. Go to the right edge of the selection box.

3. Hold down the right mouse button while you drag the box to the right.

C	D	E	F	G
Profit	GP%			
164,599	44.5%			
515,469	41.3%			
273,935	45.2%			
218,470	44.5%			
145,571	44.2%			
221,591	43.9%		F2:F14	
206,861	45.0%			

3

4. Keep holding down the right mouse button while you drag the box back to the original location.

5. When you release the right mouse button, in the menu that pops up, select Copy Here As Values Only.

How does anyone ever randomly discover right-click, drag right, drag left, let go? It is not something that you would ever accidentally do.

It turns out the menu is called the Alternate Drag-and-Drop menu. You get this menu any time you right-drag a selection somewhere.

GP%
44.5%
41.3%
45.2%
44.5%
44.2%
43.9%
45.0%
44.2%
44.3%
43.8%

Move Here
Copy Here
Copy Here as Values Only
Copy Here as Formats Only
Link Here
Create Hyperlink Here
Shift Down and Copy

In this case, you want the values to cover the original formulas, so you have to drag right and then back to the left.

For Those Who Prefer Using Keyboard Shortcuts

I love keyboard shortcuts. I can Ctrl+C, Alt+E, S, V, Enter faster than you can blink. But starting in Excel 2010, there is a faster way. Look at the bottom row of your keyboard. To the left of the Spacebar, you usually have Ctrl, Windows, Alt. To the right of the Spacebar is Alt, *Something*, and Ctrl.

What is that key between the right Alt and the right Ctrl? It has a picture of a mouse pointer and a pop-up menu. Its official name is the Application key. I've heard it called the Program key, the Menu key, the Context Menu key, and the Right-Click key. I don't care what you call it, but here is a picture of it:

Here is the fastest keyboard shortcut for copying and pasting values. Press Ctrl+C. Press and release the Program/Application/Right-Click key. Press V.

Again, this only works in Excel 2010 or newer.

And, if you have a Lenovo laptop, it is likely that you don't even have this key. On a keyboard without this key, you can press Shift+F10 instead.

Bonus Tip: Skip Blanks While Pasting

A mysterious part of the Paste Special dialog is the Skip Blanks feature. What does it do? Say that you have a list of existing values. In another column, you have updates for some of those values but not all of them. In the next figure, select D2:D10 and Copy.

	A	B	C	D
1	State	Rate		Updated Rate
2	Alabama	92		87
3	Alaska	51		
4	Arizona	10		14
5	Arkansas	13		
6	California	21		
7	Colorado	17		16
8	Connecticut	51		
9	Delaware	39		
10	Florida	20		15

Select the original values in B2:B10. Do a Paste Special and select Skip Blanks.

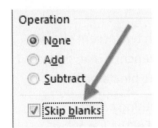

The 87 in D2 overwrites the 92 in B2, but Excel does not clear out the 51 in B3.

	A	B
1	State	Rate
2	Alabama	87
3	Alaska	51
4	Arizona	14
5	Arkansas	13
6	California	21
7	Colorado	16
8	Connecticut	51
9	Delaware	39
10	Florida	15

Thanks to Ed Bott, Ken McLean, Melih Met, and Bryony Stewart-Seume for suggesting this feature. Laura Lewis suggested the Skip Blanks trick.

3

#42 See All Formulas at Once

You inherit a spreadsheet from a former co-worker and you need to figure out how the calculations work. You could visit each cell, one at a time, and look at the formula in the formula bar. Or you could quickly toggle between pressing F2 and Esc to see the formula right in the cell.

	A	B	C	D
1	Vendor	Last Year	Growth	Next Year
2	adaept information management	190,716	7%	204,100
3	Orange County Health Department	188,874	8%	204,000
4	MrExcel.com	188,173	5%	197,600
5	Access Analytic	177,972	7%	190,400
6	Excelerator BI	185,529	4%	193,000
7	MyOnlineTrainingHub.com	181,901	6%	192,800
8	Cambia Factor	153,609	6%	162,800
9	data2impact	154,605	8%	117,000
10	Blockhead Data Consultants	121,751	8%	131,500
11	Bits of Confetti	100,308	8%	108,300
12	Total	1,643,438		1,701,500

But there is a faster way. On most U.S. keyboards, just below the Esc key is a key with two accent characters: the tilde from Spanish and the grave accent from French. It is an odd key. I don't know how I would ever use this key to actually type piñata or frère .

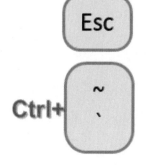

If you hold down Ctrl and this key, you toggle into something called Show Formulas mode. Each column gets wider, and you see all of the formulas.

B	C	D
Last Year	Growth	Next Year
190716	=RANDBETWEEN(4,8)/100	=ROUND(B2*(1+C2),-2)
188874	=RANDBETWEEN(4,8)/100	=ROUND(B3*(1+C3),-2)
188173	=RANDBETWEEN(4,8)/100	=ROUND(B4*(1+C4),-2)
177972	=RANDBETWEEN(4,8)/100	=ROUND(B5*(1+C5),-2)
185529	=RANDBETWEEN(4,8)/100	=ROUND(B6*(1+C6),-2)
181901	=RANDBETWEEN(4,8)/100	=ROUND(B7*(1+C7),-2)
153609	=RANDBETWEEN(4,8)/100	=ROUND(B8*(1+C8),-2)
154605	=RANDBETWEEN(4,8)/100	=ROUND(B9*(1+C9),-2)-50000
121751	=RANDBETWEEN(4,8)/100	=ROUND(B10*(1+C10),-2)
100308	=RANDBETWEEN(4,8)/100	=ROUND(B11*(1+C11),-2)
1643438		=SUM(D2:D11)

This gives you a view of all the formulas at once. It is great for spotting "plug" numbers (B9) or when someone added the totals with a calculator and typed the number instead of using =SUM(). You can see that the co-worker left RANDBETWEEN functions in this model.

Note: Here is another use for the Tilde key. Say you need to use the Find dialog to search for a wildcard character (such as the * in "Wal*Mart" or the ? in "Hey!?" Precede the wildcard with a tilde. Search for Wal~*Mart or Hey!~?.

Tip: To type a lowercase n with a tilde above, hold down Alt while pressing 164 on the number keypad. Then release Alt.

Bonus Tip: Highlight All Formula Cells

If you are going to be auditing the worksheet, it would help to mark all of the formula cells. Here are the steps:

1. Select any blank cell in the worksheet.

2. Choose Home, Find & Select, Formulas.

3. All of the formula cells will be selected. Mark them in a different font color, or, heck, use Home, Cell Styles, Calculation.

To mark all of the input cells, use Home, Find & Select, Go To Special, Constants. I prefer to then uncheck Text, Logical, and Errors, leaving only the numeric constants. Click OK in the Go To Special dialog.

Why Is the F1 Key Missing from Your Keyboard?

Twice I have served as a judge for the ModelOff Financial Modeling Championships in New York. On my first visit, I was watching contestant Martijn Reekers work in Excel. He was constantly pressing F2 and Esc with his left hand. His right hand was on the arrow keys, swiftly moving from cell to cell. F2 puts a cell in Edit mode so you can see the formula in the cell. Esc exits Edit mode and shows you the number. Martijn would press F2 and Esc at least three times every second.

But here is the funny part: What dangerous key is between F2 and Esc? F1. If you accidentally press F1, you will have a 10-second delay while Excel loads online Help. If you are analyzing three cells a second, a 10-second delay is a disaster. You might as well go to lunch. So, Martijn had pried the F1 key from his keyboard so he would never accidentally press it.

Photo Credit: Mary Ellen Jelen

Bonus Tip: Trace Precedents to See What Cells Flow into a Formula

If you need to see which cells flow into a formula, you can use the Trace Precedents command in the Formula Auditing group on the Formulas tab. In the following figure, select D6. Choose Trace Precedents. Blue lines will draw to each cell referenced by the formula in D6.

The dotted line leading to a symbol in B4 means there is at least one precedent on another worksheet. If you double-click the dotted line, Excel shows you a list of the off-sheet precedents.

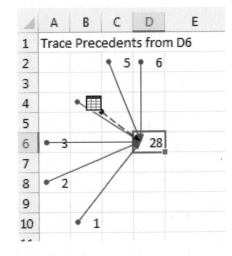

If you stay in cell D6 and choose Trace Precedents a few more times, you will see the second-level precedents, then the third-level precedents, and so on. When you are done, click Remove Arrows.

Bonus Tip: See Which Cells Depend on the Current Cell

Sometimes you have the opposite problem: You want to see which cells rely on the value in the current cell. Choose any cell and click Trace Dependents to see which cells directly refer to the active cell.

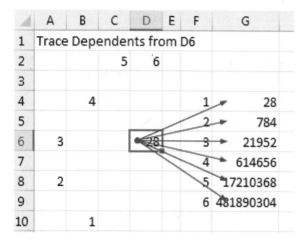

#43 Audit a Worksheet With Spreadsheet Inquire

There is about a 20% chance that you have some amazing tools in your Excel that you've never seen. Well, wait…there is a 100% chance that you've never seen everything in Excel; there are things in Excel that I have never seen, I consider knowing everything Excel to be my job. The 20% that I mentioned before refers to one particular set of tools, called Spreadsheet Inquire.

Inquire was developed by a company called Prodiance that offered the slick Spreadsheet Compare tool for $145 per person per year. The Excel team liked it so much that Microsoft bought out Prodiance and gave the tool for free to anyone who is on Pro Plus, Professional Plus, or Enterprise Level E3.

In classic Microsoft fashion, they kept the tool hidden so even if you have it, you don't know that it is there. If you've ever seen a Power Pivot tab in your Ribbon, you likely have Inquire. It is at least worth the minute to figure out if you have it.

If you have the Developer tab in the Ribbon, click the COM Add-Ins button and continue to step 3 below. Otherwise, follow these steps:

1. Go to File, Options. In the left bar of Excel Options, choose Add-ins (near the bottom of the list).

2. Go all the way to the bottom of the dialog, next to Manage. Open the dropdown and change from Excel Add-Ins to COM Add-ins. After choosing COM Add-ins, click Go….

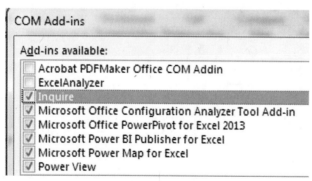

3. If you have Inquire in the list, check the box next to it, click OK, and keep reading. If you don't have Inquire in your list, jump ahead to "#44 Discover New Functions by Using fx" on page 113.

Once you enable Inquire, you have a new tab in the Ribbon called Inquire that provides the following options.

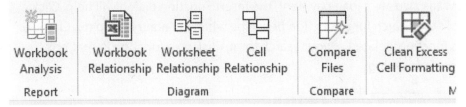

- The Workbook Analysis takes from a few seconds to a few minutes to build a report about your worksheet. It tells you the number of formulas, hidden sheets, linked workbooks, external data connections, and array formulas, as well as how many formulas result in errors. Click any category for a list of the various items.

- The next three icons allow you to draw diagrams showing relationships between workbooks, worksheets, or cells. The diagram below shows all inbound and outbound dependencies for cell D6. You can see the second-level precedents. Each node can be collapsed or expanded.

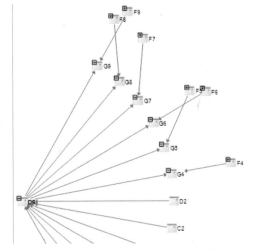

- Compare Files helps you find all changes between two open files. It does a really good job. You can foil most comparison tools by deleting a row in the second file. But Inquire detects that row 8 was deleted and keeps comparing row 9 in one file to row 8 in the other file.

- Clean Excess Cell Formatting locates the last non blank cell in a worksheet and deletes all conditional formatting beyond that cell. You might want to do this, for example, if someone selects an entire row or column and applies conditional formatting.

Thanks to Ron Armstrong, Olga Kryuchkova, and Sven Simon for suggesting this feature.

#44 Discover New Functions by Using fx

There are 400+ functions in Excel. I have room for only 120 tips this book, so there is no way I can cover them all. But instead of taking 450 pages to describe every function, I am going to teach you how to find the function that you need.

The Excel 2007 formulas tab introduced a huge *fx* Insert Function icon. But you don't need to use the one on the Formulas tab; the same icon has been to the left of the formula bar ever since I can remember.

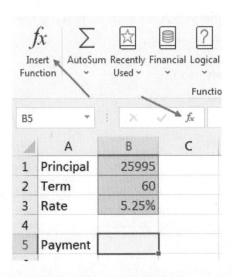

If you are trying to figure out how to calculate a loan payment, the Insert Function dialog will help. Click the icon next to the formula bar. In the Search for a Function box, type what you are trying to do. Click Go. The Select a Function box shows functions related to your search term. Click on a function in that box to see the description at the bottom of the dialog.

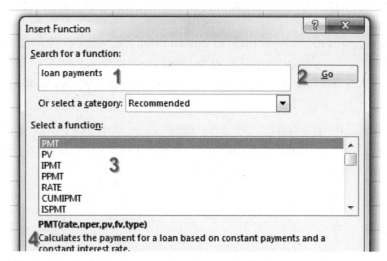

When you find the correct function and click OK, Excel takes you into the Function Arguments dialog. This is an amazing tool when you are new to a function. As you click in each argument box, help appears at the bottom of the window, with specifics on that argument.

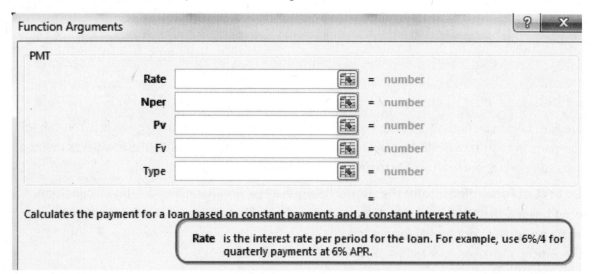

Personally, I could never get the PMT function to work correctly because I always forgot that the rate had to be the interest rate per period. Instead of pointing to the 5.25% in B3, you have to point to B3/12. Below, the help for Nper explains that it is the total number of payments for the loan, also known as the term, from B2.

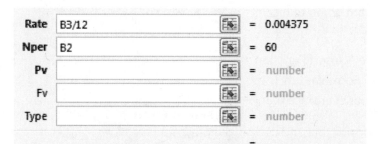

PV is the loan amount. Since I never write a check for negative $493, I want the answer from PMT to be positive instead of negative. That is why I always use –B1 for the PV argument. If you use B1 instead, you will get the correct $493.54065 answer, but it will appear as negative in your worksheet. Think of the original $25,995 as money leaving the bank; that is why the PV is negative.

Rate	B3/12	📊	= 0.004375
Nper	B2	📊	= 60
Pv	-B1|	📊	= -25995
Fv		📊	= number
Type		📊	= number

= 493.54065

Calculates the payment for a loan based on constant payments and a constant interest rate.

Pv is the present value: the total amount that a series of future payments is worth now.

Formula result = 493.54065

Help on this function   OK   Cancel

Notice in the above figure that three argument names are bold. These are the required arguments. Once you finish the required arguments, the Function Arguments dialog shows you the answer in two places. I always use this as a sanity check. Does this answer sound like a typical car payment?

This one topic really covered three things: how to calculate a loan payment, how to use the *fx* icon to discover new functions, and how to use the Function Arguments dialog to get help on any function. If you are in a situation where you remember the function name but still want to use the Function Arguments dialog, type =PMT(with the opening parenthesis and then press Ctrl+A.

#45 Use Function Arguments for Nested Functions

The Function Arguments dialog shown above is cool, but in real life, when you have to nest functions, how would you use this dialog?

Say that you want to build a formula to do a two-way lookup:

=INDEX(B2:E16,MATCH(G2,A2:A16,0),MATCH(H2,B1:E1,0))

	A	B	C	D	E	F	G	H	I
1		Jan	Feb	Mar	Apr		Acct	Month	Result
2	C221	4	6	8	10		E106	Apr	20
3	C236	6	9	12	15				
4	E106	8	12	16	20				
5	C116	10	15	20	25				
6	E220	12	18	24	30				
7	C129	14	21	28	35				

You would start out using the Function Arguments dialog box for INDEX. In the Row_num argument box, type MATCH(. Using the mouse, go up to the formula bar and click anywhere inside the word MATCH.

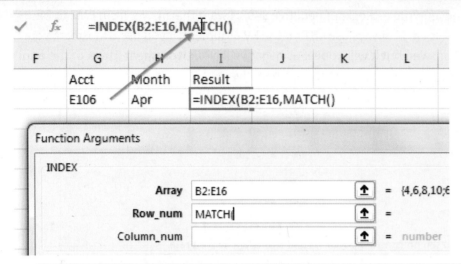

Caution: Don't click the formula in the cell. You have to click the formula in the formula bar.

The Function Arguments dialog switches over to MATCH. When you are finished building the MATCH function, go up to the formula bar and click anywhere in the word INDEX.

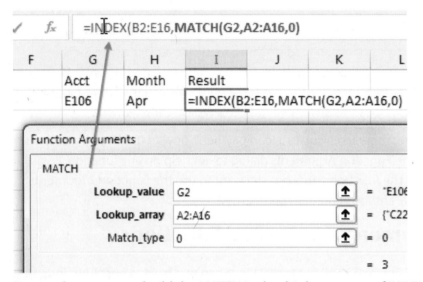

Repeat these steps to build the MATCH in the third argument of INDEX. Make sure to click back in the word INDEX in the formula bar when you are done with the second MATCH.

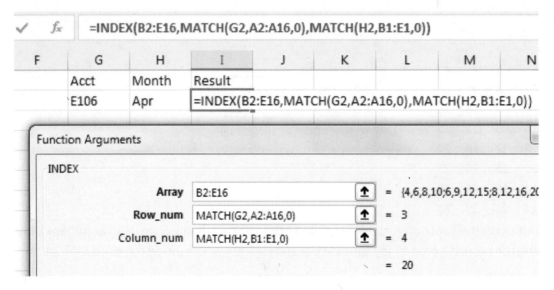

It turns out that the Function Arguments dialog can be fooled into building an invalid function. Type a well-formed but nonsensical function in the formula bar. Using the mouse, click inside the fake function name in the formula bar and click the fx icon.

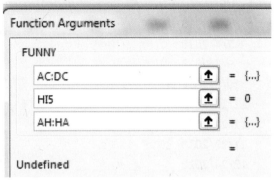

Thanks to Tony DeJonker and Cat Parkinson for suggesting the Function Arguments dialog trick.

#46 Calculate Nonstandard Work Weeks

In my live Power Excel seminars, it is pretty early in the day when I show how to right-click the Fill Handle, drag a date, and then choose Fill Weekdays. This fills Monday through Friday dates. I ask the audience, "How many of you work Monday through Friday?" A lot of hands go up. I say, "That's great. For everyone else, Microsoft clearly doesn't care about you." Laughter.

It certainly seems that if you work anything other than Monday through Friday or have a year ending any day other than December 31, a lot of things in Excel don't work very well.

However, two functions in Excel show that the Excel team does care about people who work odd work weeks: NETWORKDAYS.INTL and WORKDAY.INTL.

But let's start with their original Monday–Friday antecedents. The following figure shows a start date in column B and an end date in column C. If you subtract =C5-B5, you will get the number of days between the two dates. To figure out the number of weekdays, you use =NETWORKDAYS(B2,C2).

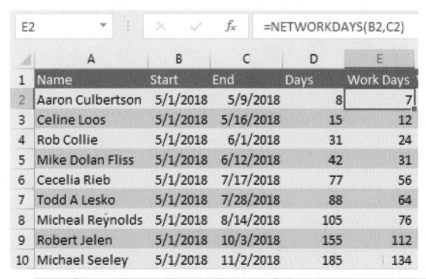

Note: If you subtract Monday August 14 from Friday August 18, Excel will tell you that there are 4 days between the two dates. Excel does not count the end date. But, NETWORKDAYS counts both the first and last date in the range.

It gets even better. NETWORKDAYS allows for an optional third argument where you specify work holidays. In the next figure, the list of holidays in H3:H15 allows the Work Days Less Holidays calculation in column F.

`=NETWORKDAYS(B4,C4,$H$3:$H$15)`

	D	E	F	G	H
	Days	**Work Days**	**Work Days less Holidays**		
'2018	8	7	7		**Holidays**
'2018	15	12	12		5/28/2018
'2018	31	24	23		7/4/2018
'2018	42	31	30		9/3/2018
'2018	77	56	54		10/8/2018
'2018	88	64	62		11/12/2018
'2018	105	76	74		11/22/2018
'2018	155	112	109		11/23/2018
'2018	185	134	130		12/24/2018
'2018	192	139	135		12/25/2018
'2018	206	149	142		1/1/2019
'2019	350	251	239		1/21/2019
					2/18/2019
					5/27/2019

Prior to Excel 2007, the NETWORKDAYS and WORKDAY functions were available if you enabled the Analysis ToolPak add-in that shipped with every copy of Excel. For Excel 2007, those add-ins were made a core part of Excel. In Excel 2007, Microsoft added INTL versions of both functions with a new Weekend argument. This argument allowed for any two consecutive days as the weekend and also allowed for a one-day weekend.

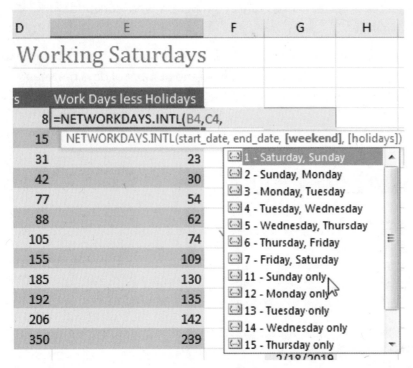

Plus, there are several countries with weekends that don't fall on Saturday and Sunday. All of the countries shown below except Brunei Darussalem gained functionality with NETWORKDAYS.INTL and WORKDAY. INTL.

However, there are still cases where the weekend does not meet any of the 14 weekend definitions added in Excel 2007.

For example, the Hartville Marketplace is open Monday, Thursday, Friday, and Saturday. That means their weekend is Tuesday, Wednesday, and Sunday.

Starting in Excel 2010, instead of using 1-7 or 11-17 as the weekend argument, you can pass 7-digit binary text to indicate whether a company is open or closed on a particular day. It seems a bit unusual, but you use a 1 to indicate that the store is closed for the weekend and a 0 to indicate that the store is open. After all, 1 normally means On and 0 normally means Off. But the name of the argument is Weekend, so 1 means it is a day off, and 0 means you don't have the day off.

Thus, for the Monday, Thursday, Friday, Saturday schedule at the Hartville Marketplace, you would use "0110001". Every time I type one of these text strings, I have to silently say in my head, "Monday, Tuesday, Wednesday…" as I type each digit.

Marion Coblentz at the Hartville Marketplace could use the following formula to figure out how many Marketplace days there are between two dates.

C8			×	✓	f_x	=NETWORKDAYS.INTL(A8,B8,"0110001")		
	A	B		C	D	E	F	G
1	Hartville Marketplace and Flea Market							
2	Open Monday, Thursday, Friday, Saturday							
3	Closed Tuesday, Wednesday, Sunday							
4	7 Binary Digits, starting with Monday							
5	1=Weekend, 0=Open							
6								
7	Start	End		Work Days				
8	5/1/2018	5/9/2018		4	=NETWORKDAYS.INTL(A8,B8,"0110001")			
9	5/1/2018	5/16/2018		8				
10	5/1/2018	6/1/2018		18				
11	5/1/2018	6/12/2018		24				
12	5/1/2018	7/17/2018		44				
13	5/1/2018	7/28/2018		51				

By the way, I did not use the optional Holidays argument above because Memorial Day, July 4, and Labor Day are the biggest customer days in Hartville.

If you are ever in northeastern Ohio, you need to stop by Hartville to see the 100% American-Made house inside of the Hartville Hardware and to try the great food at the Hartville Kitchen.

Bonus Tip: Use WORKDAY.INTL for a Work Calendar

While NETWORKDAYS calculates the work days between two dates, the WORKDAY function takes a starting date and a number of days, and it calculates the date that is a certain number of work days away.

One common use is to calculate the next work day. In the following figure, the start date is the date on the previous row. The number of days is always 1. To generate a class schedule that meets on Monday, Wednesday, and Friday, specify a weekend of "0101011".

1	Fill Monday, Wednesday, Friday Dates	
2	Mon, 1/4/2021	
3	Wed, 1/6/2021	=WORKDAY.INTL(A2,1,"0101011")
4	Fri, 1/8/2021	=WORKDAY.INTL(A3,1,"0101011")
5	Mon, 1/11/2021	=WORKDAY.INTL(A4,1,"0101011")

3

#47 Turn Data Sideways with a Formula

Someone built this lookup table sideways, stretching across C1:N2. I realize that I could use HLOOKUP instead of VLOOKUP, but I prefer to turn the data back to a vertical orientation.

Copy C1:N2. Right-click in A4 and choose the Transpose option under the Paste Options. Transpose is the fancy Excel word for "turn the data sideways."

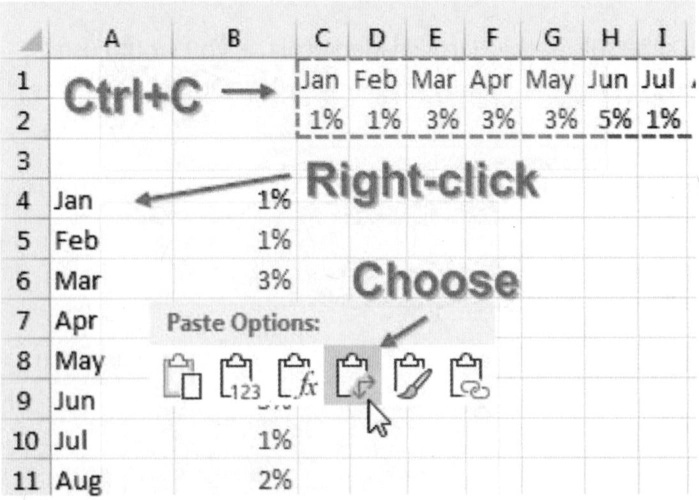

I transpose a lot. But I use Alt+E,S,E,Enter to transpose instead of the right-click.

There is a problem, though. Transpose is a one-time snapshot of the data. What if you have formulas in the horizontal data? Is there a way to transpose with a formula?

The first way is a bit bizarre. If you are trying to transpose 12 horizontal cells, you need to select 12 vertical cells in a single selection. Start typing a formula such as =TRANSPOSE(C2:N2) in the active cell but do not press Enter. Instead, hold down Ctrl+Shift and then press Enter. This puts a single array formula in the selected cells. This TRANSPOSE formula is going to return 12 answers, and they will appear in the 12 selected cells, as shown below.

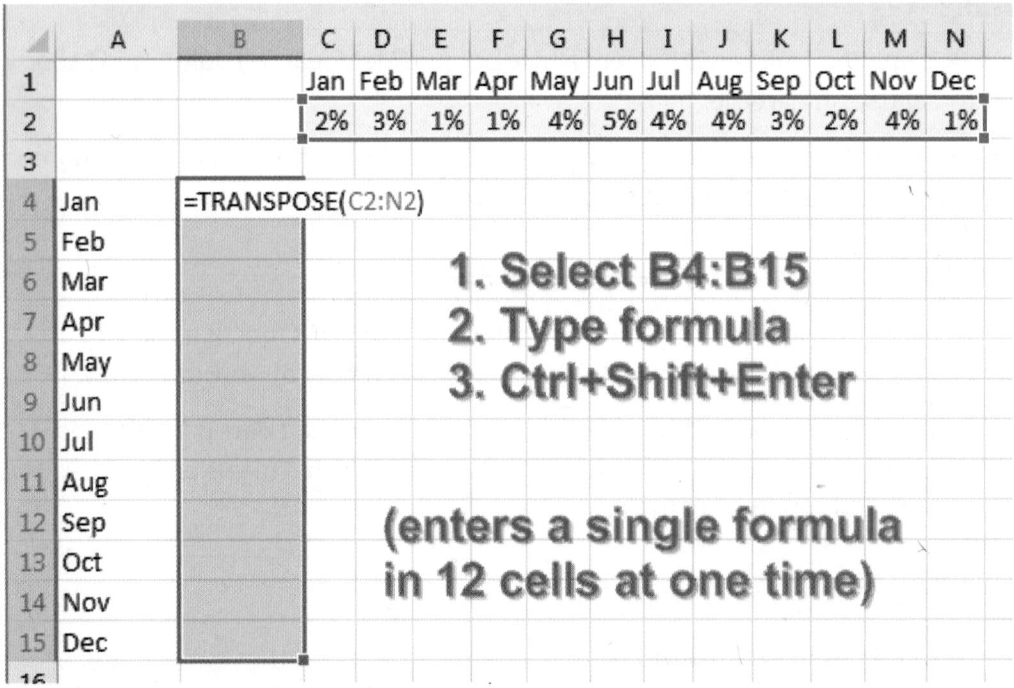

As the data in the horizontal table changes, the same values appear in your vertical table, as shown below.

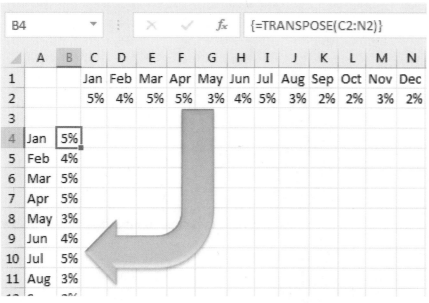

But array formulas are not well known. Some spreadsheet rookie might try to edit your formula and forget to press Ctrl+Shift+Enter.

To avoid using the array formula, use a combination of INDEX and ROW, as shown in the figure below. =ROW(1:1) is a clever way of writing the number 1. As you copy this formula down, the row reference changes to 2:2 and returns a 2.

The INDEX function says you are getting the answers from C2:N2, and you want the *n*th item from the range.

	A	B	C	D	E	F	G	H	I
1			Jan	Feb	Mar	Apr	May	Jun	Jul
2			1%	1%	4%	4%	1%	2%	2%
3									
4	Jan	1%	=INDEX($C$2:$N$2,ROW(1:1))						
5	Feb								

In the figure below, =FORMULATEXT in column C shows how the formula changes when you copy down.

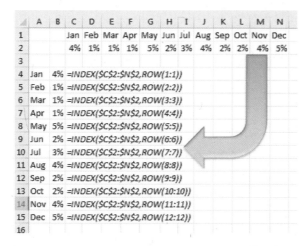

Bonus Tip: Protect Rows with an Array Formula

Here is an odd use for an array formula: Say that you don't want anyone to delete or insert any rows in one section of a worksheet. Scroll far to the right, off the screen, and build an array in those rows. Select Z1:Z9. Type =2 and press Ctrl+Shift+Enter. You can use any number, =0, =1, =2, and so on.

3

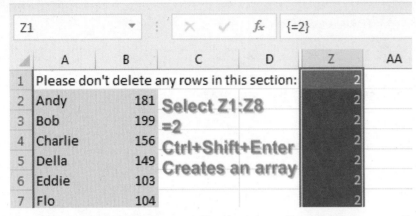

If someone tries to delete a row, Excel prevents it and shows a cryptic message about arrays, shown below.

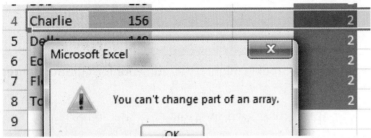

Thanks to Excel Ace and Tracia Williams for suggesting this feature.

#48 Handle Multiple Conditions in IF

When you need to do a conditional calculation, the IF function is the answer. It works like this: If <something is true>, then <this formula>; otherwise <that formula>. In the following figure, a simple IF calculates a bonus for your sales of more than $20,000.

| D4 | | f_x | =IF(B4>=20000,0.02*B4,0) |

	A	B	C	D	E
1	Pay a 2% bonus for sales > 20000				
2					
3	Sales Rep	Revenue	GP%	Bonus	
4	Richard B Lanza	22810	45.9%	456.2	
5	David Haggarty	2257	54.0%	0	
6	Anthony J. LoBello Jr.	18552	46.3%	0	
7	Jon Higbed	9152	50.5%	0	
8	David Colman	8456	46.1%	0	
9	Eddie Stephen	21730	54.4%	434.6	

But what happens when two conditions need to be met? Most people will nest one IF statement inside another, as shown below:

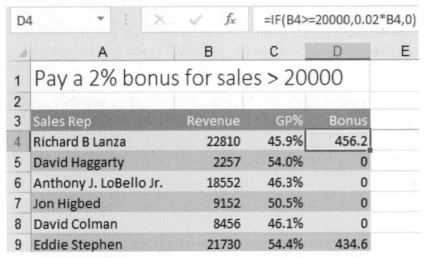

	Sales Rep	Revenue	GP%	Bonus
1	Bonus for sales > 20000 + GP%>50%			
2	=IF(B4>20000,IF(C4>0.5,0.02*B4,0),0)			
3	Sales Rep	Revenue	GP%	Bonus
4	Richard B Lanza	22810	45.9%	0
5	David Haggarty	2257	54.0%	0
6	Anthony J. LoBello Jr.	18552	46.3%	0
7	Jon Higbed	9152	50.5%	0
8	David Colman	8456	46.1%	0

But this nesting gets out of hand if you have many conditions that have to be met. Use the AND function to shorten and simplify the formula. =AND(Test,Test,Test,Test) is True only if all of the logical tests evaluate to True. The following example shows a shorter formula with the same results.

	A	B	C	D
1	Bonus for sales > 20000 + GP%>50%			
2	=IF(AND(B4>20000,C4>0.5),0.02*B4,0)			
3	Sales Rep	Revenue	GP%	Bonus
4	Richard B Lanza	22810	45.9%	0
5	David Haggarty	2257	54.0%	0
6	Anthony J. LoBello Jr.	18552	46.3%	0
7	Jon Higbed	9152	50.5%	0
8	David Colman	8456	46.1%	0
9	Eddie Stephen	21730	54.4%	434.6
10	Mike excelisfun Girvir	16416	48.2%	0
11	Leonard LaFrenier	21438	52.0%	428.76
12	Victor E. Scelba II	6267	53.7%	0

If you like AND, you might find a use for OR and NOT. =OR(Test,Test,Test,Test) is True if any one of the logical tests are True. NOT reverses an answer, so =NOT(True) is False, and =NOT(False) is True. If you ever have to do something fancy like a NAND, you can use NOT(AND(Test,Test,Test,Test)).

Caution: Although Excel 2013 introduced XOR as an Exclusive Or, it does not work the way that accountants would expect. =XOR(True,False,True,True) is True for reasons that are too complicated to explain here. XOR counts whether you have an odd number of True values. Odd. Really odd.

Bonus Tip: Use Boolean Logic

I always cover IF in my seminars. And I always ask how people would solve the two-conditions problem. The results are often the same: 70–80% of people use nested IF, and 20–30% use AND. Just one time, in Virginia, a woman from Price Waterhouse offered the formula shown below:

	A	B	C	D
1	Bonus for sales > 20000 + GP%>50%			
2	=B4*0.02*(B4>20000)*(C4>0.5)			
3	Sales Rep	Revenue	GP%	Bonus
4	Richard B Lanza	22810	45.9%	0
5	David Haggarty	2257	54.0%	0
6	Anthony J. LoBello Jr.	18552	46.3%	0
7	Jon Higbed	9152	50.5%	0
8	David Colman	8456	46.1%	0
9	Eddie Stephen	21730	54.4%	434.6
10	Mike excelisfun Girvir	16416	48.2%	0

It works. It gives the same answer as the other formulas. Calculate the bonus .02*B4. But then multiply that bonus by logical tests in parentheses. When you force Excel to multiply a number by True or False, the True becomes 1, and the False becomes 0. Any number times 1 is itself. Any number times 0 is 0. Multiplying the bonus by the conditions ensures that only rows that meet both conditions are paid.

It is cool. It works. But it seems confusing when you first see it. My joke in my seminar is, "If you are leaving your job next month and you hate your co-workers, start using this formula."

3

#49 Troubleshoot VLOOKUP

VLOOKUP is my favorite function in Excel. If you can use VLOOKUP, you can solve many problems in Excel. But there are things that can trip up a VLOOKUP. This topic talks about a few of them.

But first, the basics of VLOOKUP in plain English.

The data in A:C came from the IT department. You asked for sales by item and date. They gave you item number. You need the item description. Rather than wait for the IT department to rerun the data, you find the table shown in column F:G.

	A	B	C	D	E	F	G	H
1	Item	Date	Qty	Description				
2	W25-6	8/1/2018	878			SKU	Description	
3	CR 50-4	8/1/2018	213			BG33-3	14K Gold Bangle Bracelet with Vin
4	CR 50-4	8/2/2018	744			CR50-3	14K Gold Cross with Onyx
5	BR26-3	8/3/2018	169			RG75-3	14K Gold RAY OF LIGHT Onyx Me
6	CR50-6	8/3/2018	822			RG78-25	14K Gold Ballerina Ring w/ Blue &

You want VLOOKUP to find the item in A2 while it searches through the first column of the table in $F$3:$G$30. When VLOOKUP finds the match in F7, you want VLOOKUP to return the description found in the second column of the table. Every VLOOKUP that is looking for an exact match has to end in False (or zero, which is equivalent to False). The formula below is set up properly.

D2	▼	:	✕ ✓	f_x	=VLOOKUP(A2,$F$3:$G$30,2,FALSE)

	A	B	C	D	E	F	
1	Item	Date	Qty	Description			
2	W25-6	8/1/2018	878	18K Italian Gold Women's Watch		SKU	Descri
3	CR 50-4	8/1/2018	213	14K Gold Onyx Cross		BG33-3	14K G
4	CR 50-4	8/2/2018	744	14K Gold Onyx Cross		CR50-3	14K G
5	BR26-3	8/3/2018	169	18K Italian Gold Men's Bracelet		RG75-3	14K G
6	CR50-6	8/3/2018	822	14K Gold Onyx Cross with White		RG78-25	14K G
7	ER46-14	8/3/2018	740	14K Gold Fish Hoop Earrings		W25-6	18K Ita

Notice that you use F4 to add four dollar signs to the address for the lookup table. As you copy the formula down column D, you need the address for the lookup table to remain constant. There are two common alternatives: You could specify the entire columns F:G as the lookup table. Or, you could name F3:G30 with a name such as ItemTable. If you use =VLOOKUP(A2,ItemTable,2,False), the named range acts like an absolute reference.

Any time you do a bunch of VLOOKUPs, you need to sort the column of VLOOKUPs. Sort ZA, and any #N/A errors come to the top. In this case, there is one. Item BG33-9 is missing from the lookup table. Maybe it is a typo. Maybe it is a brand-new item. If it is new, insert a new row anywhere in the middle of your lookup table and add the new item.

	A	B	C	Sort ZA	E	F
1	Item	Date	Qty	Description		
2	BG33-9	8/19/2018	37	#N/A		SKU
3	W25-6	8/1/2018	878	18K Italian Gold Women's Watch		BG33-3
4	W25-6	8/21/2018	254	18K Italian Gold Women's Watch		CR50-3
5	W25-6	8/22/2018	832	18K Italian Gold Women's Watch		RG75-3
6	W25-6	8/29/2018	581	18K Italian Gold Women's Watch		RG78-25
7	BR26-3	8/3/2018	169	18K Italian Gold Men's Bracelet		W25-6
8	BR26-3	8/5/2018	541	18K Italian Gold Men's Bracelet		BR26-3
9	BR26-3	8/6/2018	849	18K Italian Gold Men's Bracelet		BR15-3
10	BR26-3	8/10/2018	881	18K Italian Gold Men's Bracelet		BG33-8
11	BR26-3	8/12/2018	737	18K Italian Gold Men's Bracelet		BG33-17

It is fairly normal to have a few #N/A errors. But in the figure below, exactly the same formula is returning nothing but #N/A. When this happens, see if you can solve the first VLOOKUP. You are looking up the BG33-8 found in A2. Start cruising down through the first column of the lookup table. As you can see, the matching value clearly is in F10. Why can you see this, but Excel cannot see it?

D2			fx	=VLOOKUP(A2,$F$3:$G$30,2,FALSE)

	A	B	C	D	E	F	G
1	Item	Date	Qty	Description			
2	BG33-8	8/1/2018	580	#N/A		SKU	Description
3	Cross50-5	8/1/2018	422	#N/A		BG33-3	14K Gold Bar
4	RG78-25	8/2/2018	638	#N/A		CR50-3	14K Gold Cro
5	BG33-8	8/3/2018	775	#N/A		RG75-3	14K Gold RA'
6	BG33-8	8/3/2018	331	#N/A		RG78-25	14K Gold Bal
7	ER46-7	8/3/2018	140	#N/A		W25-6	18K Italian Gc
8	RG75-3	8/3/2018	231	#N/A		BR26-3	18K Italian Gc
9	W25-6	8/4/2018	878	#N/A		BR15-3	14K Gold Ony
10	CR50-6	8/4/2018	571	#N/A		BG33-8	14K Gold Bar
11	ER41-4	8/4/2018	208	#N/A		BG33-17	14K Gold Bar

Go to each cell and press the F2 key. The figure below shows F10. Note that the insertion cursor appears right after the 8.

W25-6	14
BR26-3	18
BR15-3	14
BG33-8	14
BG33-17	14
CR 50-4	14
CR50-2	14

The following figure shows cell A2 in Edit mode. The insertion cursor is a couple of spaces away from the 8. This is a sign that at some point, this data was stored in an old COBOL data set. Back in COBOL, if the Item field was defined as 10 characters and you typed only 6 characters, COBOL would pad it with 4 extra spaces.

	A	
1	Item	D
2	BG33-8	
3	Cross50-5	
4	RG78-25	
5	BG33-8	
6	BG33-8	

The solution? Instead of looking up A2, look up TRIM(A2).

| D2 | | | | | f_x | =VLOOKUP(TRIM(A2),$F$3:$G$30,2,FALSE) |

	A	B	C	D	E	F	G
1	Item	Date	Qty	Description			
2	BG33-8	8/1/2018	580	14K Gold Bangle	SKU		Description
3	Cross50-5	8/1/2018	422	14K Gold Onyx C	BG33-3		14K Gold Bangle Br
4	RG78-25	8/2/2018	638	14K Gold Ballerir	CR50-3		14K Gold Cross with
5	BG33-8	8/3/2018	775	14K Gold Bangle	RG75-3		14K Gold RAY OF L
6	BG33-8	8/3/2018	331	14K Gold Bangle	RG78-25		14K Gold Ballerina F

The TRIM() function removes leading and trailing spaces. If you have multiple spaces between words, TRIM converts them to a single space. In the figure below there are spaces before and after both names in A1. =TRIM(A1) removes all but one space in A3.

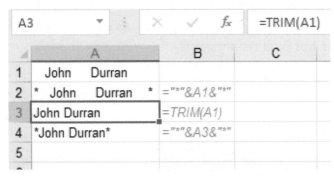

| A3 | | | | | f_x | =TRIM(A1) |

	A	B	C
1	John Durran		
2	* John Durran *	="*"&A1&"*"	
3	John Durran	=TRIM(A1)	
4	*John Durran*	="*"&A3&"*"	
5			

By the way, what if the problem had been trailing spaces in column F instead of column A? Add a column of TRIM() functions to E, pointing to column F. Copy those and paste as values in F to make the lookups start working again.

The other very common reason that VLOOKUP won't work is shown here. Column F contains real numbers. Column A holds text that looks like numbers.

| D2 | | | | | f_x | =VLOOKUP(A2,$F$3:$G$30,2,FALSE) |

	A	B	C	D	E	**Numbers**	G
1	Item	Date	Qty	Description			
2	4399	8/1/2018	580	#N/A		SKU	Description
3	4250	8/1/2018	422	#N/A		6041	14K Gold Ban
4	3712	8/2/2018	638	#N/A		2304	14K Gold Cros
5	4399	8/3/2018	775	#N/A		1242	14K Gold RAY
6	4399	8/3/2018	331	#N/A		3712	14K Gold Balle
7	3363	8/3/2018	140	#N/A		5805	18K Italian Go
8	1242	8/3/2018	231	#N/A		1995	18K Italian Go
9	5805	8/4/2018	878	#N/A		2619	14K Gold Ony
10	2925	8/4/2018	571	#N/A		4399	14K Gold Ban
11	3270	8/4/2018	208	#N/A		4101	14K Gold Ban
12	3270	8/5/2018	429	#N/A		5403	14K Gold Ony

??   **Text**

Select all of column A. Press Alt+D, E, F. This does a default Text to Columns operation and converts all text numbers to real numbers. The lookup starts working again.

Alt+D, E, F

	A	B	C	D	E
1	Item	Date	Qty	Description	
2	4399	8/1/2018	580	14K Gold Bangle Bra	
3	4250	8/1/2018	422	14K Gold Onyx Cross	
4	3712	8/2/2018	638	14K Gold Ballerina Ri	

If you want the VLOOKUP to work without changing the data, you can use =VLOOKUP(1*A2,...) to handle numbers stored as text or =VLOOKUP(A2&"",...) when your lookup table has text numbers.

#50 Use a Wildcard in VLOOKUP

You can do a sort of fuzzy match with VLOOKUP. If you aren't sure if your lookup table will contain Apple, Apple Computer, or Apple Computer Inc, you can use =VLOOKUP("Apple*",Table,2,False), and Excel will find the first item in the lookup table that starts with Apple. (Thanks to -Khalif John Clark)

> **Tip**: Microsoft Labs offers a free Fuzzy Lookup add-in for Excel. See "#52 Use the Fuzzy Lookup Tool from Microsoft Labs" on page 129

Bonus Tip: VLOOKUP to Two Tables

You want to try to find a match in Table1. If a match is not found, then do a lookup to Table2. You can use =IFNA(Formula,Value if NA). =IFNA(VLOOKUP(A2,Table1,3,False),VLOOKUP(A2,Table2,3,False)).

#51 Replace Columns of VLOOKUP with a Single MATCH

The following figure shows a situation in which you have to do 12 VLOOKUP functions for each account number.

| B4 | | | | f_x | =VLOOKUP($A4,$O$4:$AA$227,2,FALSE) |

	A	B	C	D	E	F	G	H	I	J	K	L	M	N		O	P	Q	R	S	T	U	V	W	X	Y	Z	AA
1																												
2																												
3	Acct	Jan	Feb	Mar	Apr	May	Jun	Jul	Aug	Sep	Oct	Nov	Dec			Acct	J	F	M	A	M	J	J	A	S	O	N	D
4	A308	6														A101	5	2	0	8	3	1	1	0	6	1	4	7
5	A219															A102	3	0	7	0	4	9	4	3	5	3	7	1
6	A249															A103	1	4	9	0	3	4	3	3	8	0	5	6

VLOOKUP is powerful, but it takes a lot of time to do calculations. Plus, the formula has to be edited in each cell as you copy across. The third argument has to change from 2 to 3 for February, then 4 for March, and so on.

| C4 | | | | f_x | =VLOOKUP($A4,$O$4:$AA$227,3,FALSE) |

	A	B	C	D	E	F	G	H	I	J	K	L	M	N	O
1															
2															
3	Acct	Jan	Feb	Mar	Apr	May	Jun	Jul	Aug	Sep	Oct	Nov	Dec		Acct
4	A308	6	1												A101
5	A219														A102

One workaround is to add a row with the column numbers. Then, the third argument of VLOOKUP can point to this row, as shown below. At least you can copy the same formula from B4 and paste to C4:M4 before copying the 12 formulas down.

| G4 | | | | f_x | =VLOOKUP($A4,$O$4:$AA$227,G$1,FALSE) |

	A	B	C	D	E	F	G	H	I	J	K	L	M	N	O	P
1		2	3	4	5	6	7	8	9	10	11	12	13			
2																
3	Acct	Jan	Feb	Mar	Apr	May	Jun	Jul	Aug	Sep	Oct	Nov	Dec		Acct	J
4	A308	6	1	9	2	9	1	5	4	4	4	7	3		A101	5
5	A219	0	0	5	0	2	8	8	7	8	3	0	0		A102	3

But here is a much faster approach: add a new column B with Where? as the heading. Column B contains a MATCH function. This function is very similar to VLOOKUP: You are looking for the value in A4 in the column P4:P227. The 0 at the end is like the False at the end of VLOOKUP. It specifies that you want an exact match. Here is the big difference: MATCH returns where the value is found. The answer 208 says that A308 is the 208th cell in the range P4:P227. From a recalc time perspective, MATCH and VLOOKUP are about equal.

B4	f_x	=MATCH(A4,$P$4:$P$227,0)

	A	B	C	D	E	F	G	H	I	J	K	L	M
1													
2													
3	Acct	Where?	Jan	Feb	Mar	Apr	May	Jun	Jul	Aug	Sep	Oct	No
4	A308	208											
5	A219	119											
6	A249	149											
7	A154	54											

I can hear what you are thinking: "What good is it to know where something is located? I've never had a manager call up and ask, 'What row is that receivable in?'"

While humans rarely ask what row something is in, it can be handy for the INDEX function to know that position. The formula in the following figure tells Excel to return the 208th item from Q4:Q227.

SUM	f_x	=INDEX(Q$4:Q$227,$B4)

	A	B	C	D	E	F	G	H	I	J	K	L	M	N	O	P	Q	R	S	T
1																				
2																				
3	Acct	Where?	Jan	Feb	Mar	Apr	May	Jun	Jul	Aug	Sep	Oct	Nov	Dec			Acct	J	F	M A
4	A308	208	=INDEX(Q$4:Q$227,$B4)														A101	5	2	0 8
5	A219	119															A102	3	0	7 0
6	A249	149															A103	1	4	9 0
7	A154	54															A104	0	4	2 5
8	A128	28															A105	9	4	8 1
9	A229	129															A106	6	3	6 2

As you copy this formula across, the array of values moves across the lookup table as shown below. For each row, you are doing one MATCH and 12 INDEX functions. The INDEX function is incredibly fast compared to VLOOKUP. The entire set of formulas will calculate 85% faster than 12 columns of VLOOKUP.

SUM	f_x	=INDEX(Y$4:Y$227,$B4)

	A	B	C	D	E	F	G	H	I	J	K	L	M	N	O	P	Q	R	S	T	U	V	W	X	Y	Z	AA	AB
1																												
2																												
3	Acct	Where?	Jan	Feb	Mar	Apr	May	Jun	Jul	Aug	Sep	Oct	Nov	Dec			Acct	J	F	M	A	M	J	J	A	S	O	N	D
4	A308	208	6	1	9	2	9	1	5	4	=INDEX(Y$4:Y$227,$B4)							5	2	0	8	3	1	1	0	6	1	4	7
5	A219	119	0	0	5	0	2	8	8	7	8	3	0	0				A102	3	0	7	0	4	9	4	3	5	3	7	1
6	A249	149	1	7	1	3	2	9	6	7	1	2	9	5				A103	1	4	9	0	3	4	3	3	8	0	5	6
7	A154	54	2	5	8	0	3	3	5	5	2	8	9	3				A104	0	4	2	5	0	0	9	7	6	8	8	5
8	A128	28	4	1	8	6	2	5	7	8	4	0	9	5				A105	9	4	8	1	3	4	5	7	7	7	9	7

Note: In late 2018, Office 365 introduced new logic for VLOOKUP that makes the calculation speed as fast as the INDEX/MATCH shown here.

#52 Use the Fuzzy Lookup Tool from Microsoft Labs

When you use VLOOKUP, HLOOKUP, or INDEX/MATCH, Excel is expecting an exact match. But in real life, data is messy. Several years ago, the research team at Microsoft Labs released a free Fuzzy Lookup add-in. The functionality was never added to Excel, but later showed up in SQL Server. However, the free tool is still available from https://mrx.cl/fuzzylookup.

Download and install the add-in. The last step of the install process lets you open the install folder where you will you will find a ReadMe document and a sample Excel file.

Open the sample file. On the Fuzzy Lookup tab, choose Fuzzy Lookup. In the panel that opens, choose the Left Table, the Right Table, and the columns in common.

Optionally, choose that you want to see the best 2 or best N matches. Although it is more work, I always ask for at least two matches because Fuzzy Matches are never perfect.

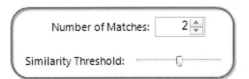

Here are the results. Note if you had asked for only 1 match, you would not see the choice between Coca-Cola Company and Coca-Cola Enterprises. Also - beware of Fuzzy Match algorithms: ATT Corp and ITT Corporation are very similar and could be reported as a match. Someone should always review the matches to determine if they are accurate.

	E	H	I	R
2	Company	Ticker	Company	Similarity
3	AMAZON COM INC STK	AMZN	Amazon.com Inc.	94.1%
4	MOTOROLA	MSI	Motorola Solutions, Inc.	90.0%
5	MOTOROLA	MMI	Motorola Mobility Holdings, Inc.	87.1%
6	ATT CORP	T	AT&T, Inc.	81.4%
7	ATT CORP	ITT	ITT Corporation	50.8%
8	BERSHIER HATHWAY	BRK-B	Berkshire Hathaway Inc.	90.9%
9	MICROSOFT	MSFT	Microsoft Corporation	95.0%
10	COCACOLA	KO	The Coca-Cola Company	90.7%
11	COCACOLA	CCE	Coca-Cola Enterprises Inc.	90.1%
12	DR PEPPER CORP	DPS	Dr Pepper Snapple Group, Inc.	78.6%
13	AUTO DESK INC COM STK NPV	ADSK	Autodesk, Inc.	84.7%
14	MELLON BANK	BK	The Bank of New York Mellon Corporation	86.7%

When you look at the sample workbook in the installation folder, check out the Transformations table where you can identify synonyms specific to your data set. For example, your system might use A/G as a synonym for Associate Grocers.

3

#53 Lookup to the Left with INDEX/MATCH

What if your lookup value is to the right of the information that you want VLOOKUP to return? Conventional wisdom says VLOOKUP cannot handle a negative column number in order to go left of the key.

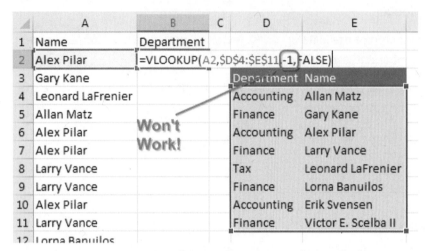

One solution is =VLOOKUP(I7,CHOOSE({1,2},G1:G5,F1:F5),2,0). However, I prefer to use MATCH to find where the name is located and then use INDEX to return the correct value.

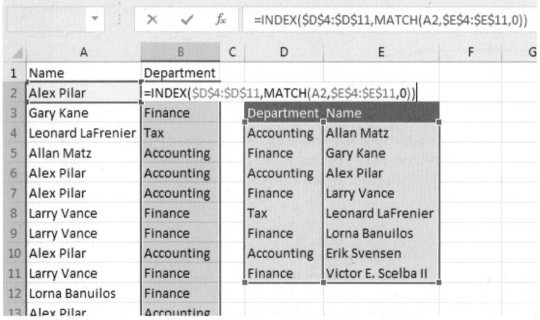

VLOOKUP was suggested by Rod Apfelbeck, Patty Hahn, John Henning, @ExcelKOS, and @tomatecaolho. The INDEX/MATCH trick came from Mark Domeyer, Jon Dow, Justin Fishman, Donna Gilliland, Alex Havermans, Jay Killeen, Martin Lucas, Patrick Matthews, Mike Petry, Michael Tarzia, and @beatexcel. Thanks to all of you.

A VALUE TO THE LEFT....

VLOOKUP'S KRYPTONITE

This message brought to you by:

INDEX & MATCH

=INDEX(X2:X99,MATCH(A2,Z2:Z99,0))

YOUR **1** STOP FOR EXCEL SOLUTIONS

mrExcel.com

3

Poster Credit: Bobby Rosenstock
justAjar Design Press, http://www.justajar.com/

#54 Preview What Remove Duplicates Will Remove

The new Remove Duplicates tool added in Excel 2010 was a nice addition.

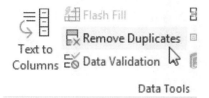

Data Tools

However, the tool does remove the duplicates. Sometimes, you might want to see the duplicates before you remove them. And the Home, Conditional Formatting, Highlight Cells, Duplicate Values marks both instances of Andy instead of just the one that will be removed. The solution is to create a conditional formatting rule using a formula. Select A2:B14. Home, Conditional Formatting, New Rule, Use a Formula. The formula should be: `=COUNTIF($A$1:$A1,$A2)>0`.

► Use a formula to determine which cells to format

Edit the Rule Description:

Format values where this formula is true:

`=COUNTIF($A$1:$A1,$A2)>0`   ⬆

Preview: AaBbCcYyZz   Format...

It is hard to visualize why this will work. Notice that there is a dollar sign missing from $A$1:$A1. This creates an expanding range. In English the formula says "Look at all of the values from A1 to A just above the current cell and see if they are equal to the current cell". Only cells that return >0 will be formatted.

I've added the formula to column C below so you can see how the range expands. In Row 5, the COUNTIF checks how many times Andy appears in A1:A4. Since there is one match, the cell is formatted.

	A	B	C
1	Name	Amount	Formula
2	Andy	36.80	=COUNTIF($A$1:$A1,$A2)>0
3	Barb	36.90	=COUNTIF($A$1:$A2,$A3)>0
4	Chris	92.25	=COUNTIF($A$1:$A3,$A4)>0
5	Andy	85.15	=COUNTIF($A$1:$A4,$A5)>0
6	Diane	85.65	=COUNTIF($A$1:$A5,$A6)>0
7	Ed	78.35	=COUNTIF($A$1:$A6,$A7)>0
8	Chris	69.75	=COUNTIF($A$1:$A7,$A8)>0
9	Hank	62.90	=COUNTIF($A$1:$A8,$A9)>0
10	Gary	95.60	=COUNTIF($A$1:$A9,$A10)>0
11	Chris	47.25	=COUNTIF($A$1:$A10,$A11)>0
12	Flo	91.80	=COUNTIF($A$1:$A11,$A12)>0
13	Flo	94.35	=COUNTIF($A$1:$A12,$A13)>0
14	Hank	61.90	=COUNTIF($A$1:$A13,$A14)>0

#55 Replace Nested IFs with a Lookup Table

A long time ago, I worked for the vice president of sales at a company. I was always modeling some new bonus program or commission plan. I became pretty used to commission plans with all sorts of conditions. The one shown in this tip is pretty tame.

The normal approach is to start building a nested IF formula. You always start at either the high end or the low end of the range. "If sales are over $500K, then the discount is 20%; otherwise,...."The third argument of the IF function is a whole new IF function that tests for the second level: "If sales are over $250K, then the discount is 15%; otherwise,...."

These formulas get longer and longer as there are more levels. The toughest part of such a formula is remembering how many closing parentheses to put at the end of the formula.

Mini Bonus Tip: Match the Parentheses

Excel cycles through a variety of colors for each new level of parentheses. While Excel reuses the colors, it uses black only for the opening parenthesis and for the matching closing parenthesis. As you are finishing the formula below, just keep typing closing parentheses until you type a black parenthesis.

	A	B	C	D
1	Next Year Discount Level Rules			
2	Based on last year's revenue:			
3	Anyone over $500K: 20% discount		=IF(B10>500000,20%,	
4	Anyone over $250K: 15% discount		IF(B10>250000,15%,	
5	Anyone over $100K: 10% discount		IF(B10>100000,10%,	
6	Anyone over $50K: 5% discount		IF(B10>50000,5%,	
7	Anyone over $10K: 1% Discount		IF(B10>10000,1%,0)))))	
9	Customer	Revenue	Future Discount	
10	SpringBoard	550000	20%	
11	LaFrenier Sons Septic	503500	20%	

Tip: In Office 365, you could use the following formula to solve the discount presented above:
=IFS(B10>500000,20%,B10>250000,15%,B10>100000,10%,B10>50000,5%,B10>10000,1%,TRUE,0)

Back to the Nested Formula Tip

If you're using Excel 2003, your formula is already nearing the limit. With that version, you cannot nest more than 7 IF functions. It was an ugly day when the powers that be changed the commission plan and you needed a way to add an eighth IF function. Today, you can nest 64 IF functions. You should never nest that many, but it is nice to know there is no problem nesting 8 or 9.

Rather than use the nested IF function, try using the VLOOKUP function. When the fourth argument of VLOOKUP changes from False to True, the function is no longer looking for an exact match. Well, first VLOOKUP tries to find an exact match. But if an exact match is not found, Excel settles into the row just less than what you are searching for.

Consider the table below. In cell C13, Excel will be looking for a match for $28,355 in the table. When it can't find 28355, Excel will return the discount associated with the value that is just less—in this case, the 1% discount for the $10K level.

When you convert the rules to the table in E13:F18, you need to start from the smallest level and proceed to the highest level. Although it was unstated in the rules, if someone is below $10,000 in sales, the discount will be 0%. You need to add this as the first row in the table.

	A	B	C	D	E	F
5						
6		=VLOOKUP(B10,$E$13:$F$18,2,TRUE				
7						
8						
9	Customer	Revenue	Future Discount			
10	SpringBoard	550000	20%		Lookup Table	
11	LaFrenier Sons Septic	503500	20%			
12	myexcelonline.com	18699	1%		Sales	Discount
13	California Blazing Chile Farms	28355	1%		0	0%
14	Cambia Factor	4860	0%		10000	1%
15	All Systems Go Consulting	123750	10%		50000	5%
16	Vertex42	201250	10%		100000	10%
17	Mary Maids	255750	15%		250000	15%
18	leanexcelbooks.com	328250	15%		500000	20%
19	MN Excel Consulting	444050	15%			

Caution: When you are using the "True" version of VLOOKUP, your table has to be sorted ascending. Many people believe that all lookup tables have to be sorted. But a table needs to be sorted only for an approximate match.

What if your manager wants a completely self-contained formula and does not want to see the bonus table off to the right? After building the formula, you can embed the table right into the formula. Put the formula in Edit mode by double-clicking the cell or by selecting the cell and pressing F2. Use the cursor to select the entire second argument: $E$13:$F$18.

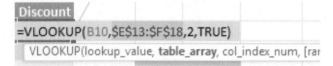

Discount
=VLOOKUP(B10,$E$13:$F$18,2,TRUE)
  VLOOKUP(lookup_value, table_array, col_index_num, [ra

Press the F9 key. Excel embeds the lookup table as an array constant. In the array constant, a semicolon indicates a new row, and a comma indicates a new column. See "Bonus Tip: Understanding Array Constants" on page 145

P(B10,{0,0;10000,0.01;50000,0.05;100000,0.1;250000,0.15;500000,0.2},:

Press Enter. Copy the formula down to the other cells.

You can now delete the table. The final formula is shown below.

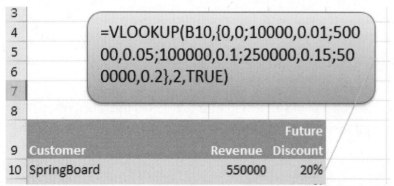

=VLOOKUP(B10,{0,0;10000,0.01;500 00,0.05;100000,0.1;250000,0.15;50 0000,0.2},2,TRUE)

9	Customer	Revenue	Future Discount
10	SpringBoard	550000	20%

Thanks to Mike Girvin for teaching me about the matching parentheses. The VLOOKUP technique was suggested by Danny Mac, Boriana Petrova, Andreas Thehos, and @mvmcos.

#56 Suppress Errors with IFERROR

Formula errors are common. If you have a data set with hundreds of records, a divide-by-zero and an #N/A errors are bound to pop up now and then.

In the past, preventing errors required Herculean efforts. Nod your head knowingly if you've ever knocked out =IF(ISNA(VLOOKUP(A2,Table,2,0)),"Not Found",VLOOKUP(A2,Table,2,0)). Besides being really long to type, that solution requires twice as many VLOOKUPs. First, you do a VLOOKUP to see if the VLOOKUP is going to produce an error. Then you do the same VLOOKUP again to get the non-error result.

Excel 2010 introduced the greatly improved =IFERROR(Formula,Value If Error). I know that IFERROR sounds like the old ISERROR, ISERR, and ISNA functions, but it is completely different.

This is a brilliant function: =IFERROR(VLOOKUP(A2,Table,2,0),"Not Found"). If you have 1,000 VLOOKUPs and only 5 return #N/A, then the 995 that worked require only a single VLOOKUP. Only the 5 VLOOKUPs returned #N/A that need to move on to the second argument of IFERROR.

Oddly, Excel 2013 added the IFNA() function. It is just like IFERROR but only looks for #N/A errors. One might imagine a strange situation where the value in the lookup table is found, but the resulting answer is a division by 0. If you want to preserve the divide-by-zero error for some reason, you can use IFNA() to do this.

B4			f_x	=IFNA(VLOOKUP(A4,Table,4,0),"Not Found")			

	A	B	C	D	E	F	G
1	Handle	Average					
2	Bluefeather8989	539		Handle	Qty	Revenue	Avg Price
3	MikeAsHimself	582		aBoBoBook	895	521785	583
4	MrExcel	#DIV/0!		Bluefeather8989	989	533071	539
5	ExcelisFun	Not Found		INDZARA	1124	611456	544
6	Bluefeather8989	539		Kazmdav	1019	507462	498
7	McGunigales	527		McGunigales	921	485367	527
8				MikeAsHimself	843	490626	582
9				MrExcel	0	0	#DIV/0!
10				Symons	972	562788	579

Of course, the person who built the lookup table should have used IFERROR to prevent the division by zero in the first place. In the figure below, the "n.m." is a former manager's code for "not meaningful."

		f_x	=IFERROR(F9/E9,"n.m.")	

D	E	F	G
Handle	Qty	Revenue	Avg Price
aBoBoBook	895	521785	583
Bluefeather8989	989	533071	539
INDZARA	1124	611456	544
Kazmdav	1019	507462	498
McGunigales	921	485367	527
MikeAsHimself	843	490626	582
MrExcel	0	0	n.m.
Symons	972	562788	579

Thanks to Justin Fishman, Stephen Gilmer, and Excel by Joe.

#57 Handle Plural Conditions with SUMIFS

Did you notice the "S" that got added to the end of SUMIF starting in Excel 2007? While SUMIF and SUMIFS sound the same, the new SUMIFS can run circles around its elder sibling.

The old SUMIF and COUNTIF have been around since Excel 97. In the figure below, the formula tells Excel to look through the names in B2:B22. If a name is equal to the name in F4, then sum the corresponding cell from the range starting in D2:D22. (While the third argument could be the first cell of the sum range D2, it will make the function volatile, causing the worksheet to calculate more slowly.)

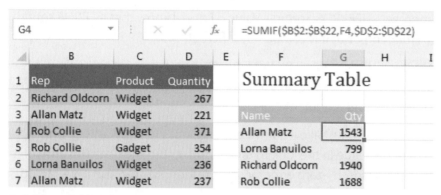

SUMIF and COUNTIF were great with only one condition. But with two or more things to check, you had to switch over to SUMPRODUCT, as shown below. (I realize most people would replace my multiplication signs with commas and add a double-minus before the first two terms, but my version works, too.)

SUMIFS allows for up to 127 conditions. Because you might have an indeterminate number of conditions in the function, the numbers that you are adding up move from the third argument to the first argument. In the following formula, you are summing D2:D22, but only the rows where column B is Allen Matz and column C is Widget. The logic of "Sum this if these conditions are true" is logical in SUMIFS.

		fx	=SUMIFS($D$2:$D$22,$B$2:$B$22,$F4,$C$2:$C$22,G$3)				
	A	B	C	D	E	F	G	H

	Invoice	Rep	Product	Quantity		Summary Table		
1	Invoice	Rep	Product	Quantity				
2	1001	Richard Oldcorn	Widget	267				
3	1002	Allen Matz	Widget	221		Name	Widget	Gadget
4	1003	Rob Collie	Widget	371		Allen Matz	1290	253
5	1004	Rob Collie	Gadget	354		Lorna Banuilos	799	0
6	1005	Lorna Banuilos	Widget	236		Richard Oldcorn	1355	585
7	1006	Allen Matz	Widget	237		Rob Collie	1334	354

Excel 2007 also added plural versions of COUNTIFS and AVERAGEIFS. All these "S" functions are very efficient and fast.

Thanks to Nathi Njoko, Abshir Osman, Scott Russell, and Ryan Sitoy.

#58 Geography & Stock Data Types in Excel

In the past, Excel did not really handle data types. Yes, you could format some cells as Date or Text, but the new data types provide a whole new entry point for new data types now and in the future.

Start with a column of City names. For large cities like Madison Wisconsin, you can just put Madison. For smaller towns, you might enter Madison, FL.

From the Data tab, select Geography.

Excel searches the Internet and finds a city for each cell. A folded map appears next to each cell. Notice that you lose the state that was in the original cell.

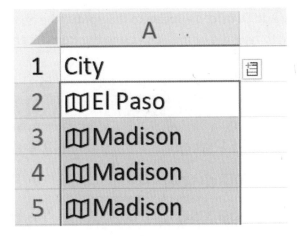

Click on the Map icon and a data card appears with information about the city.

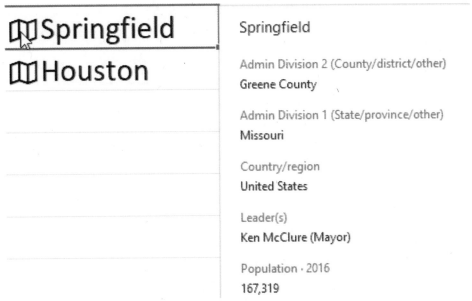

The best part: for any data in the card, you can use a formula to pull that data into a cell. Enter =A2.Population in cell B2 and Excel returns the population of El Paso. Double click the Fill Handle in B2 and Excel returns the population for each city.

	A	B
1	City	Population
2	📖El Paso	683,080
3	📖Madison	2,853
4	📖Madison	47,959
5	📖Madison	2,853
6	📖Paris	9,840
7	📖Springfield	167,319
8	📖Houston	2,303,482

Caution: These new formulas might return a #FIELD! error. This means, Excel (or more correctly Bing, does not know the answer to this yet, but it may do so at some time in the future. It is not an error with the formula or the table, just a lack of knowledge currently.

The Geography and Stock data types have extra features if you format as a table using Ctrl+T.

A new Add Data icon appears to the right of the heading. Use this drop-down menu to add fields without having to type the formulas. Clicking the icon will enter the formula for you.

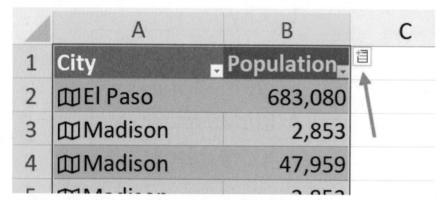

You can also sort the data by any field, even if it is not in the Excel grid. Open the drop-down menu for the City column. Use the new Display Field drop-down to choose Longitude.

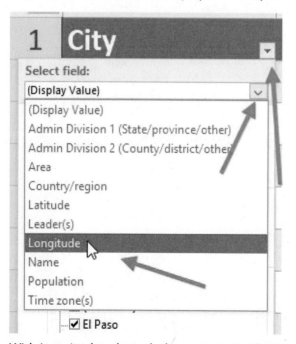

With Longitude selected, choose sort Smallest to Largest.

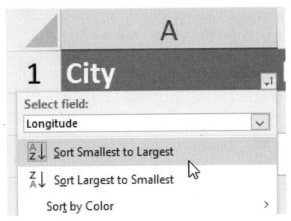

The result: data is sorted west to east.

	A	B	C	D
1	City	Population	Admin Div	Admin Division 2 (Ce
2	El Paso	683,080	Texas	El Paso County
3	Houston	2,303,482	Texas	Harris County
4	Springfield	167,319	Missouri	Greene County
5	Madison	252,551	Wisconsin	Dane County
6	Madison	47,959	Alabama	Madison County
7	Paris	9,840	Kentucky	Bourbon County
8	Madison	2,853	Florida	Madison County

Bonus Tip: Use Data, Refresh All to Update Stock Data

The other data type available is Stock data. Enter some publicly held companies:

	A
1	Company
2	Microsoft
3	Netflix
4	Southwest Airlines
5	Coca Cola

Choose, Data, Stocks. An icon of a building with Roman columns should appear next to each company You can add fields such as CEO, Price, Volume, High, Low, Previous Close.

	A	B	C	D
1	Company	CEO	Price	
2	Microsoft Corp	Mr. Satya Nadella	$ 106.12	
3	Netflix Inc	Mr. Reed Hastings	$ 353.19	
4	Southwest Airlines Co	Gary C. Kelly	$ 50.59	
5	Coca-Cola Co	Mr. James Robert Quincey	$ 47.06	

In contrast to Geography, where population might only be updated once a year, the stock price will be constantly changing throughout the trading day. Rather than go out to the Internet with every recalc, Excel will only updated the data from these Linked Data Types when you choose Refresh.

One easy way to update the stock prices is to use the Refresh All icon on the Data tab.

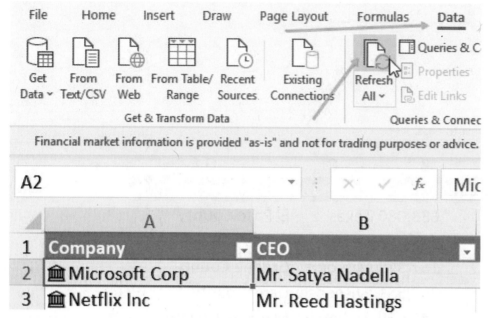

As the name implies, Refresh All will update everything in your workbook, including any Power Query data connections which might take a long time to update. If you want to only refresh the current block of linked data, right-click on A2, choose Data Types, Refresh.

#59 Dynamic Arrays Can Spill

Introduced in 2019, the new Dynamic Arrays represent a major change to the Excel calculation engine. While the old Ctrl+Shift+Enter array formulas could return several results into a pre-selected range, these new formulas do not require Ctrl+Shift+Enter and you don't have to pre-select the range.

For example, let's say you type =B2:B8*C1 into cell C2. In the past, this formula would have required dollar signs around $C$1. You would copy the formula to all 7 cells and something called implicit intersection would make sure the numbers were correct.

	A	B	C	
1	Product	Amount	10%	
2	Apple	5460	=B2:B8*C1	
3	Banana	4370		
4	Cherry	1520		
5	Date	1410		
6	Elderberry	5470		
7	Fig	1620		
8	Guava	2330		
9				

But now, with Dynamic Arrays, one formula in cell C2 will spill over and return results into many cells.

| C2 | ▼ | ⋮ | ✕ | ✓ | *fx* | =B2:B8*C1 |

	A	B	C	D
1	Product	Amount	10%	
2	Apple	2060	206	
3	Banana	1530	153	
4	Cherry	2560	256	
5	Date	2760	276	
6	Elderberry	4450	445	
7	Fig	4790	479	
8	Guava	3940	394	
9				

When you select any cell from C2:C8, a blue outline appears around the cells to let you know that the values are the result of a single formula. That single formula only exists in C2. If you select any other cell in the range, the formula appears in the formula bar, but it is greyed out.

| ✕ | ✓ | *fx* | =B2:B8*C1 |

B	C	D
Amount	10%	
2060	206	
1530	153	
2560	256	

If the range B2:B8 grows (by someone inserting rows in the middle), the spilled results will grow as well. However, simply typing new values in A9:B9 will not cause the formula to extend, unless you format the whole range with Ctrl+T before adding values.

What if a formula can not spill? What if there are non-empty cells in the way? Rather than return partial results, the formula will return the new #SPILL! error.

B	C	
Amount	10%	
1⊙0	#SPILL!	
2420		
2060	stuff	
4030	in	
4740	the	
1490	way	

Open the yellow dropdown to the left of the error and you can select the obstructing cells.

B	C	D
ount	10%	
1 ! ▼	#SPILL!	
2	Spill range isn't blank	
2	Help on this Error	
4	Select Obstructing Cells	
4	Show Calculation Steps...	
1	Ignore Error	
3	Edit in Formula Bar	
	Error Checking Options...	

Once you clear the obstructing cells, the answers will appear again.

#60 Sorting with a Formula

Sorting data in Excel is easy. Unless, you are building a dashboard for your manager's manager. You can't ask that person to select C3, go to the Data tab and click the AZ button every time they want an updated report. The new SORT and SORTBY functions allow you to easily sort with a formula.

You can pass three arguments to the SORT function. The first is the range to be sorted. Leave the headings out of this argument. Next, which column do you want to sort by. If your data is in B:D and you want to sort by column D, you would specify column 3 as the sort column. The third argument is a 1 for ascending or -1 for descending.

In this figure, the data is sorted by Amount descending:

F3				f_x	=SORT(B3:D9,3,-1)		

	A	B	C	D	E	F	G	H
1	**Sort by Amount (column 3), descending (-1)**							
2		Product	Team	Amount				
3		Apple	Red	1220		Elderberry	Red	4740
4		Banana	Blue	2420		Lime	Blue	4030
5		Cherry	Red	2060		Guava	Red	3890
6		Elderberry	Red	4740		Banana	Blue	2420
7		Fig	Blue	1490		Cherry	Red	2060
8		Guava	Red	3890		Fig	Blue	1490
9		Lime	Blue	4030		Apple	Red	1220

What if you want to do a two-level sort? You can specify an array constant for both the second and third argument. In this case, the data is sorted by Team ascending and Amount descending. For the sort column, specify {2;3}. For the sort order, specify {1,-1}.

F3				f_x	=SORT(B3:D9,{2;3},{1;-1})		

	A	B	C	D	E	F	G	H
1	**Sort by Team ascending and Amount descending**							
2		Product	Team	Amount				
3		Apple	Red	1220		Lime	Blue	4030
4		Banana	Blue	2420		Banana	Blue	2420
5		Cherry	Red	2060		Fig	Blue	1490
6		Elderberry	Red	4740		Elderberry	Red	4740
7		Fig	Blue	1490		Guava	Red	3890
8		Guava	Red	3890		Cherry	Red	2060
9		Lime	Blue	4030		Apple	Red	1220

The Excel Calc team also gave you the SORTBY function. Say you want to return a list of products but not the associated amounts. You want the products to be sorted by the amount. The formula below says to return the products from B3:B9 sorted descending by the amounts in D3:D9.

F3				f_x	=SORTBY(B3:B9,D3:D9,-1)		

	A	B	C	D	E	F	G	H
1	Sort products by amount, but only show products							
2		Product	Team	Amount				
3		Apple	Red	1220		Elderberry		
4		Banana	Blue	2420		Lime		
5		Cherry	Red	2060		Guava		
6		Elderberry	Red	4740		Banana		
7		Fig	Blue	1490		Cherry		
8		Guava	Red	3890		Fig		
9		Lime	Blue	4030		Apple		

#61 Filter with a Formula

The FILTER function is new as part of the dynamic arrays feature. There are three arguments: array, include, and an optional [if empty].

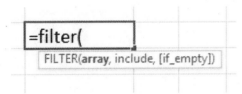

```
=filter(
    FILTER(array, include, [if_empty])
```

Say you want to be able to enter a team name in G1 and extract all of the records for that team. Use a formula of =FILTER(B3:E9,C3:C9=G1).

G3				f_x	=FILTER(B3:E9,C3:C9=G1)				

	A	B	C	D	E	F	G	H	I	J
1	Filter to Red Team						Red			
2		Product	Team	Status	Amount					
3		Apple	Red	O	1220		Apple	Red	O	1220
4		Banana	Blue	C	2420		Cherry	Red	C	2060
5		Cherry	Red	C	2060		Elderberry	Red	O	4740
6		Date	Blue	O	4030		Guava	Red	C	3890
7		Elderberry	Red	O	4740					
8		Fig	Blue	C	1490					
9		Guava	Red	C	3890					
10										

If cell G1 changes from Red to Blue, the results change to show you the blue team records.

F	G	H	I	J
	Blue			
	Banana	Blue	C	2420
	Date	Blue	O	4030
	Fig	Blue	C	1490

In the above examples, the optional [If Empty] argument is missing. If someone is allowed to enter the wrong team name in G1, then you will get a #CALC! error.

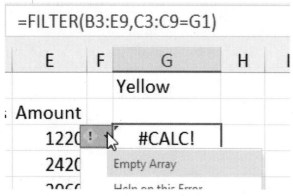

```
=FILTER(B3:E9,C3:C9=G1)
```

E	F	G	H	I
		Yellow		
Amount				
1220	!	#CALC!		
2420		Empty Array		
2060		Help on this Error		

To avoid the #CALC! error, add a third argument.

```
=FILTER(B3:E9,C3:C9=G1,"None Found")
```

E	F	G	H	I
		Yellow		
Amount				
1220		None Found		
2420				

You can specify an array constant for the third argument if you want to fill each column of the answer array.

```
=FILTER(B3:E9,C3:C9=G1,{"No","Team","O",0})
```

E	F	G	H	I	J
		Green			
Amount		Product		Team	Statu Amount
1220		No		Team	O	0
2420					

To filter to records where multiple conditions are met, multiply the conditions together.

| G3 | ▼ | ⋮ | ✕ | ✓ | ƒx | | =FILTER(B3:E9,(C3:C9=G1)*(D3:D9="O"),"None |

	A	B	C	D	E	F	G	H	I	J
1		Filter to Red Team & Status=O					Red			
2		Product	Team	Status	Amount					
3		Apple	Red	O	1220		Apple	Red	O	122(
4		Banana	Blue	C	2420		Elderberry	Red	O	474(
5		Cherry	Red	C	2060					
6		Date	Blue	O	4030					
7		Elderberry	Red	O	4740					
8		Fig	Blue	C	1490					
9		Guava	Red	C	3890					

Bonus Tip: Understanding Array Constants

You've just seen a few examples that included an array constant. Here is a simple way to understand them. A comma inside an array constant means to move to the next column. A semi-colon means to move to the next row. How do you remember which is which? The semi-colon on your keyboard is located near the Enter or Return key which also goes to the next row.

| A4 | ▼ | ⋮ | ✕ | ✓ | ƒx | | ={1;2 |

	A	B	C
1	Separators in an Array Co		
2			
3	Semi-colons (located near Ente		
4	1		
5	2		

When you see an array constant with a mix of commas and semi-colons, remember that each semi-colon moves to a new row.

| ✓ | ƒx | | ={1,2,3;4,5,6} |

	G	H	I	J
	Separators in an Array Constant			
	Columns and rows:			
	1	2	3	
	4	5	6	

3

#62 Formula for Unique or Distinct

The UNIQUE function will provide either a list of unique or distinct values.

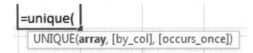

If you ask me for the list of unique values from this list: Apple, Apple, Banana, Cherry, Cherry, I would tell you that the list of unique values is Apple, Banana, Cherry. If you ask 100 accountants, about 92 of them would agree with me. But there is a segment of the population who disagrees and says that the only unique thing in the list is Banana because it is the only item that appears once.

This unusual definition of "unique" comes from the SQL Server world, where database pros would say that "Apple, Banana, Cherry" is a list of distinct values and Banana is the only unique value.

The new UNIQUE function will return either list. If you simply ask for =UNIQUE(R5:R9), you get my definition of all values that occur one or more times. But, if you are a database pro or Casey Kasem, then you can put a True as the third argument.

	R	S	T	U	V	W
3	Unique or Distinct?					
4						
5	Apple		Apple		Banana	
6	Apple		Banana			
7	Banana		Cherry			
8	Cherry					
9	Cherry					
10			=UNIQUE(R5:R9)			
11				=UNIQUE(R5:R9,,TRUE)		

Here is a list of all the Billboard Top 10 Hits from 1979 - 1993.

	A	B	C	D
1	Top 10 Hits 1979-1993			
3	ID	Artist	Track	Genre
4	1979_001	Knack, The	My Sharona	Rock
5	1979_002	Donna Summer	Bad Girls	Rock
6	1979_003	Rod Stewart	Do Ya Think I'm Sexy?	Rock
7	1979_004	Peaches & Herb	Reunited	Rock
8	1979_005	Donna Summer	Hot Stuff	Rock
9	1979_006	Gloria Gaynor	I Will Survive	Rock
10	1979_007	Rupert Holmes	Escape (The Pina Colad	Rock

To get a list of genres, use =UNIQUE()

```
=UNIQUE(D4:D6132)
```

E	F	G
	List of all Genres	
	Rock	
	Easy	
	Vocal	
	Pop	
	R&B	
	Country	
	Folk	

Bonus Tip: Use # "The Spiller" to Refer to All Array Results

In the previous screenshot, the UNIQUE function is in cell F5. You never really know how many results that formula will return. To refer to "the entire array returned by the formula in F5", you would write F5#. There is no official name for this notation, so I am using an idiom coined by Excel MVP Ingeborg Hawighorst: The Spiller.

#63 Other Functions Can Now Accept Arrays as Arguments

Once you see the list of genres, you might want to know how frequently each genre appears. That would normally require a series of COUNTIF or COUNTIFS formulas. For example, =COUNTIF(D$4:D$6132,"Rock") would count how many songs were in the Rock genre. But rather than entering a bunch of COUNTIF functions, you could enter a single COUNTIF function and pass an array as the second argument. The formula below uses The Spiller syntax to ask Excel to repeat the COUNTIF for each answer in the UNIQUE function in F5.

```
=COUNTIF(D4:D6132,F5#)
```

E	F	G
	List of all Genres	
	Rock	4608
	Easy	18
	Vocal	69
	Pop	25

#64 One Hit Wonders with UNIQUE

For me, I can't imagine why I would ever need a list of items that have been sold exactly once. My only example is the One-Hit Wonders segment on Casey Kasem's American Top 40 radio show.

To get a list of artists who had exactly one hit, use =UNIQUE(B4:B6132..True). In the figure below, the UNIQUE function is wrapped in a SORT function so the resulting list is alphabetical.

```
=SORT(UNIQUE(B4:B6132,FALSE,TRUE))
```

	I
	List of One-Hit Wonders
	1 Of The Girls
	10cc
	1927
	2 Hyped Brothers & A Dog

To get the titles in column J, a VLOOKUP uses an array as the first argument. This is pretty wild - one VLOOKUP formula is actually doing over 1000 lookups and returning all 1000 results.

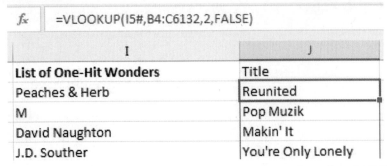

f_x =VLOOKUP(I5#,B4:C6132,2,FALSE)

I	J
List of One-Hit Wonders	**Title**
Peaches & Herb	Reunited
M	Pop Muzik
David Naughton	Makin' It
J.D. Souther	You're Only Lonely

Another approach is to use a FILTER function combined with IFERROR and MATCH.

```
=FILTER(A4:D6132,
IFERROR(MATCH(B4:B6132,
UNIQUE(B4:B6132,FALSE,TRUE),0),FALSE))
```

L	M	N	O	P
	1979_004	Peaches & Herb	Reunited	Rock
	1979_015	M	Pop Muzik	Pop
	1979_047	David Naughton	Makin' It	Rock

#65 SEQUENCE inside of other Functions such as IPMT

After SORT, SORTBY, FILTER, and UNIQUE, the SEQUENCE and RANDARRAY functions seem pretty tame. SEQUENCE will generate a sequence of numbers.

	A	B	C	D
1	=SEQUENCE(			
2	SEQUENCE(**rows**, [columns], [start], [step])			

It does not seem like this is very interesting. Who needs to generate a list of numbers?

	A	B	C	D
1	=SEQUENCE(5)		=SEQUENCE(5,2,3,9)	
2				
3	1		3	12
4	2		21	30
5	3		39	48
6	4		57	66
7	5		75	84

Try putting SEQUENCE inside other functions. Here, IPMT calculates the interest in the 7th month of a loan:

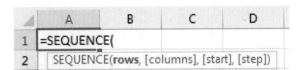

	G	H	I
1	How much interest will be paid		
2	during month 7 of this loan?		
3	Principal	250000	
4	Term	60	
5	Rate	5%	
6			
7	($948.80)	=IPMT(H5/12,7,H4,H3)	

Thanks to SEQUENCE, this formula calculates the interest paid during 12 months starting in month 7:

	G	H	I	J	K	L
1	How much interest will be paid					
2	during months 7-18 of this loan?					
3	Principal	250000				
4	Term	60				
5	Rate	5%				
7	($10,334.60)	=SUM(IPMT(H5/12,SEQUENCE(12,1,7),H4,H3))				
8						
9		**12 numbers starting with 7**				

Two formulas create a forward-looking calendar:

	A	B	C	D	E	F	G
1	**Tue**	**Wed**	**Thu**	**Fri**	**Sat**	**Sun**	**Mon**
2	Jan-29	Jan-30	Jan-31	Feb-1	Feb-2	Feb-3	Feb-4
3	Feb-5	Feb-6	Feb-7	Feb-8	Feb-9	Feb-10	Feb-11
4	Feb-12	Feb-13	Feb-14	Feb-15	Feb-16	Feb-17	Feb-18
5	Feb-19	Feb-20	Feb-21	Feb-22	Feb-23	Feb-24	Feb-25
6	Feb-26	Feb-27	Feb-28	Mar-1	Mar-2	Mar-3	Mar-4
7	A1: =TEXT(A2:G2,"DDD") B1: =SEQUENCE(5,7,TODAY())						

#66 Replace a Pivot Table with 3 Dynamic Arrays

As the co-author of *Pivot Table Data Crunching*, I love a good pivot table. But Excel Project Manager Joe McDaid and Excel MVP Roger Govier both pointed out that the three formulas shown here simulate a pivot table and do not have to be refreshed.

To build the report, **=SORT(UNIQUE(C2:C392))** provides a vertical list of customers starting in **F6**. Then, **=TRANSPOSE(SORT(UNIQUE(A2:A392)))** provides a horizontal list of products starting in **G5**.

When you specify **F6#** and **G5#** in arguments of **SUMIFS**, Excel returns a two-dimensional result: **=SUMIFS(D2:D392,C2:C392,F6#,A2:A392,G5#)**.

G6			fx	=SUMIFS(D2:D392,C2:C392,F6#,A2:A392,G5#)				

	A	B	C	D	E	F	G	H	I
1	Product	Date	Customer	Revenue		F6: =SORT(UNIQUE(C2:C392))			
2	DEF	2/8/2017	ABC Stores	20610		G5: =TRANSPOSE(SORT(UNIQUE(A2:A392)))			
3	DEF	2/23/2017	ABC Stores	8116		G6: =SUMIFS(D2:D392,C2:C392,F6#,A2:A392,G5#)			
4	DEF	8/16/2017	ABC Stores	7032					
5	DEF	5/2/2018	ABC Stores	18290			ABC	DEF	XYZ
6	XYZ	1/6/2017	AT&T	2401		ABC Stores	0	54,048	0
7	XYZ	3/2/2017	AT&T	6765		AT&T	0	271,339	227,598
8	DEF	3/9/2017	AT&T	21357		BankUnited	406,326	0	0

Bonus Tip: Replace Ctrl+Shift+Enter with Dynamic Arrays.

Before dynamic arrays, people would use these crazy Ctrl+Shift+Enter formulas.

Say that you have a friend who is superstitious about Friday the 13th. You want to illustrate how many Friday the 13ths your friend has lived through. Before Dynamic Arrays, you would have to use the formula below.

	A	B	C	D	E
1	Birth Date	2/17/1965			
2	Today	6/12/2018			
3					
4	Number of Friday the 13th's				
5	that you've survived:				
6		91			
7					
8	=SUMPRODUCT(				
9	--(DAY(ROW(INDIRECT(B1&":"&B2)))=13),				
10	--(WEEKDAY(ROW(INDIRECT(B1&":"&B2)),2)=5))				
11					

The same formula after dynamic arrays is still complicated, but less intimidating:

B5   fx   =SUMPRODUCT(
(DAY(SEQUENCE(B4,,B3))=13)*
(WEEKDAY(SEQUENCE(B4,,B3),2)=5))

	A	B	C	D	E	F	G
1	Start	2/17/1965					
2	End	6/12/2018					
3	Start as a number	23790					
4	# of Days	19474	=B2-B1+1				
5	# Friday the 13ths	91					
6							

Another example from Mike Girvin's Ctrl+Shift+Enter book is to get a unique list.

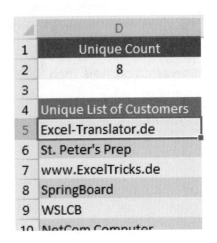

Here is the formula. I won't try to explain it to you.

```
{=IF(ROWS(D$5:D5)>$D$2,"",
INDEX($B$2:$B$146,
SMALL(IF(FREQUENCY(IF($B$2:$B$146<>"",
MATCH($B$2:$B$146,$B$2:$B$146,0)),
ROW($B$2:$B$146)-1),
ROW($B$2:$B$146)-1),
ROWS(D$5:D5)))))}
```

The replacement formula with dynamic arrays is =UNIQUE(B2:B146).

#67 Dependent Validation using Dynamic Arrays

The Data Validation feature lets you choose from a dropdown list in Excel. It works great until someone wants to have two lists. The items in the second list are dependent on what is chosen in the first list. This is called dependent validation.

In the figure below, the items for the first dropdown list appear in **D4#**, thanks to =SORT(UNIQUE(B4:B23)). The validation in **H3** points to =D4#. The list for the second validation appears in **E4#** because of the formula =SORT(FILTER(A4:A23,B4:B23=H3,"Choose Class First")). The validation in **H5** uses =E4#.

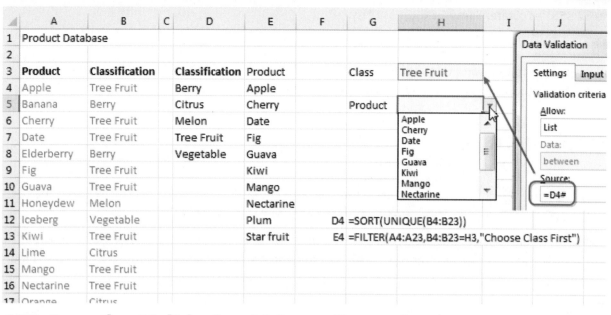

	A	B	C	D	E	F	G	H	I	J
1	Product Database									Data Validation
2										
3	**Product**	**Classification**	**Classification**	Product			Class	Tree Fruit		Settings / Input
4	Apple	Tree Fruit	Berry	Apple						Validation criteria
5	Banana	Berry	Citrus	Cherry			Product			Allow: List
6	Cherry	Tree Fruit	Melon	Date						Data: between
7	Date	Tree Fruit	Tree Fruit	Fig						Source: =D4#
8	Elderberry	Berry	Vegetable	Guava						
9	Fig	Tree Fruit		Kiwi						
10	Guava	Tree Fruit		Mango						
11	Honeydew	Melon		Nectarine						
12	Iceberg	Vegetable		Plum		D4	=SORT(UNIQUE(B4:B23))			
13	Kiwi	Tree Fruit		Star fruit		E4	=FILTER(A4:A23,B4:B23=H3,"Choose Class First")			
14	Lime	Citrus								
15	Mango	Tree Fruit								
16	Nectarine	Tree Fruit								
17	Orange	Citrus								

#68 Complex Validation Using a Formula

The method above is fine if you have Dynamic Arrays. But a lot of people running perpetual versions of Excel won't have Dynamic Arrays for years. Other published methods for Dependent Validation require a new named range for every possible choice in the first and second drop-down.

I was doing a seminar in Mobile, Alabama and several people there wanted to set up a three-level validation, but they did not care about having drop-downs to choose from. "I just want to validate that people are typing the correct values."

Rather than use the option to allow a list, you can set up custom validation using a formula. Say that you have a table with hundreds of valid selections.

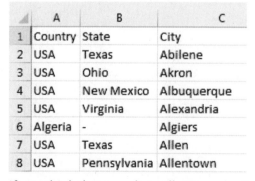

	A	B	C
1	Country	State	City
2	USA	Texas	Abilene
3	USA	Ohio	Akron
4	USA	New Mexico	Albuquerque
5	USA	Virginia	Alexandria
6	Algeria	-	Algiers
7	USA	Texas	Allen
8	USA	Pennsylvania	Allentown

If you think that your list will grow over time, format it as a Table using Ctrl+T.

Set up a named range for each of the three columns. This step is necessary so you can refer to each column and the names will grow as the table grows.

Select A2:A551. In the Name Box, type cCountry and press enter.

cCountry			fx	USA	
	Country	State		City	
2	USA	Texas		Abilene	
3	USA	Ohio		Akron	
4	USA	New Mexico		Albuquerque	
5	USA	Virginia		Alexandria	
6	Algeria	-		Algiers	
7	USA	Texas		Allen	

3

Name B2:B551 as cState. Name C2:C551 as cCity.

Here is the area where you want people to type a Country, State, and City.

It is always easier to build and test your formulas for conditional formatting and validation in a cell first. Take a look at the formulas shown below to test each of the entries.

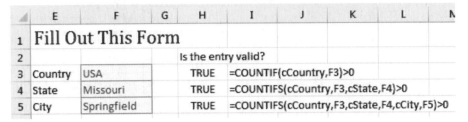

	E	F	G	H	I	J	K	L	N
1	**Fill Out This Form**								
2				Is the entry valid?					
3	Country	USA		TRUE	=COUNTIF(cCountry,F3)>0				
4	State	Missouri		TRUE	=COUNTIFS(cCountry,F3,cState,F4)>0				
5	City	Springfield		TRUE	=COUNTIFS(cCountry,F3,cState,F4,cCity,F5)>0				

Once those formulas are working, edit cell H3. Using the mouse, select the characters in the formula bar and press Ctrl+C to copy. Select F3 and press Alt+D L to open the Data Validation drop-down. In the Allow box, choose Custom. This will reveal a Formula box. Paste your formula in that box.

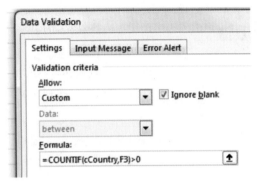

Optionally, fill out an Input Message and Error Alert. Repeat to put the H4 formula as the validation for F4 and the H5 formula for validation for F5. The result: it will prevent a wrong entry.

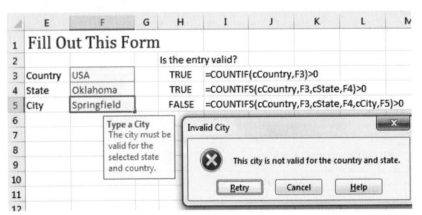

	E	F	G	H	I	J	K	L	N
1	**Fill Out This Form**								
2				Is the entry valid?					
3	Country	USA		TRUE	=COUNTIF(cCountry,F3)>0				
4	State	Oklahoma		TRUE	=COUNTIFS(cCountry,F3,cState,F4)>0				
5	City	Springfield		FALSE	=COUNTIFS(cCountry,F3,cState,F4,cCity,F5)>0				

#69 Use A2:INDEX() as a Non-Volatile OFFSET

There is a flexible function called OFFSET. It can point to a different-sized range that is calculated on-the-fly. In the image below, if someone changes the # Qtrs dropdown in H1 from 3 to 4, the fourth argument of OFFSET will make sure that the range expands to include four columns.

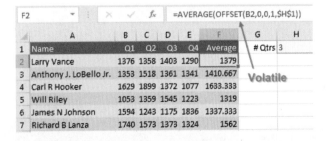

	A	B	C	D	E	F	G	H
	F2			fx	=AVERAGE(OFFSET(B2,0,0,1,$H$1))			
1	Name	Q1	Q2	Q3	Q4	Average	# Qtrs	3
2	Larry Vance	1376	1358	1403	1290	1379		
3	Anthony J. LoBello Jr.	1353	1518	1361	1341	1410.667	Volatile	
4	Carl R Hooker	1629	1899	1372	1077	1633.333		
5	Will Riley	1053	1359	1545	1223	1319		
6	James N Johnson	1594	1243	1175	1836	1337.333		
7	Richard B Lanza	1740	1573	1373	1324	1562		

Spreadsheet gurus hate OFFSET because it is a volatile function. If you go to a completely unrelated cell and enter a number, all of the OFFSET functions will calculate—even if that cell has nothing to do with H1 or B2. Most of the time, Excel is very careful to only spend time calculating the cells that need to calculate. But once you introduce OFFSET, all of the OFFSET cells, plus everything downline from the OFFSET, starts calculating after every change in the worksheet.

In the formula below, there is a colon before the INDEX function. Normally, the INDEX function shown below would return the 1403 from cell D2. But when you put a colon on either side of the INDEX function, it starts returning the cell address D2 instead of the contents of D2. It is wild that this works.

F2			f_x	=AVERAGE(B2:INDEX(B2:E2,$H$1))		
	A	**B**	**C**	**D**	**E**	**F**	**G**	**H**
1	Name	Q1	Q2	Q3	Q4	Average	# Qtrs	3
2	Larry Vance	1376	1358	1403	1290	1379	Index	
3	Anthony J. LoBello Jr.	1353	1518	1361	1341	1410.667	returns	
4	Carl R Hooker	1629	1899	1372	1077	1633.333	D2	
5	Will Riley	1053	1359	1545	1223	1319		
6	James N Johnson	1594	1243	1175	1836	1337.333		

Why does this matter? INDEX is not volatile. You get all of the flexible goodness of OFFSET without the time-sucking recalculations over and over.

I first learned this tip from Dan Mayoh at Fintega. Thanks to Access Analytic for suggesting this feature.

#70 Subscribe to Office 365 for Monthly Features

From 1997 to 2013, there was a predictable release cycle for Microsoft Office. A new version would come out every three years. Your IT department would wait one year for the Service Pack to come out and then would consider upgrading.

All of the Office apps had to ship on the same day. This created pressure on each individual team to have their features ready in time. No one wanted to be the person who caused the Office release date to slip. Some great Excel features got ripped out of the product because the team wasn't sure they could complete those features in time. If a feature did not make it into an Excel version, there would not be another opportunity for three years for that feature to make it into the product.

Today, the paradigm has changed. The Excel team has an opportunity to release a new feature to Office 365 on any given Tuesday. If a feature is not quite done this Tuesday, it only slips seven days, until the next Tuesday. There is no pressure to have 15 new features all ready on a certain day.

The net result is that Office 365 subscribers are getting access to many more features. While it can be annoying that this book is obsolete the Tuesday after it prints, I appreciate getting great new features every month instead of every three years.

Your IT department still has a measure of control over when you get the features. There are several channels for distributing features:

- People who are not doing mission-critical work and want to test the latest bits can sign up for the Insider channel. On any given Tuesday, my Excel can experience bizarre bugs. One day, the Pivot Table Fields List stopped updating.

- People who like to see new features but who don't want to find themselves without Office can sign up for the Monthly Channel (Targeted) channel. Features appear in this channel about four weeks after they appear in the Insider channel. By that point, any bugs discovered by the Insider people have been resolved. You get new features quickly, but you won't see bugs that cause parts of Excel to stop working.

- Your IT department is likely going to have you on the semi-annual channel. These people get features every 26 weeks. The features have been tested by millions of other customers and are safe to use.

So a feature can be used by all Office 365 customers about 6 months after it is released. This beats the 3-year wait for a new version of Office and then the 12-month wait for your IT department to see the Service Pack and know it is safe to install.

Caution: Microsoft still sells a perpetual version of Office 2019. You pay once and never pay a monthly fee. But you will not get the new features. I feel bad for the people who paid $400 for Office 2019 but are not getting all of the new features such as Dynamic Arrays and Geography Data Types.

Note: Office 365 does not mean you are running Office in the cloud. When you subscribe to Office 365, you agree to pay a monthly or annual fee, and you are using the real version of Office for Windows. As part of the bundle, you can also run Office on an iPad, or an Android, or in a web browser. For most people, those are not where most work gets done.

Here are some of the features that are only available to Office 365 subscribers:

- Pivot Table defaults: I want all future pivot tables to appear in Tabular layout instead of Compact.

- You now have access to Funnel chart, Map charts, the Insert Icons feature, and the ability to insert 3D models with full rotation ability.

- Co-authoring: Your whole team can now be editing the same Excel workbook at the same time.

- The black theme in Excel is available for people who like to work in the dark.

- The new functions MAXIFS, MINIFS, IFS, SWITCH, CONCAT, and TEXTJOIN: I hate to sound superlative, but the freaking awesomeness of =TEXTJOIN(", ",True,A2:A99) is truly life-changing, particularly since the third argument can handle arrays to create a criteria-based TEXTJOIN.

- Excel will not nag you twice when you want to save as CSV. Trust me, for the people who had to create 100 CSV files a day to feed data into some other system, the constant nagging of "Are you sure? You will lose some features if you go with CSV" were annoying.

- A new Superscript and Subscript icon have been added.

- Improved function autocomplete: If you start to type =LOOKUP, the tooltip will offer VLOOKUP, HLOOKUP, and LOOKUP.

- Power Query has new features, including the ability for Split Columns (think: Text to Columns) to split at a delimiter but put each item in a new row. It also adds Column by Example, similar to Flash Fill.

- The ability to turn off the newly introduced Pivot Table Date Grouping feature.

- You can now copy cells and they stay on the clipboard, even if you insert some rows or columns.

- Dynamic Arrays and new functions like SORT, SORTBY, UNIQUE, and FILTER.

- Picture transparency is now controlled with a slider on the Picture Tools tab.

- Artificial Intelligence with Ideas.

By the time you read this book, several more new features will have been added.

#71 Find Largest Value That Meets One or More Criteria

One of the new Office 365 functions added in February 2016 is the MAXIFS function. This function, which is similar to SUMIFS, finds the largest value that meets one or more criteria: You can either hard-code the criterion as in row 7 below or point to cells as in row 9. A similar MINIFS function finds the smallest value that meets one or more criteria.

	A	B	C	D	E	F	G	H
1	Largest	$99,876.41	=MAX($D$12:$D$125)					
2	2nd Largest	$99,588.23	=LARGE($D$12:$D$125,2)					
3	3rd Largest	$98,469.33	=LARGE($D$12:$D$125,3)					
4	3rd Smallest	$14,691.12	=SMALL($D$12:$D$125,3)					
5	2nd Smallest	$14,469.75	=SMALL($D$12:$D$125,2)					
6	Smallest	$13,593.04	=MIN($D$12:$D$125)					
7	Smallest Widget	$13,593.04	=MINIFS($D$12:$D$125,$B$12:$B$125,"Widget")					
8	Choose Criteria:	Widget	Central ▼					
9	Largest with Criteria	$90,861.70	=MAXIFS($D$12:$D$125,$B$12:$B$125,B8,$C$12:$C$125,C8)					
10								
11	Name	Item	Region	Amount				
12	Peter Albert	Gadget	East	$40,292.39				
13	Amy Andrae	Whatzit	Central	$28,872.16				
14	Frank Arendt-Theilen	Gadget	West	$88,640.58				
15	Fr Tony Azzarto	Gadget	East	$49,898.29				
16	Lorna Banuilos	Widget	Central	$90,861.70				

While most people have probably heard of MAX and MIN, but how do you find the second largest value? Use LARGE (rows 2 and 3) or SMALL (rows 4 and 5).

What if you need to sum the top seven values that meet criteria? The orange box below shows how to solve with the new Dynamic Arrays. The green box is the Ctrl+Shift+Enter formula required previously.

	A	B	C	D
1		Item	Gadget	Top
2	Choose Criteria:	Widget	Central	7
3	Sum Top N meeting Criteria	486268.16		
4				
5	=SUM(LARGE(FILTER(D13:D126,			
6	(B13:B126=B2)*(C13:C126=C2)),			
7	SEQUENCE(D2)))			
8				
9	{=SUM(AGGREGATE(14,4,($B$13:$B$126=$B$2) *($C$13:$C$126=$C$2) *($D$13:$D$126), ROW(INDIRECT("1:"&D2)))))}			
10				
11				
12	Name	Item	Region	Amount
13	Peter Albert	Gadget	East	$40,292.39
14	Amy Andrae	Whatzit	Central	$28,872.16

Bonus Tip: Concatenate a Range by Using TEXTJOIN

My favorite new calculation function in Office 365 is TEXTJOIN. What if you needed to concatenate all of the names in A1:A10? The formula =A1&A2&A3&A4&A5&A6&A7&A8&A9&A10 would jam everyone together like AndyBobCaroleDaleEdFloGloriaHelenIkeJill. By using TEXTJOIN, you can specify a delimiter such as ", ". The second argument lets you specify if blank cells should be ignored. =TEXTJOIN(", ",True,A1:A10) would produce Andy, Bob, Carole, and so on.

Tip: TEXTJOIN works with arrays. The array formula shown in A7 uses a criterion to find only the people who answered Yes. Make sure to hold down Ctrl + Shift while pressing Enter to accept this formula. The alternate formula shown in A8 uses the Dynamic Array FILTER function and does not require Ctrl+Shift+Enter.

	A	B
1	List of invitees:	
2	Zack Barresse, Jeremy Bartz, Simon Benninga, Caroline Bonner, Melanie Breden, Derek Brown, Brian Canes, John Cockerill, Rob Collie	
3	=TEXTJOIN(", ",TRUE,$A$10:$A$18)	
5	List where RSVP is Yes:	
6	Zack Barresse, Melanie Breden, John Cockerill, Rob Collie	
7	{=TEXTJOIN(", ",TRUE,IF(B10:B18="Yes",A10:A18,""))}	
8	=TEXTJOIN(", ",TRUE,FILTER(A10:A18,B10:B18="Yes"))	
9	Name	RSVP
10	Zack Barresse	Yes
11	Jeremy Bartz	No
12	Simon Benninga	No
13	Caroline Bonner	No
14	Melanie Breden	Yes
15	Derek Brown	No
16	Brian Canes	No
17	John Cockerill	Yes
18	Rob Collie	Yes

#72 Less CSV Nagging and Better AutoComplete

Some people have to create CSV files hundreds of times per day. Excel used to hassle you when you saved a CSV file: "Some features in your workbook might be lost if you save as CSV." People who have to export as CSV understand this and wanted Excel to stop hassling them. Starting in 2017, people with Office 365 are no longer hassled for choosing to save as CSV.

Another small change in Office 365: If you type an equals sign and start to type a function name, the tooltip offers partial matching. Type LOOK, and you will see all three functions that contain the text LOOK.

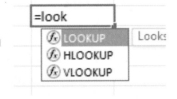

#73 Speed Up VLOOKUP

VLOOKUP is a relatively expensive function. When you are looking for an exact match, Excel has to look through the lookup table one row at a time. Previous editions of this book demonstrated a Charles Williams formula to make VLOOKUP faster. Starting in 2018, Office 365 includes a re-engineered VLOOKUP that is as fast as the Charles Williams trick.

=IF(VLOOKUP(A2,Table,1)=A2,VLOOKUP(A2,Table,1),"Not Found")

#74 Protect All Formula Cells

The use of worksheet protection in Excel is a little strange. Using the steps below, you can quickly protect just the formula cells in your worksheet.

It seems unusual, but all 16 billion cells on a worksheet start out with their Locked property set to True. You need to unlock all of the cells first:

1. Select all cells by using the icon above and to the left of cell A1.

2. Press Ctrl+1 (that is the number 1) to open the Format Cells dialog.

3. In the Format Cells dialog, go to the Protection tab. Uncheck Locked. Click OK.

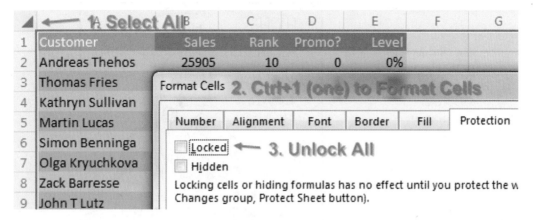

While all cells are still selected, select Home, Find & Select, Formulas.

At this point, only the formula cells are selected. Press Ctrl+1 again to display the Format Cells dialog. On the Protection tab, choose Locked to lock all of the formula cells.

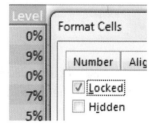

Locking cells does nothing until you protect the worksheet. On the Review tab, choose Protect Sheet. In the Protect Sheet dialog, choose if you want people to be able to select your formula cells or not.

> **Note:** Scroll down a few rows in the Protect Sheet dialog box to reveal popular choices: Use AutoFilter and Use PivotTable & PivotChart. If you want allow people to interact with these features, scroll down and select them.

> **Caution:** Don't bother putting in a password. Passwords are easily broken and easily lost. You will find yourself paying $39 to the Estonians who sell the Office password-cracking software.

#75 Back into an Answer by Using Goal Seek

Do you remember from ""#44 Discover New Functions by Using fx" on page 113, that I showed you how to calculate a loan payment by using the Insert Function dialog? Back in that example, the monthly loan payment was going to be $493.54. I did not mention it at the time, but my monthly budget for car payments is $425.

If you are about the same age as me and spent your summers watching TV, you might remember a crazy game show called *The Price Is Right*. Long before Drew Carey, the venerable Bob Barker would give away prizes using a variety of games. One that I recall is the Hi Lo game. Bob would give you the car if you could state the price of the car. You would guess. Bob would shout "Higher" or "Lower." I think you had 20 seconds to narrow your guesses to the exact price.

4

A lot of times, I feel like those summers watching Bob Barker trained me to find answers in Excel. Have you ever found yourself plugging in successively higher and lower values into an input cell, hoping to arrive at a certain answer?

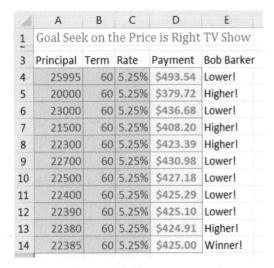

Illustration: Chad Thomas

A tool that is built in to Excel does exactly this set of steps. Select the cell with the Payment formula. On the Data tab, in the Data Tools group, look for the What-If Analysis dropdown and choose Goal Seek….

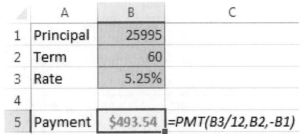

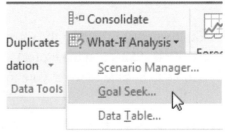

The figure below shows how you can try to set the payment in B5 to $425 by changing cell B1

Goal Seek finds the correct answer within a second.

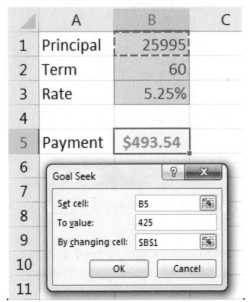

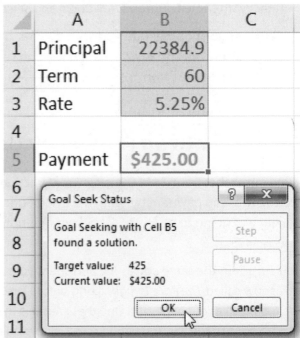

Note that the formula in B5 stays intact. The only thing that changes is the input value typed in B1.

Also, with Goal Seek, you are free to experiment with changing other input cells. You can still get the $425 loan payment and the $25,995 car if your banker will offer you a 71.3379-month loan!

	A	B
1	Principal	25995
2	Term	71.3379
3	Rate	5.25%
4		
5	Payment	$425.00

Thanks to Jon Wittwer of Vertex42.com and to @BizNetSoftware for suggesting this Goal Seek trick.

#76 Do 60 What-If Analyses with a Sensitivity Analysis

Goal Seek lets you find the set of inputs that lead to a particular result. Sometimes, you want to see many different results from various combinations of inputs. Provided that you have only two input cells to change, the Data Table feature will do a sensitivity analysis.

Using the loan payment example, say that you want to calculate the price for a variety of principal balances and for a variety of terms.

	A	B	C	D	E	F
1	Principal	25995	Test from $20,995 to $29,995			
2	Term	60	Test from 36 to 72			
3	Rate	5.25%				
4						
5	Payment	$494				

Make sure that the formula you want to model is in the top-left corner of a range. Put various values for one variable down the left column and various values for another variable across the top.

B5 | | × | ✓ | f_x | =PMT(B3/12,B2,-B1)

	A	B	C	D	E	F	G	H
5	Payment	$494	36	48	54	60	66	72
6		20,995						
7		21,995						
8		22,995						

From the Data tab, select What-If Analysis, Data Table....

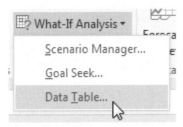

What-If Analysis ▾
Forec
Scenario Manager...
Goal Seek...
Data Table...

4

You have values along the top row of the input table. You want Excel to plug those values into a certain input cell. Specify that input cell for Row Input Cell.

You have values along the left column. You want those plugged into another input cell. Specify that cell for the Column Input Cell.

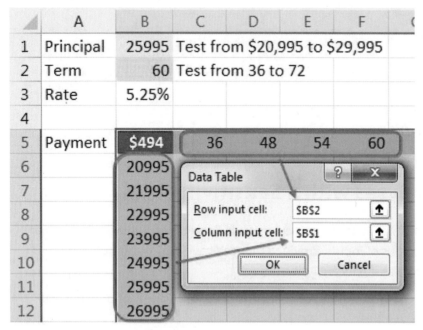

When you click OK, Excel repeats the formula in the top-left column for all combinations of the top row and left column. In the image below, you see 60 different loan payments, based on various inputs.

$494	36	48	54	60	66	72
20,995	632	486	437	399	367	341
21,995	662	509	458	418	384	357
22,995	692	532	479	437	402	373
23,995	722	555	500	456	419	389
24,995	752	578	521	475	437	405
25,995	782	602	542	494	454	422
26,995	812	625	562	513	472	438
27,995	842	648	583	532	489	454
28,995	872	671	604	550	507	470
29,995	902	694	625	569	524	487

Note: I formatted the table results to have no decimals and used Home, Conditional Formatting, Color Scale to add the red/yellow/green shading.

Here is the great part: This table is "live." If you change the input cells along the left column or top row, the values in the table recalculate. Below, the values along the left are focused on the $23K to $24K range.

$494	48	51	54	57	60	63
22,995	532	504	479	457	437	418
23,095	534	506	481	459	438	420
23,195	537	508	483	461	440	422

Tip: You can build far more complex models and still use a data table. In my podcast 2141 "Will Asteroid Bennu Strike the Earth" on YouTube, I had a model with 100K NORM.INV and 100K VLOOKUP. Those 200,000 formulas were sent to a SUM function that summarized them. I used a Data Table to run those 200,001 formulas 100 times. The whole thing recalcs in about 11 seconds.

Thanks to Owen W. Green for suggesting this tables technique.

Bonus Tip: Create a Data Table from a Blank Cell

Note: If you took a class on financial modeling in college, you likely used a textbook written by Professor Simon Benninga. He showed me this cool Excel trick.

Simon Benninga tells a story of a game called Penny Pitching. You and another student would each flip a penny. If you get one head and one tail, you win the penny. If the coins match (heads/heads or tails/tails), the other student gets the penny.

It is simple to model this game in Excel. If RAND()>.5, you win a penny. Otherwise, you lose a penny. Do that for 25 rows and chart the result. Press F9 to play 25 more rounds.

This is known as a Random Walk Down Wall Street. Simon would point out a result like the one below, where a hot young stock analyst is on fire with a series of wins, but then a series of losses wipe out the gain. This is why they say that past results are not a guarantee of future returns.

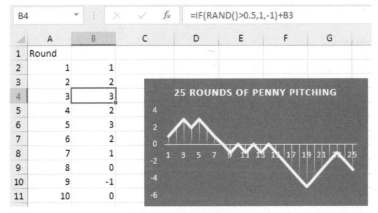

Instead of 25 trials, extend your table in columns A and B to run 250 trials. This would be like playing one round of penny pitching every work day for a year. Build a row of statistics about that year, as shown below.

	G	H	I	J	K	L
	Max	Min	Average	Win Streak	Lose Streak	Final
	3	-30	-14.7	6	8	-30

Create an odd data table where the blank cell in column F is the corner cell. Leave Row Input Cell blank. Specify any blank cell for Column Input Cell.

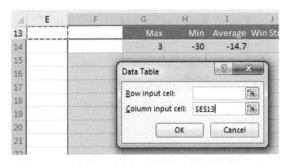

4

When you create the table, Excel runs the 250 coin flips, once per row. This 30-row table models the entire career of a stock analyst. Every time you press F9, Excel runs the 250-row model for each of 30 years. You can watch an entire 30-year career be modeled with the simple press of F9.

	G	H	I	J	K		L
13	Max	Min	Average	Win Streak	Lose Streak		Final
14	2	-16	-5.412	6	9	▼	-12
15	3	-26	-14.028	5	6	▼	-22
16	21	-5	6.772	12	7	▲	+14
44	19	-3	9.78	12	7	▭	0

Note: The download file for this chapter shows a few different ways to calculate the Win Streak and Loss Streak.

Thanks to Professor Simon Benninga for showing me this technique.

#77 Find Optimal Solutions with Solver

Excel was not the first spreadsheet program. Lotus 1-2-3 was not the first spreadsheet program. The first spreadsheet program was VisiCalc in 1979. Developed by Dan Bricklin and Bob Frankston, VisiCalc was published by Dan Fylstra. Today, Dan runs Frontline Systems. His company wrote the Solver used in Excel. Frontline Systems has also developed a whole suite of analytics software that works with Excel.

If you have Excel, you have Solver. It may not be enabled, but you have it. To enable Solver in Excel, press Alt+T followed by I. Add a checkmark next to Solver Add-in.

To successfully use Solver, you have to build a worksheet model that has three elements:

- There has to be a single Goal cell. This is a cell that you either want to minimize, maximize, or set to a particular value.

- There can be many input cells. This is one fundamental improvement over Goal Seek, which can deal with only one input cell.

- There can be constraints.

Your goal is to build the scheduling requirements for an amusement park. Each employee will work five straight days and then have two days off. There are seven different possible ways to schedule someone for five straight days and two off days. These are shown as text in A4:A10 in the figure below. The blue cells in B4:B10 are the input cells. This is where you specify how many people you have working each schedule.

The Goal cell is total Payroll/Week, shown in B17. This is straight math: Total People from B11 times $68 salary per person per day. You will ask Solver to find a way to minimize the weekly payroll.

The red box shows values that will not change. This is how many people you need working the park on each day of the week. You need at least 30 people on the busy weekend days—but as few as 12 on Monday and Tuesday. The orange cells use SUMPRODUCT to calculate how many people will be scheduled each day, based on the inputs in the blue cells.

The icons in row 15 indicate whether you need more people or fewer people or whether you have exactly the right number of people.

First, I tried to solve this problem without Solver. I went with 4 employees each day. That was great, but I did not have enough people on Sunday. So, I started increasing schedules to get more Sunday employees. I ended up with something that works: 38 employees and $2,584 of weekly payroll.

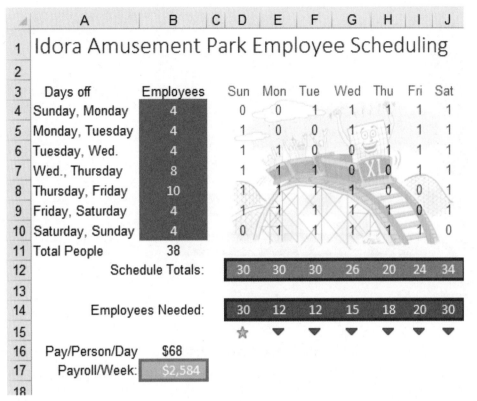

	Days off	Employees		Sun	Mon	Tue	Wed	Thu	Fri	Sat
3				Sun	Mon	Tue	Wed	Thu	Fri	Sat
4	Sunday, Monday	4		0	0	1	1	1	1	1
5	Monday, Tuesday	4		1	0	0	1	1	1	1
6	Tuesday, Wed.	4		1	1	0	0	1	1	1
7	Wed., Thursday	8		1	1	1	0	0	1	1
8	Thursday, Friday	10		1	1	1	1	0	0	1
9	Friday, Saturday	4		1	1	1	1	1	0	1
10	Saturday, Sunday	4		0	1	1	1	1	1	0
11	Total People	38								
12	Schedule Totals:			30	30	30	26	20	24	34
13										
14	Employees Needed:			30	12	12	15	18	20	30
15				☆	▼	▼	▼	▼	▼	▼
16	Pay/Person/Day	$68								
17	Payroll/Week:	$2,584								

(Title row: **Idora Amusement Park Employee Scheduling**)

Of course, there is an easier way to solve this problem. Click the Solver icon on the Data tab. Tell Solver that you are trying to set the payroll in B17 to the minimum. The input cells are B4:B10.

Constraints fall into obvious and not-so-obvious categories.

The first obvious constraint is that D12:J12 has to be >= D14:J14.

But, if you tried to run Solver now, you would get bizarre results with fractional numbers of people and possibly a negative number of people working certain schedules.

While it seems obvious to you that you can't hire 0.39 people, you need to add constraints to tell Solver that B4:B10 are >= 0 and that B4:B10 are integers.

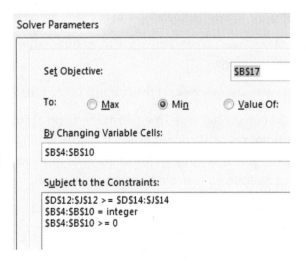

Solver Parameters

Set Objective: $B$17

To: ○ Max ● Min ○ Value Of:

By Changing Variable Cells:
$B$4:$B$10

Subject to the Constraints:
$D$12:$J$12 >= $D$14:$J$14
$B$4:$B$10 = integer
$B$4:$B$10 >= 0

Choose Simplex LP as the solving method and click Solve. In a few moments, Solver presents one optimal solution.

4

Solver finds a way to cover the amusement park staffing by using 30 employees instead of 38. The savings per week is $544—or more than $7000 over the course of the summer.

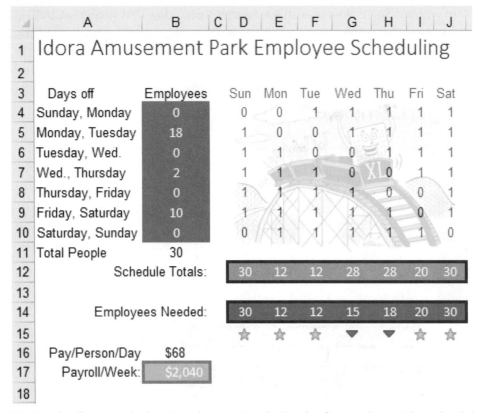

	A	B	C D	E	F	G	H	I	J
1	Idora Amusement Park Employee Scheduling								
2									
3	Days off	Employees	Sun	Mon	Tue	Wed	Thu	Fri	Sat
4	Sunday, Monday	0	0	0	1	1	1	1	1
5	Monday, Tuesday	18	1	0	0	1	1	1	1
6	Tuesday, Wed.	0	1	1	0	0	1	1	1
7	Wed., Thursday	2	1	1	1	0	0	1	1
8	Thursday, Friday	0	1	1	1	1	0	0	1
9	Friday, Saturday	10	1	1	1	1	1	0	1
10	Saturday, Sunday	0	0	1	1	1	1	1	0
11	Total People	30							
12	Schedule Totals:		30	12	12	28	28	20	30
13									
14	Employees Needed:		30	12	12	15	18	20	30
15			☆	☆	☆	▼	▼	☆	☆
16	Pay/Person/Day	$68							
17	Payroll/Week:	$2,040							
18									

Notice the five stars below Employees Needed in the figure above. The schedule that Solver proposed meets your exact needs for five of the seven days. The by-product is that you will have more employees on Wednesday and Thursday than you really need.

I can understand how Solver came up with this solution. You need a lot of people on Saturday, Sunday, and Friday. One way to get people there on those day is to give them Monday and Tuesday off. That is why Solver gave 18 people Monday and Tuesday off.

But just because Solver came up with an optimal solution does not mean that there are not other equally optimal solutions.

When I was just guessing at the staffing, I didn't really have a good strategy.

Now that Solver has given me one of the optimal solutions, I can put on my logic hat. Having 28 college-age employees on Wednesday and Thursday when you only need 15 or 18 employees is going to lead to trouble. There won't be enough to do. Plus, with exactly the right head count on five days, you will have to call in someone for overtime if someone else calls in sick.

I trust Solver that I need to have 30 people to make this work. But I bet that I can rearrange those people to even out the schedule and provide a small buffer on other days.

For example, giving someone Wednesday and Thursday off also ensures that the person is at work Friday, Saturday, and Sunday. So, I manually move some workers from the Monday, Tuesday row to the Wednesday, Thursday row. I keep manually plugging in different combinations and come up with the solution shown below which has the same payroll expense as Solver but better intangibles. The overstaff situation now exists on four days instead of two. That means you can handle absences on Monday through Thursday without having to call in someone from their weekend.

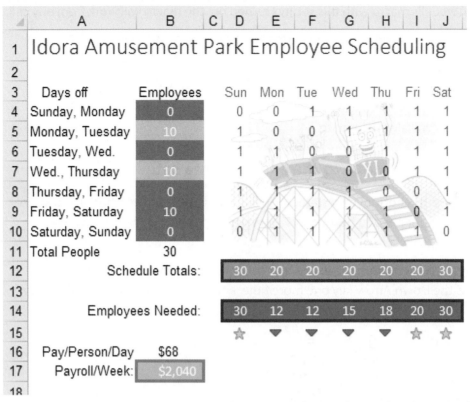

Days off	Employees	Sun	Mon	Tue	Wed	Thu	Fri	Sat
Sunday, Monday	0	0	0	1	1	1	1	1
Monday, Tuesday	10	1	0	0	1	1	1	1
Tuesday, Wed.	0	1	1	0	0	1	1	1
Wed., Thursday	10	1	1	1	0	0	1	1
Thursday, Friday	0	1	1	1	1	0	0	1
Friday, Saturday	10	1	1	1	1	1	0	1
Saturday, Sunday	0	0	1	1	1	1	1	0
Total People	30							
Schedule Totals:		30	20	20	20	20	20	30
Employees Needed:		30	12	12	15	18	20	30
Pay/Person/Day	$68							
Payroll/Week:	$2,040							

Row 1: Idora Amusement Park Employee Scheduling

Is it bad that I was able to come up with a better solution than Solver? No. The fact is that I would not have been able to get to this solution without using Solver. Once Solver gave me a model that minimized costs, I was able to use logic about intangibles to keep the same payroll.

If you need to solve problems that are more complex than Solver can handle, check out the premium Excel solvers available from Frontline Systems: mrx.cl/solver77.

Thanks to Dan Fylstra and Frontline Systems for this example. Walter Moore illustrated the XL roller coaster.

#78 Improve Your Macro Recording

I loved the 1985 version of the Macro Recorder in Lotus 1-2-3. The code was hard to understand, but it worked. There are some defaults in the Excel Macro Recorder that cause misery for anyone trying to record macros. Here are three tips to make the macro experience possibly better.

Tip 1: Turn on Relative Reference for Every Macro.

Say that you start in A2 and record a simple macro that moves to A4. I would call that macro MoveDownTwoCells. But if you run this macro while the cell pointer is in J10, the macro will move to cell A4. This is rarely what you want to have happen. But you can change the behavior of the macro recorder by selecting View, Macros, Use Relative References before you record the macro.

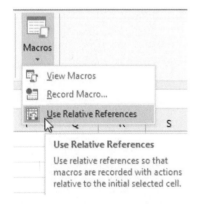

4

If you record the MoveDownTwoCells macro with this setting turned on, the macro will work from any cell.

Caution: The setting stays turned on only until you close Excel. Tomorrow, you will have to turn it back on again.

Tip: What if you actually need to record a macro that always jumps to cell A4? Even with Relative References enabled, you could press F5 for Go To and use the Go To dialog to go to A4. The macro recorder will record code that will always jump to A4.

Tip 2: Use Ctrl+Shift+Arrow to move to the end of a data set.

Say that you want to add a total at the bottom of yesterday's invoice register. You want the total to appear in row 9 today, but tomorrow, it might need to be in row 17 or row 5, depending on how many rows of data you have.

Find a column that is reliably 100% filled. From the top of that column, record the action of pressing Ctrl+Shift+Down Arrow. Press the Down Arrow key one more time, and you will know you are in the row where the totals should be.

	A	B	C	D	E
1	InvoiceDate	InvoiceNun	SalesRepl	Customer	ProductRe
2	5/8/2021	123829	S21	C8754	21000
3	5/8/2021	123830	S45	C3390	188100
4	5/8/2021	123831	S54	C2523	510600
5	5/8/2021	123832	S21	C5519	86200
6	5/8/2021	123833	S45	C3245	800100
7	5/8/2021	123834	S54	C7796	339000
8	5/8/2021	123835	S21	C1654	161000
9		**Ctrl+Shift+↓**			
10					

Tip 3: Type =SUM(E$2:E8) instead of pressing the AutoSum button

The macro recorder will not record the intent of AutoSum. When you press AutoSum, you will get a sum function that starts in the cell above and extends up to the first non-numeric cell. It does not matter if you have Relative References on or off; the macro recorder will hard-code that you want to sum the seven cells above the active cell.

Instead of using the AutoSum icon, type a SUM function with a single dollar sign before the first row number: =SUM(E$2:E8). Use that formula while recording the macro, and the macro will reliably sum from the cell above the active cell all the way up to row 2, as shown below.

=SUM(E$2:E8)

	E	
ier	ProductRe	Servi
	21000	
	188100	
	510600	
	86200	
	800100	
	339000	
	161000	
	2106000	

#79 Clean Data with Power Query

Power Query is built in to Windows versions of Office 365, Excel 2016, Excel 2019 and is available as a free download in Windows versions of Excel 2010 and Excel 2013. The tool is designed to extract, transform, and load data into Excel from a variety of sources. The best part: Power Query remembers your steps and will play them back when you want to refresh the data. This means you can clean data on Day 1 in 80% of the normal time, and you can clean data on Days 2 through 400 by simply clicking Refresh.

I say this about a lot of new Excel features, but this really is the best feature to hit Excel in 20 years.

I tell a story in my live seminars about how Power Query was invented as a crutch for SQL Server Analysis Services customers who were forced to use Excel in order to access Power Pivot. But Power Query kept getting better, and every person using Excel should be taking the time to learn Power Query.

Get Power Query

You may already have Power Query. It is in the Get & Transform group on the Data tab.

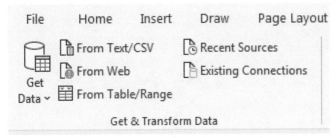

But if you are in Excel 2010 or Excel 2013, go to the Internet and search for Download Power Query. Your Power Query commands will appear on a dedicated Power Query tab in the Ribbon.

Clean Data the First Time in Power Query

To give you an example of some of the awesomeness of Power Query, say that you get the file shown below every day. Column A is not filled in. Quarters are going across instead of down the page.

To start, save that workbook to your hard drive. Put it in a predictable place with a name that you will use for that file every day.

	A	B	C	D	E	F
1	Product	Customer	Q1	Q2	Q3	Q4
2	Apple	SkyWire, Inc.	225	151	126	183
3		Tennessee Moo	156	185	150	273
4		SlinkyRN Excel I	284	111	130	281
5		University of No	185	230	259	123
6		Spain Enterprise	223	281	242	159
7		SkyWire, Inc.	267	174	213	204
8	Banana	Steve Comer	176	252	143	214
9		The Lab with Le(	295	198	134	172
10		Steve Comer	132	234	193	255

In Excel, select Get Data, From File, From Workbook.

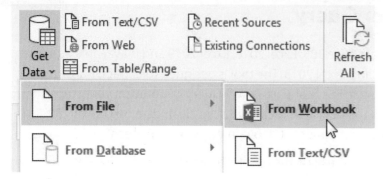

Browse to the workbook. In the Preview pane, click on Sheet1. Instead of clicking Load, click Edit. You now see the workbook in a slightly different grid—the Power Query grid.

Now you need to fix all the blank cells in column A. If you were to do this in the Excel user interface, the unwieldy command sequence is Home, Find & Select, Go To Special, Blanks, Equals, Up Arrow, Ctrl+Enter.

	A^B_C Product		A^B_C Customer
1	Apple		SkyWire, Inc.
2		null	Tennessee Moon
3		null	SlinkyRN Excel Instruction and Consulting
4		null	University of North Carolina

In Power Query, select Transform, Fill, Down.

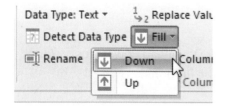

All of the null values are replaced with the value from above. With Power Query, it takes three clicks instead of seven.

Next problem: The quarters are going across instead of down. In Excel, you can fix this with a Multiple Consolidation Range pivot table. This requires 12 steps and 23+ clicks.

In Power Query select the two columns that are not quarters. Open the Unpivot Columns dropdown on the Transform tab and choose Unpivot Other Columns, as shown below.

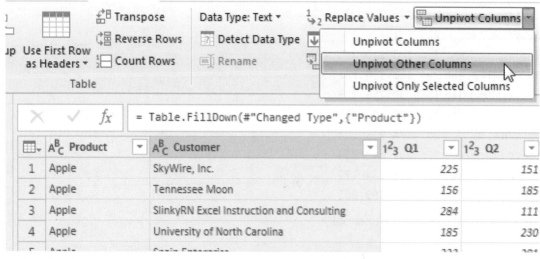

Right-click on the newly created Attribute column and rename it Quarter instead of Attribute. Twenty-plus clicks in Excel becomes five clicks in Power Query.

	Product	Customer	Quarter	Value
1	Apple	SkyWire, Inc.	Q1	225
2	Apple	SkyWire, Inc.	Q2	151
3	Apple	SkyWire, Inc.	Q3	126
4	Apple	SkyWire, Inc.	Q4	183
5	Apple	Tennessee Moon	Q1	156
6	Apple	Tennessee Moon	Q2	185

Now, to be fair, not every cleaning step is shorter in Power Query than in Excel. Removing a column still means right-clicking a column and choosing Remove Column. But to be honest, the story here is not about the time savings on Day 1.

But Wait: Power Query Remembers All of Your Steps

Look on the right side of the Power Query window. There is a list called Applied Steps. It is an instant audit trail of all of your steps. Click any gear icon to change your choices in that step and have the changes cascade through the future steps. Click on any step for a view of how the data looked before that step.

When you are done cleaning the data, click Close & Load as shown below.

> **Tip**: If your data is more than 1,048,576 rows, you can use the Close & Load dropdown to load the data directly to the Power Pivot Data Model, which can accommodate 995 million rows if you have enough memory installed on the machine.

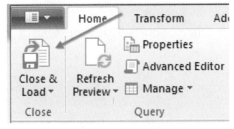

In a few seconds, your transformed data appears in Excel. Awesome.

	Product	Customer	Quarter	Value
7	Apple	Tennessee Moon	Q2	185
8	Apple	Tennessee Moon	Q3	150
9	Apple	Tennessee Moon	Q4	273
10	Apple	SlinkyRN Excel Instruction and Consulting	Q1	284
11	Apple	SlinkyRN Excel Instruction and Consulting	Q2	111
12	Apple	SlinkyRN Excel Instruction and Consulting	Q3	130

4

The Payoff: Clean Data Tomorrow With One Click

But again, the Power Query story is not about the time savings on Day 1. When you select the data returned by Power Query, a Queries & Connections panel appears on the right side of Excel, and on it is a Refresh button. (We need an Edit button here, but because there isn't one, you have to right-click the original query to view or make changes to the original query).

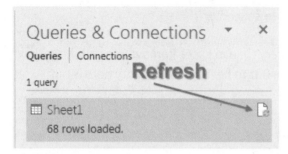

It is fun to clean data on Day 1. I love doing something new. But when my manager sees the resulting report and says "Beautiful. Can you do this every day?" I quickly grow to hate the tedium of cleaning the same data set every day.

So, to demonstrate Day 400 of cleaning the data, I have completely changed the original file. New products, new customers, smaller numbers, more rows, as shown below. I save this new version of the file in the same path and with the same filename as the original file.

	A	B	C	D	E	F
1	Product	Customer	Q1	Q2	Q3	Q4
17		leanexcelbooks.	12	95	42	62
18		Mary Maids	65	80	15	52
19	Guava	MAU Workforce	26	34	91	69
20		MN Excel Consu	89	61	44	37
21		MrExcel.com	57	54	55	42
22		myexcelonline.(	83	51	80	76
23		MyOnlineTrainir	55	21	20	73
24		MySpreadsheetl	78	49	50	73
25	**More rows**					
26	**New Customers**					
27						
~~	**Different Numbers**					

If I open the query workbook and click Refresh, in a few seconds, Power Query reports 92 rows instead of 68 rows.

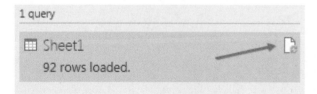

Cleaning the data on Day 2, Day 3, Day, 4,...Day 400,...Day Infinity now takes two clicks.

89	Guava	MyOnlineTrainingHub.com	Q4	73
90	Guava	MySpreadsheetLab	Q1	78
91	Guava	MySpreadsheetLab	Q2	49
92	Guava	MySpreadsheetLab	Q3	50
93	Guava	MySpreadsheetLab	Q4	73
94				

This one example only scratches the surface of Power Query. If you spend two hours with the book, *M is for (Data) Monkey* by Ken Puls and Miguel Escobar, you will learn about other features, such as these:

- Combining all Excel or CSV files from a folder into a single Excel grid

- Converting a cell with Apple;Banana;Cherry;Dill;Eggplant to five rows in Excel

- Doing a VLOOKUP to a lookup workbook as you are bringing data into Power Query

- Making a single query into a function that can be applied to every row in Excel

For a complete description of Power Query, check out *M Is for (Data) Monkey* by Ken Puls and Miguel Escobar. By late 2019, the retitled second edition, *Master Your Data*, will be available.

Thanks to Miguel Escobar, Rob Garcia, Mike Girvin, Ray Hauser, and Colin Michael for nominating Power Query.

#80 Render Excel Data on an iPad Dashboard Using Power BI

Power BI provides a new way of creating interactive modern dashboards using data from Excel.

To get started, sign up for a free account at http://powerbi.microsoft.com. You need to sign up with a work e-mail address; you can't use Gmail, Yahoo mail, or other third-party e-mail providers.

Then download the free app called Power BI Desktop.

In Power BI Desktop, start with the Get Data button.

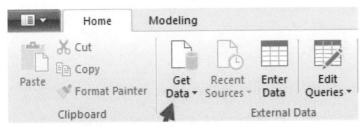

The experience will be exactly like with Power Query, as discussed in ""#79 Clean Data with Power Query"." You can also define relationships between tables, as in ""#37 Eliminate VLOOKUP with the Data Model" on page 93, and define new calculations, as discussed in "Bonus Tip: Portable Formulas" on page 97.

Once you have your data loaded into Power Query, choose a visualization from the top right and drag fields to the various drop zones.

After you design several dashboard tiles, you can publish your dashboard. Anyone that you invite will be able to view the dashboard in a browser or on an iPhone, iPad, or Android device.

#81 Build a Pivot Table on a Map Using 3D Maps

3D Maps (née Power Map) is available in the Office 365 versions of Excel 2013 and all versions of Excel 2016. Using 3D Maps, you can build a pivot table on a map. You can fly through your data and animate the data over time.

3D Maps lets you see five dimensions: latitude, longitude, color, height, and time. Using it is a fascinating way to visualize large data sets.

3D Maps can work with simple one-sheet data sets or with multiple tables added to the Data Model. Select the data. On the Insert tab, choose 3D Map. (The icon is located to the right of the Charts group.) If you have Excel 2013 you might have to download Power Map Preview from Microsoft to use the feature.

Next, you need to choose which fields are your geography fields. This could be Country, State, County, Zip Code, or even individual street addresses.

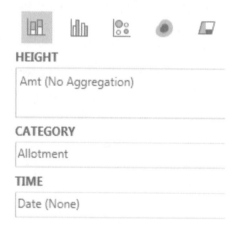

You are given a list of the fields in your data set and drop zones named Height, Category, and Time.

Hover over any point on the map to get details such as last sale date and amount.

In the default state of 3D Maps, each data point occupies about one city block. To be able to plot many houses on a street, select the Gear Wheel, Layer Options and change the thickness of the point to 10%.

To get the satellite imagery, open the Themes dropdown and use the second theme.

3D Maps provides a completely new way to look at your data. It is hard to believe that this is Excel.

Here is a map of Merritt Island, Florida. The various colors are different housing allotments. Each colored dot on the map is a house with a dock, either on a river or one of many canals dredged out in the 1960s and 1970s.

Using the time slider, you can go back in time to any point. Here is the same area at the time when NASA landed the first man on the Moon. The NASA engineers had just started building waterfront homes here, a few miles south of Kennedy Space Center.

Use the wheel mouse to scroll in. You can actually see individual streets, canals, and driveways.

Hold down the Alt key and drag sideways to rotate the map. Hold down the Alt key and drag up to tip the map so your view is closer to the ground.

Thanks to Igor Peev and Scott Ruble at Microsoft for this cool new feature.

4

#82 The Forecast Sheet Can Handle Some Seasonality

Before Excel 2016, Excel offered a few forecasting tools that did not fit in every situation. If your sales data included some seasonality, the old forecasting tools would do a bad job. Consider a movie theatre where sales peak on the weekend and plummet on Monday. Using the old linear trendline, Excel shows an R-Squared of 0.02, meaning that the trendline is doing a horrible job of predicting the future.

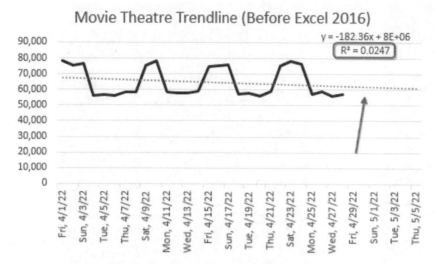

Excel 2016 introduced a new set of forecasting functions and an icon on the Data tab of the Ribbon to create a Forecast Sheet. If you have data with Date in column A and Sales in column B, select the data and choose Data, Forecast Sheet.

In the Create Forecast Worksheet dialog, click Options and review the Seasonality and ask for stats. Click Create and Excel inserts a new worksheet with FORECAST.ETS functions to create a forecast. The 3% error shown means that this forecast is explaining most of the variability.

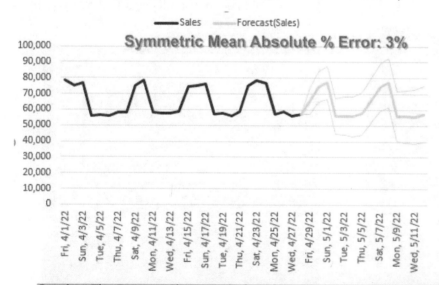

Caution: The Forecast Sheet works fine if you have one level of seasonality: More movie-goers on Friday or more gift buyers in November and December. But if your real-life data calls for <u>both</u> a December boom and a Saturday/Sunday peak, the FORECAST.ETS won't handle it.

#83 Perform Sentiment Analysis in Excel

It is easy to quantify survey data when it is multiple choice: You use a pivot table to figure out the percentage for each answer. But what about free-form text answers? These are hard to process if you have hundreds or thousands of them.

Sentiment analysis is a machine-based method for predicting if an answer is positive or negative. Microsoft offers a tool that does sentiment analysis in Excel. It is called Azure Machine Learning.

Traditional sentiment analysis requires a human to analyze and categorize 5% of the statements. Excel uses MPQA Subjectivity Lexicon. This generic dictionary includes 5,097 negative and 2,533 positive words. Each word is assigned a strong or weak polarity. This works great for short sentences, such as tweets or Facebook posts.

Look in the Add-ins group of the Insert tab. The first icon used to be called Store and now is called My Apps. Click that icon and search for Azure Machine Learning.

Specify an input range and two blank columns for the output range.

The heading for the input range has to match the schema tweet_text.

The results show positive, negative, or neutral and a percentage score. Items near 99% are very likely positive. Items near 0% are very likely negative.

	A	B	C
1	tweet_text	Sentiment	Score
2	Hello, I'm having trouble working this one. In col	positive	98.800%
3	OK, so it's Monday morning and I obviously cann	neutral	51.651%
4	Hi all, There has been a post previous to this reg	negative	0.000%
5	hi, would like to have a formula or vb code for th	positive	97.175%
6	Hi, I need to collect data (selected range) from	positive	95.626%

#84 Fill in a Flash

Excel 2013 added a new data-cleansing tool called Flash Fill.

In the figure below, you see full names in column A. You want to get the person's first initial and last name in column B. Rather than try to puzzle out =PROPER(LEFT(A2,1)&" "&MID(A2,FIND(" ",A2)+1,50)), you simply type a sample of what you want in B2.

	A	B
1	Name	First Initial Last Name
2	ALEX PILAR	A. Pilar
3	GARY KANE	
4	DENNIS P. JANCSY	
5	ALLAN MATZ	
6	MIKE GIRVIN	
7	CAROLINE BONNER	
8	GRAHAM STENT	

Type the first initial in B3. Excel sees what you are doing and "grays in" a suggested result.

	A	B
1	Name	First Initial L
2	ALEX PILAR	A. Pilar
3	GARY KANE	G. Kane
4	DENNIS P. JANCSY	D. Jancsy
5	ALLAN MATZ	A. Matz
6	MIKE GIRVIN	M. Girvin
7	CAROLINE BONNER	C. Bonner
8	GRAHAM STENT	G. Stent
9	MARTHA K. WENDEL	M. Wendel
10	PETER SUSEN	P. Susen

Press Enter to accept the suggestion. Bam! All of the data is filled in.

4

Look carefully through your data for exceptions to the rule. Two people here have middle initials listed. Do you want the middle initials to appear? If so, correct the suggestion for Dennis P. Jancsy in cell B4. Flash Fill will jump into action and fix Martha K. Wendel in B9 and any others that match the new pattern. The status bar will indicate how many changes were made.

In the above case, Excel gurus could figure out the formula. But Flash Fill is easier. In the example shown below, it would be harder to write a formula to get the last word from a phrase that has a different number of words and more than one hyphen.

	A	B
1	Customer	Type
2	900 bradedgar.com - consulting	Consulting
3	1164 Frontline Systems - applications	
4	1156 California Blazing Chile Farms - retail	
5	1175 Safety Elements Ltd. - services	
6	918 Hybrid Software - applications	
7	947 IMA Houston Chapter - associations	
8	1048 Fintega Financial Modelling - consulting	
9	1001 Roto-Rooter - services	
10	1103 MN Excel Consulting - consulting	
11	1145 Open Sky Martial Arts - training	

Flash Fill makes this easy. Go to cell B3 and press Ctrl+E to invoke Flash Fill.

	A	B
1	Customer	Type
2	900 bradedgar.com - consulting	Consulting
3	1164 Frontline Systems - applications	Applications
4	1156 California Blazing Chile Farms - retail	Retail
5	1175 Safety Elements Ltd. - services	Services
6	918 Hybrid Software - applications	Applications
7	947 IMA Houston Chapter - associations	Associations
8	1048 Fintega Financial Modelling - consulting	Consulting

Note: Flash Fill will not automatically fill in numbers. If you have numbers, you might see Flash Fill temporarily "gray in" a suggestion but then withdraw it. This is your signal to press Ctrl+E to give Flash Fill permission to fill in numbers.

Thanks to Chad Rothschiller at Microsoft for building this feature. Thanks also to Olga Kryuchkova.

#85 Format as a Façade

Excel is amazing at storing one number and presenting another number. Choose any cell and select Currency format. Excel adds a dollar sign and a comma and presents the number, rounded to two decimal places. In the figure below, cell D2 actually contains 6.42452514. Thankfully, the built-in custom number format presents the results in an easy-to-read format.

	A	B	C	D
1	Rep	Qty	Revenue	Avg Price
2	Andrew Spain	26,850	172,498.50	$6.42
3	Geoffrey G Lilley	24,458	157,921.10	$6.46
4	Kevin J Sullivan	24,754	160,180.30	$6.47
5	Peter Polakovic	24,090	143,880.50	$5.97

The custom number format code in D2 is $#,##0.00. In this code, 0s are required digits. Any #s are optional digits.

However, formatting codes can be far more complex. The code above has one format. That format is applied to every value in the cell. If you provide a code with two formats, the first format is for non-negative numbers, and the second format is for negative numbers. You separate the formats with semicolons. If you provide a code with three formats, the first is for positive, then negative, then zero. If you provide a code with four formats, they are used for positive, negative, zero, and text.

Format
Format >=0;Format<0
Positive;Negative;Zero
Positive;Negative;Zero;Text

Even if you are using a built-in format, you can go to Format Cells, Number, Custom and see the code used to generate that format. The figure below shows the code for the accounting format.

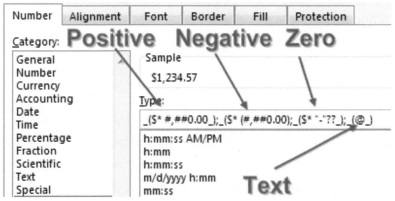

To build your own custom format, go to Format Cells, Number, Custom and enter the code in the Type box. Check out the example in the Sample box to make sure everything looks correct.

In the following example, three zones are used. Text in quotes is added to the number format to customize the message.

1	Format in C: "Please Remit "$0.00;"Credit Balance of "$0.00" (Do not pay)";"No Balance"		
2			
3	Customer	Balance	Formatted
4	Wag More Dog Store, San Antonio	-18.03	Credit Balance of $18.03 (Do not pay)
5	How To Excel At Excel.Com	192.28	Please Remit $192.28
6	SurtenExcel.com	27.72	Please Remit $27.72
7	University of North Carolina	-187.38	Credit Balance of $187.38 (Do not pay)
8	Yesenita	120.15	Please Remit $120.15

If you create a zone for zero but put nothing there, you will hide all zero values. The following code uses color codes for positive and negative. The code ends in a semicolon, creating a zone for zero values. But since the zone is empty, zero values are not shown.

4

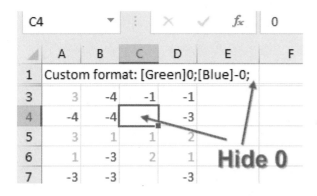

Illustration: Walter Moore

You can extend this by making all zones blank. A custom format code ;;; will hide values in the display and printout. However, you'll still be able to see the values in the formula bar. If you hide values by making the font white, the ;;; will stay hidden even if people change the fill color. The following figure includes some interesting formatting tricks.

	A	B	C
1	Value	Display	Format Code
2	123.45	********** 123.45	**0.00
3	123.45	!!!!!!!!!!!!!! 123.45	*!0.00
4	123456	123K	0,K
5	4565789	4.6M	0.0,,"M"
6	One	Enter a number!	0;-0;0;"Enter a number!"
7	62	62	[Red][<70]0;[Blue][>90]0;0
8	85	85	[Red][<70]0;[Blue][>90]0;0
9	99	99	[Red][<70]0;[Blue][>90]0;0
10	1234	1 2 3 4	0_W_W0_N0_i0

In B2 and B3, if you put ** before the number code, Excel will fill to the left of the number with asterisks, like the old check writer machines would do. But there is nothing that says you have to use asterisks. Whatever you put after the first asterisk is repeated to fill the space. Row 3 uses *! to repeat exclamation points.

In B4 and B5, each comma that you put after the final zero will divide the number by 1000. The code 0,K shows numbers in thousands, with a K afterward. If you want to show millions, use two commas. The "M" code must include quotation marks, since M already means months.

In B6, add a stern message in the fourth zone to alert anyone entering data that you want a number in the cell. If they accidentally enter text, the message will appear.

In B7 to B9, the normal zones Positives, Negatives, and Zero are overwritten by conditions that you put in square brackets. Numbers under 70 are red. Numbers over 90 are blue. Everything else is black.

In B10, those odd _(symbols in the accounting format are telling Excel to leave as much space as a left parenthesis would take. It turns out that an underscore followed by any character will leave as much white space as that character. In B10, the code contains 4 zeros. But there are different amounts of space between them. The space between the 1 and 2 is the width of 2 W characters. The space between 2 and 3 is the width of an N. The space between 3 and 4 is the width of a lowercase letter i.

The following figure shows various date formatting codes.

	A	B
1	Display	Format Code
2	7/4/22	m/d/yy
3	7/4/2022	m/d/yyyy
4	07/04/2022	mm/dd/yyyy
5	20220704	YYYYMMDD
6	7	m
7	07	mm
8	Jul	mmm
9	July	mmmm
10	J	mmmmm
11	Mon	ddd
12	Monday	dddd
13	Monday the 4 of Jul	dddd" the "d" of "mmm

Note: The mmmmm format in row 8 is useful for producing J F M A M J J A S O N D chart labels.

Thanks to Dave Baylis, Brad Edgar, Mike Girvin, and @best_excel for suggesting this feature.

#86 Word Cloud using Custom Visuals in Excel

There are plans to allow you to use Power BI Custom Visuals in Excel.

Caution: This is a future feature that may never reach Excel. It was originally announced for Excel. Microsoft set up a resource page so developers could try out the feature and build a library of custom visuals. In order to test the visuals, you needed to be on the Office 365 Insider channel. The steps to building a custom visual are daunting for non-developers. But, as a sample, the Excel team provided three finished visuals: Word Cloud, Sankey Chart, and a Tornado chart. I am putting this feature near the back of the book in case you have a spare computer that can opt in to the Insider channel so you can try these charts.

To try the feature, follow some instructions at https://microsoft.github.io/PowerBI-visuals/docs/building-for-excel/overview/ After setting up the custom visuals, you will have these three tiles on a new third tab in the Charts dialog.

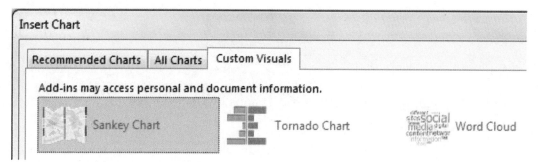

I copied the Table of Contents from this book to Excel. Select the data. Select Word Cloud. You will get an ugly word cloud like this one:

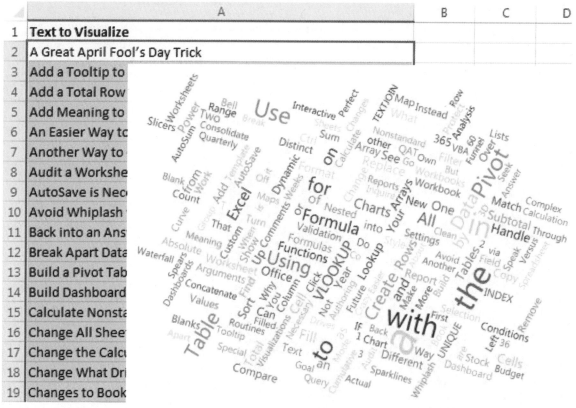

There is a less-than icon if you hover over the top-right of the chart. Open that icon and choose Select in order to get a special version of the Chart Tools Design tab in the Ribbon. Click Format.

4

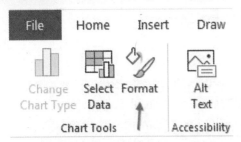

In the default word cloud, the top words in my data were The, With, To, and A. These words don't belong in the Word cloud. They are known as Stop Words. In the Format panel, choose the box for Default Stop Words.

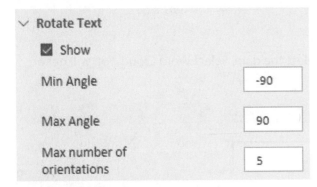

Also, the default number for Max Number of Orientations is 2. Change this to 5 or more.

⌄ **Rotate Text**	
☑ Show	
Min Angle	-90
Max Angle	90
Max number of orientations	5

Here is the improved Word Cloud:

#87 Surveys & Forms in Excel

I often start my live Excel seminars off by asking you to point your cell phone camera at a giant bar code I have projected on the screen. That QR code leads to a three-question survey. Answers automatically flow into my Excel worksheet and those answers get used in the afternoon demo of 3D Maps.

One way to use the feature is to start at Forms.Office.com. If you use OneDrive for Business, you might see a Forms icon as the fourth icon in the Insert tab. But others will see a Survey icon, which is not as robust.

A browser will open and you can build your form. Click New Question. Forms offers support for seven question types. Don't miss the useful Ranking or Likert types hidden behind the three dots.

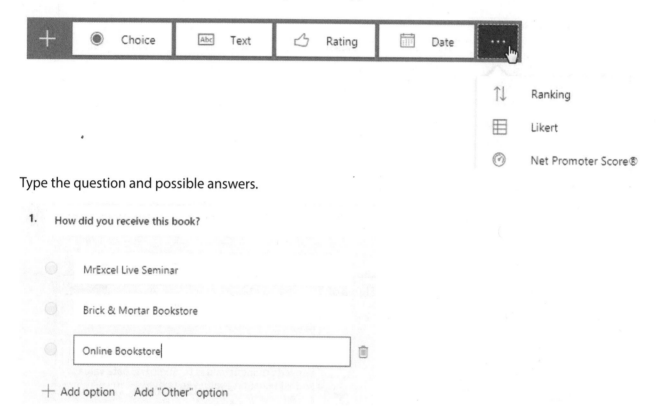

Type the question and possible answers.

1. How did you receive this book?

   ○ MrExcel Live Seminar

   ○ Brick & Mortar Bookstore

   ○ Online Bookstore|

   + Add option   Add "Other" option

When you are done with all questions, click Share in the top right corner. You can share via a link, or via e-mail, or using the QR Code. Try it: point your cell phone camera at the bar code on the right.

4

#88 Use the Windows Magnifier

If you received this book while attending one of my live Power Excel seminars, you likely saw me use the Windows Magnifier. Someone always asks how to use this, so I will write up the key steps.

First, there are three versions of the magnifier. To start the magnifier, press the Windows key and the Plus sign on the Numeric Keypad. To stop the magnifier, press the Windows key and Esc.

The first time that you use the magnifier, it opens in a view called Full Screen. Everything on the screen becomes bigger and you can use the mouse to move around. I don't like this version. Look for the floating Magnifier toolbar. Open Views and choose Lens.

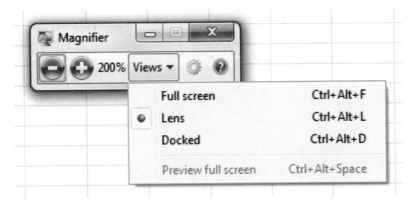

A magnifier lens follows your mouse cursor around the screen. You can use the Settings (gear wheel) icon in the toolbar to change the size of the lens.

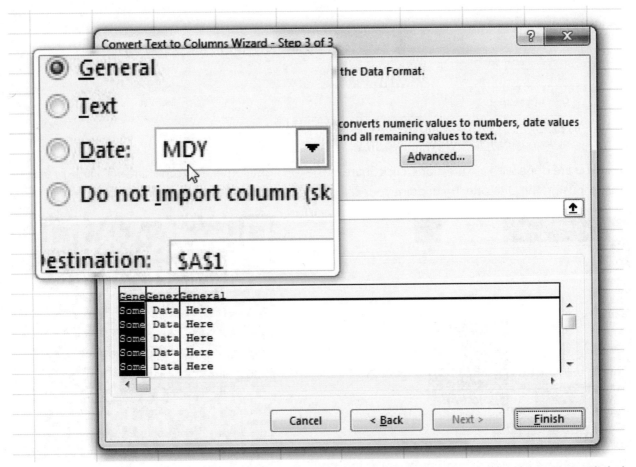

On some computers, the Magnifier toolbar starts out as an icon that looks like a magnifying glass. Click the icon to open the toolbar. More magnifier settings are in Windows, Settings, Ease of Access, Magnifier.

#89 Word for Excellers

Note: Katie Sullivan is a project manager on the Microsoft Word team. For our next-to-last tip in the book, I turn the podium over to Katie.

While Excel fans sometimes tease that Word and PowerPoint are freeware apps that come with Excel, there are times when Microsoft Word offers a feature that Excel does not. In those cases, it makes sense to copy your data from Excel, paste to Word, do the command, then copy back to Excel. Here are some examples of techniques that are better handled in Word than in Excel.

Technique 1: Convert to Upper, Lower, Proper

If you have to convert from uppercase to lowercase or proper case, Word has a keystroke shortcut. Copy the data to Word and toggle the case using Shift+F3.

Technique 2: Add Bullets

If you want to add bullets to Excel cells, it is far easier in Word than in Excel. Copy the cells to Word and apply a bullet style. Copy from Word and paste back to Excel. You might have to use the Reduce Indent icon a few times.

Tip: Since the first edition of this book, I learned of an easier way to do bullets in Excel. If you have a range of cells that contain text, select the range and press Ctrl+1 to open the Format Cells dialog. Then, on the Number tab, choose Custom from the list on the left. Click in the Type box and clear out whatever is there. Hold down the Alt key while pressing the 7 on the numeric keypad. A bullet should appear. Type a space and then an @.

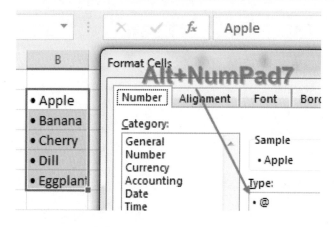

Technique 3: Visualize and Color Formulas

If you have a massively long formula, say one with 10 nested IF statements, you can paste to Word and use colors and Shift+Enter to space the formula to help make sense of it. (One rebuttal from the Excel team: You can expand the formula bar and use Alt+Enter to split a formula into many lines. Or, you can use the great RefTreeAnalyser add-in from Jan Karel Pieterse; see http://mrx.cl/jkpformula.)

Technique 4: Faster SmartArt

Word offers the Convert Text to SmartArt option. While Excel offers SmartArt, too, it is not very handy there because you have to copy the entries one at a time into the SmartArt pane.

4

Technique 5: Extract Data from a PDF

Say that someone has an Excel workbook and saves that workbook as a PDF. They send it to you. This is annoying, and clearly they don't want you to reuse the data. If you open the PDF in Acrobat Reader, copy the data, and paste to Excel, it will unwind into a single column. But here is the secret: Paste that data to Word first. The rows and columns will paste properly. You can then copy from Word and paste back into Excel. (If you are stuck in a pre-2013 version of Office, I recommend Able2Extract: mrx.cl/pdftoxl.)

The original data is shown on the left below, and you can see on the right and how it looks when you paste directly from PDF to Excel. You can see that the data "unwinds," with B1:C1 going to A2:A3 and so on.

	A	B	C
1	Trait	Dogs	Cats
2	Protective instinct	Yes	No
3	Always happy to see you when return	Yes	No
4	Spit up hairballs	No	Yes
5	Big or small	Yes	Only small
6	Chase tennis balls	Yes	No
7	Herd small children	Yes	No
8	Swim with you	Yes	No
9	Do tricks	Yes	No

	A	B
1	Trait	
2	Dogs	
3	Cats	
4	Protective instinct	
5	Yes	
6	No	
7	Always happy to see you	
8	Yes	
9	No	

Paste that same data to Word (below left), then copy from Word and paste to Excel (below right). The data stays in the original order. You can unapply Word Wrap and adjust the column widths to get back to the original data.

Trait	Dogs	Cats
Protective instinct	Yes	No
Always happy to see you when	Yes	No

Trait	Dogs	Cats
Protective e instinct	Yes	No
Always happy to see you	Yes	No

Technique 6: Change Formatting of Words Within Excel

If you have sentences of text in Excel, it is possible to select one word while in Edit mode and change the

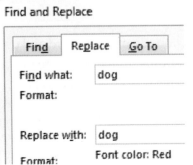

color of that word. But globally changing the color of all occurrences of the word in Excel is tedious. Instead, paste the data to Word and press Ctrl+H. Change dog to dog. Click More>> and then choose Format, Font. Choose Red. Click Replace All. Copy from Word and paste back to Excel. The figure below shows what you end up with.

▲	A	B	C	D	E	F	G	H
1	Original							
2	A dog is always happy to see you when you return home.							
3	If you have children, a dog will be protective of the children. If it is a herding dog, i							
4	Certain breeds of dog love to swim. You can not keep my dog Bella from diving in t							
5	A dog has no problems chasing a tennis ball all day.							
6								
7	After doing Replace in Word and pasting back to Excel							
8	A dog is always happy to see you when you return home.							
9	If you have children, a dog will be protective of the children. If it is a herding dog, i							
10	Certain breeds of dog love to swim. You can not keep my dog Bella from diving in t							
11	A dog has no problems chasing a tennis ball all day.							
12								

Technique 7: Replace While Keeping Character Formatting

Word also handles a similar problem: replacing text but leaving the text formatting as it is. Below is a survey about the best pet. Someone has highlighted certain words in the text.

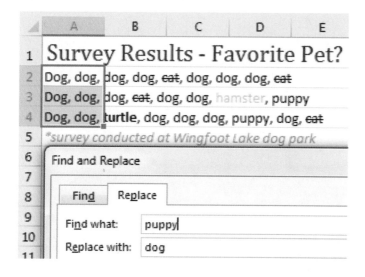

Use Ctrl+H to do a Find and Replace, as shown on the left. When you use Replace All, if a sentence was changed, your in-cell formats will be lost. In the figure below, the strikethrough remains in the first row because that row did not have an occurrence of the word *puppy* and thus was not changed.

Dog, dog, dog, dog, ~~cat~~, dog, dog, dog, ~~cat~~
Dog, dog, dog, cat, dog, dog, hamster, dog
Dog, dog, turtle, dog, dog, dog, dog, dog, cat

To keep the formatting in the original text, copy to Word. Do the replace in Word. Copy from Word and paste back to Excel.

Bonus Tip: Merge Shapes

Here's a brief plug for PowerPoint: If you need to create a shape in Excel that is a combination of other shapes, create the shapes in PowerPoint. Select all the shapes you want to include. On the Drawing Tools Format tab, choose Merge Shapes. You can then select Union, Combine, Fragment, Intersect, or Subtract to combine the shapes. (The Subtract feature lets you cut a hole in a shape.) Then copy that shape and paste to Excel (or Word).

Bonus Tip: Use the Eye Dropper

Another feature unique to PowerPoint is the eye dropper. If you want to use a particular color, you can just click the eye dropper on the color. When you open the Power Point color menu again, choose More Colors, and you can see the RGB colors. To use the eye dropper outside the PowerPoint frame, hold down the left mouse button and pick from any website or picture you have visible on your desktop.

Thanks to Katie Sullivan (a project manager on the Word team!) for contributing this tip. Katie clearly prefers dogs to cats. Thanks to Glenna Shaw and Oz du Soleil for contributing ideas to this tip. Zack Barresse and Echo Swinford pointed out the Merge Shapes option in PowerPoint. Sam Radakovitz added the eye dropper tip and noted the Subtract feature for shapes.

#90 Avoid Whiplash with Speak Cells

I hate having to hand-key data into Excel. Between the Internet and Power Query, there almost always is a way to find the data somewhere. I hate when people send a PDF where they scanned some numbers and are sending the numbers as a picture. A free trial of Able2Extract Pro (mrx.cl/ExtractPDF) will get the actual number into Excel. Even so, sometimes you end up keying data into Excel.

One of the painful parts about keying in data is that you have to proofread the numbers. So, you are looking at the sheet of paper, then the screen, then the paper, then the screen. You will end up with a sore neck. Wouldn't it be nice if you had someone to read you the screen so you can keep your eye on the paper? It's built in to Excel.

Right-click on the Quick Access Toolbar and choose Customize Quick Access Toolbar.

Change the top-left dropdown to Commands Not in the Ribbon. Scroll down to the S entries until you find Speak Cells. Add all five of these commands to the Quick Access Toolbar.

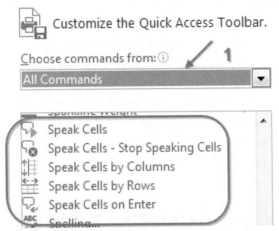

Select your range of numbers and click Speak Cells. Excel reads you the numbers.

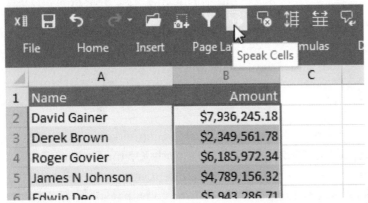

Tip: You can customize the voice in the Windows Control Panel. Search for Text to Speech. There is a setting for Voice Speed. Drag that slider to halfway between Normal and Fast to have the voice read your cells faster.

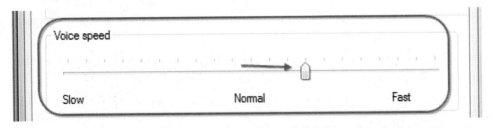

Bonus Tip: Provide Feedback with Sound

New in July 2017: Go to Excel Options. From the left category list, choose Ease of Access. Select the checkbox for Provide Feedback with Sound and choose Modern. (The other choice, Classic, should be called Annoying!)

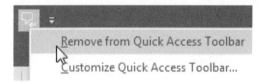

Excel now provides confirmation with gentle sounds when you do any of these tasks: Copy, Paste, Undo, Redo, AutoCorrect, Save, Insert Cells, Delete Cells.

Bonus Tip: A Great April Fool's Day Trick

Do you want a harmless prank to pull on a co-worker? When he leaves his desk to grab a cup of coffee, add the fifth icon to his Quick Access Toolbar: Speak Cells on Enter. Click the icon once, and the computer will say, "Cells will now be spoken on Enter."

Once you've turned on Speak Cells on Enter, right-click the icon in the Quick Access Toolbar and choose Remove from Quick Access Toolbar to hide any sign that you were there.

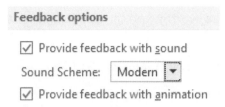

Your co-worker comes back, sits down, and starts to build a worksheet. The computer repeats back everything the co-worker types.

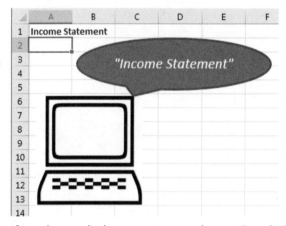

If you have a little more time and want Speak Cells on Enter with attitude, add the following macro to the code pane for the current worksheet..

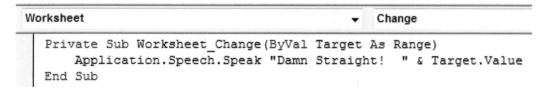

```
Private Sub Worksheet_Change(ByVal Target As Range)
    Application.Speech.Speak "Damn Straight!  " & Target.Value
End Sub
```

#91 Customize the Quick Access Toolbar

As I mentioned in "#26 Get Ideas from Artificial Intelligence" on page 57, the Excel team had not added any new features to the Home tab since January 30, 2007. Ideas is the first feature that was deemed worthy of being on the Home tab.

Even though the Excel team does not think many features are Home-tab-worthy, you can add your favorite features to the Quick Access Toolbar (hereafter called QAT).

I always like asking people what they have added to their QAT. In a Twitter poll in January 2019, I had over 70 suggestions of favorite features that could be added to the QAT.

To me, a "good" addition to the QAT is a command that you use frequently that is not already on the Home tab. Any of the features in the Commands Not In The Ribbon category are candidates if you ever have to use them.

Previously in this book, I've suggested the following icons on the QAT:

- The AutoFilter icon was used in "#3 Filter by Selection" on page 5
- Change Shape in "Bonus Tip: Old Style Comments Are Available as Notes" on page 28
- Speak Cells in "#90 Avoid Whiplash with Speak Cells" on page 186
- Speak Cells on Enter in "Bonus Tip: A Great April Fool's Day Trick" on page 187

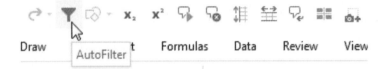

Below are more icons that you might want to add to your QAT.

The Easy Way to Add to the QAT

The easiest way to add an icon to the QAT is to right-click the icon in the Ribbon and choose Add to Quick Access Toolbar.

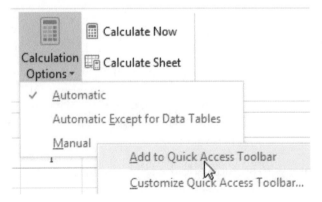

Adding Formulas, Calculation Options, Manual to the QAT gives you a clear indication of when your work-book is in Manual calculation mode:

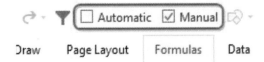

The Hard Way to Add to the QAT

Sometimes, the command you want can not be right-clicked. For example, in "Bonus Tip: Copy the Subtotal Rows" on page 53, I suggested using Alt+; as a shortcut for Visible Cells in the Go To Special dialog box.

Visible Cells Only is available to add to the QAT. But you can't add it by right-clicking in the dialog box. To make matters worse, when you follow these steps, you have to look for a command called "Select Visible Cells" instead of a command called "Visible Cells Only".

1. Right-click anywhere in the Ribbon and choose Customize Quick Access Toolbar. The Excel Options dialog box opens showing a list of Popular Commands. I reject many of these popular commands because they are already a single-click on the Home tab of the Ribbon.

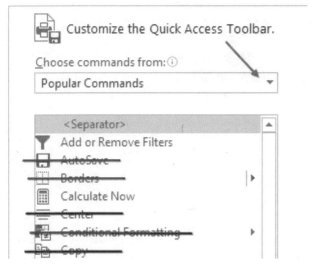

2. Open the drop-down menu to the right of Popular Commands and choose either All Commands or Commands Not In the Ribbon.

3. Scroll through the left list box to find the command.

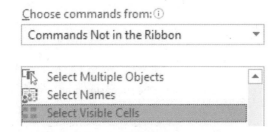

4. Click the Add>> button in the center of the screen.

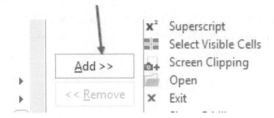

5. Click OK to close Excel Options.

6. Hover over the newly added icon to see the tooltip and possibly learn of a keyboard shortcut.

Favorite QAT Icons From Twitter

If you are looking for something to make Twitter more interesting, consider following @MrExcel. You can then play along in fun surveys like this one:

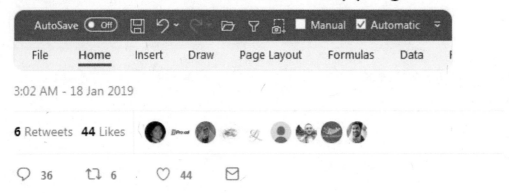

Presented below are several suggestions from people on Twitter.

Back in "#41 Quickly Convert Formulas to Values" on page 107 I had nine different ways to Paste Values. Here is a tenth way. The most popular suggestion on Twitter was the Paste Values icon.

Thanks to ExcelCity, Adam Warrington, Dan Lanning, Christopher Broas. Bonus point to AJ Willikers who suggested both Paste Values and Paste Values and Number Formatting shown to the right of Paste Values above.

Bonus Tip: Sometimes, You Don't Want the Gallery

The next most popular command to add to the QAT is Freeze Panes. Go to the View tab. Open the Freeze Panes drop-down menu. Right-click on Freeze Panes and Excel offers "Add Gallery to the Quick Access Toolbar".

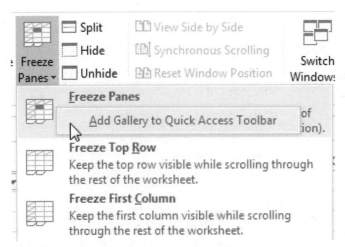

Freeze panes is a tricky command. If you want to freeze row 1 and columns A:B, you have to put the cell pointer in C2 before you invoke Freeze Panes.

	Product	Name	Jan	Feb
1	Product	Name	Jan	Feb
2	Apple	Andy	590	849
3	Banana	Barb	975	128
4	Cherry	Chris	206	920
5	Date	Diane	217	872

Active Cell: First non-frozen cell

Invoke Freeze Panes from here

Some people don't understand this, and in Excel 2007, the Excel team made the Freeze Panes gallery with choices to freeze top row and freeze first column for people who did not know to select C2 before invoking Freeze Panes.

Since you understand how Freeze Panes works, you don't want the gallery on the QAT. You just want the icon that does Freeze Panes.

When you look for commands in the Excel Options, there are two choices for Freeze Panes. The one with the arrow is the gallery. The first one is the one you want.

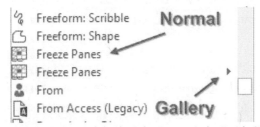

Thanks to Debra Dalgleish, Colin Foster and @Excel_City for suggesting Freeze Panes

In other cases, the Gallery version is superior to the non-gallery version. Here is an example. Jen (who apparently is a @PFChangsAddict) suggested adding Save As to the QAT. Alex Waterton suggested adding Save As Other Formats. When I initially added the non-gallery version of Save As Other Formats, I realized that both icons open the Save As dialog box.

4

Instead, use the Gallery version of Save As

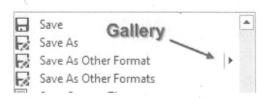

Here are those four icons in the QAT. The Save As Other Format gallery offers the most choices.

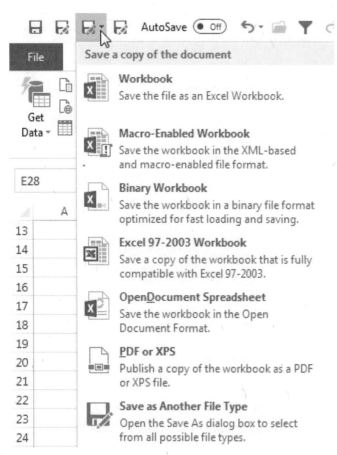

If you are planning on creating a lot of PDF files, Colin Foster suggests adding Publish as PDF or XPS to the QAT.

The First 9 Icons in QAT Have Easy Shortcut Keys

Most people who customize the QAT add new icons after the AutoSave, Save, Undo, Redo commands that are in the default QAT. But those first 9 QAT spots have super-easy keyboard shortcuts. AJ Willikers pointed out that the first 9 icons have easy short cut keys.

Press and release the Alt key. Key tips appear on each ribbon tab. So, Alt, H, S, O would sort descending. If you sort descending a lot, add the icon as one of the first 9 icons on the QAT. Press and release Alt, Then press 1 to invoke the first icon on the QAT. Note that the key tips for items 10 and beyond require you to press Alt, 0, 1 so they aren't quite as easy as the first 9 icons.

Thanks to AJ Willikers for pointing out the Alt 1-9 keyboard shortcuts.

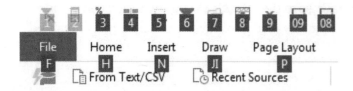

The Camera Tool versus Paste as Linked Picture

Another popular QAT command on Twitter was the Camera. This awesome hack dates back to Excel 97. It is great because it allows you to paste a live picture of cells from Sheet17 on the Dashboard worksheet. It was hard to use and Microsoft re-worked the tool in Excel 2007, rebranding it as Paste As Linked Picture. But the operation of the tool changed and some people like the old way better.

For background on the tool, see "Bonus Tip: Line Up Dashboard Sections with Different Column Widths" on page 86. Say that you wanted to paste a picture of these cells in your dashboard:

0.833	0.933	0.623
0.856	0.278	0.208
0.361	0.147	0.740
0.100	0.322	0.921
0.981	0.803	0.259

Old way: You could select the cells. Click the Camera icon. The mouse pointer changes to a cross hair. Click anywhere that you want to paste the picture of the cells.

New way: Copy the cells. Click in the new location. Choose Paste As Linked Picture. If you don't want the picture lined up with the top-left corner of the cell, drag to nudge the picture into position.

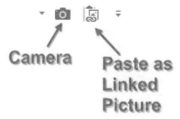

Camera   Paste as Linked Picture

Thanks to Manoel Costa, Brad Edgar, and Duncan Williamson for suggesting the Camera.

Screen Clipping to Capture a Static Image From Another Application

One of my favorite commands for the QAT is Insert Screen Clipping. Say that you want to grab a picture of a website and put it in your Excel worksheet. To effectively use the tool, you need to make sure that the web page is the most-recent window behind the Excel workbook. So - visit the web page. Then switch directly to your Excel Workbook. Choose Insert Screen Clipping and wait a few moments. The Excel screen disappears, revealing the web page. Wait for the web page to grey out, then use the mouse pointer to drag a rectangle around the portion of the web page. When you release the mouse button, a static picture of the web page (or any application) will paste in Excel. The Screen Clipping is also great for putting Excel charts in Power Point. Until you add this command to the QAT, it is hidden at the bottom of Insert, Screenshot. I don't like the Screenshot options because they put the entire full screen in Excel. Screen Clipping lets you choose just a part of the screen.

Two Icons Might Lead to the Same Place: Open Recent and Open

One of the popular QAT commands in Excel 2010 and Excel 2013 was the folder with a star - Open Recent File…. This command disappeared from Excel in Excel 2016. But people discovered that if you exported your settings from 2013 and then imported to 2016 or 2019, the icon would appear!

As I considered the prospect of dragging my Excel 2013 .tlb file around for the rest of my life, I inadvertently realized that the Open icon leads to the exact same place as the Open Recent File icon.

Thanks to Colin Foster and Ed Hansberry for suggesting Open Recent File.

Clear Filter and Reapply Filter

You hopefully already have the AutoFilter on your QAT after reading "#3 Filter by Selection" on page 5. Debra Dalgleish, Excel_City, and AJ Willikers suggests Clear Filters. This is a great way to reset your filters without visiting the Data tab.

Bathazar Lawson suggests adding Reapply Filter to the QAT. Here is how this becomes handy. Let's say you have a list of projects. You don't need to see anything where the status code is Complete. You set up a filter for this.

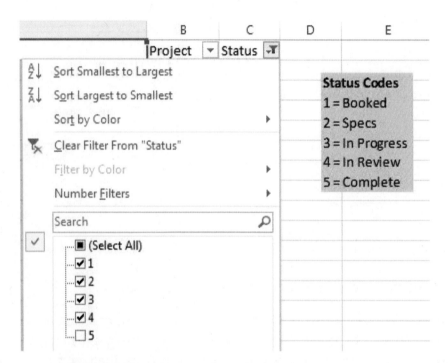

	B	C	D	E
	Project ▾	Status ▾		

- Sort Smallest to Largest
- Sort Largest to Smallest
- Sort by Color ▸
- Clear Filter From "Status"
- Filter by Color ▸
- Number Filters ▸
- Search 🔍
  - ☑ (Select All)
  - ☑ 1
  - ☑ 2
  - ☑ 3
  - ☑ 4
  - ☐ 5

Status Codes
1 = Booked
2 = Specs
3 = In Progress
4 = In Review
5 = Complete

You change the status code on some projects. Some of the projects that used to be In Review are now Complete.

B	C
Project ▾	Status ▾
Project 115	3
Project 132	5
Project 38	2
Project 94	5
Project 106	5
Project 22	3
Project 17	5

Instead of re-opening the Filter drop-down, click Reapply Filter.

Filter — ⟶ Clear
⟶ Reapply
⟶ Advanced

Sort & Filter

Excel will re-evaluate the data and hide the items which now have a 5.

B	C
Project ▾	Status ▾
Project 115	3
Project 38	2
Project 22	3
Project 21	4

Some Future Features Debut on the QAT and then Become Real Features

I was at a seminar in Topeka when Candace and Robert taught me that you could add an icon called Document Location to the QAT.

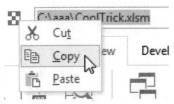

If you need to copy the document location to the clipboard, you can select the text from the QAT, right-click and choose Copy.

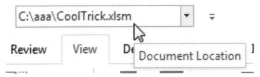

The Document Location has been available since at least Excel 2010. In early 2019, Office 365 subscribers will notice that the File, Info screen now has new equivalents of Copy Path and Open File Location.

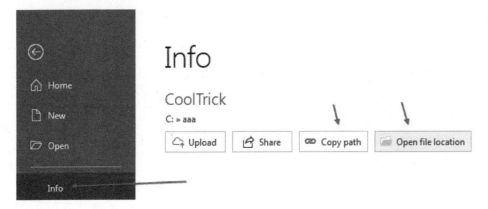

Easier Superscript and Subscripts

Add the new Superscript and Subscript icons to the QAT. As you are typing, click either icon to continue typing in subscript or superscript. This might be handy for a single character (such as the 2 in H_2O) or for several characters.

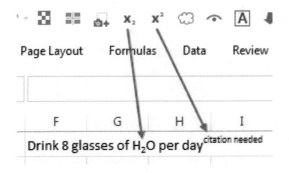

New Features from the Data Tab

The Data tab is like the Boardwalk and Park Place of the Excel ribbon. Every project manager wants to be on the Home tab, but most of the great features end up on the data tab. Excel 2016 introduced Get Data (Power Query), Relationships, and Refresh All. Add those to the QAT.

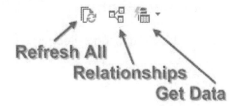

Build Formulas Without Ever Leaving the Mouse

Ha-ha! This advice flies in the face of what every Excel tipster teaches. Most people want you to build formulas without ever leaving the keyboard. But what if you hate the keyboard and want to use the mouse? You can add these operators to your QAT:

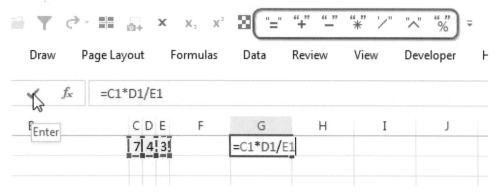

Using the mouse, you can click the Equals sign, then click on C1, then Multiply, then D1, then Divide, then E1. To complete the formula, click the green checkmark next to the formula bar to Enter. Surprisingly, Enter is not available for the QAT. But the formula bar is usually always visible, so this would work.

Those seven icons shown above are not located in one section of the Customize dialog. You have to hunt for them in the E, P, M, M, D, E, and P section of the list.

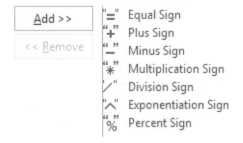

Bonus Tip: Show QAT Below the Ribbon

Right-click the Ribbon and choose Show Quick Access Toolbar Below The Ribbon. There are several advantages. First, it is a shorter mouse move to reach the icons. Second, when the QAT is above the Ribbon, you have less space until the icons run into the file name.

#92 Create Your Own QAT Routines Using VBA Macros

There are several short macros you can add to your Personal Macro Workbook and then add to the QAT. In this tip, you will see how to create the Personal Macro Workbook, type some macros, and then assign them to icons on the QAT.

Create a Personal Macro Workbook

Start from any workbook. Go to View, Macros, Record Macro. In the Record Macro dialog, type a one-word name such as HelloWorld. Choose Personal Macro Workbook. Click OK.

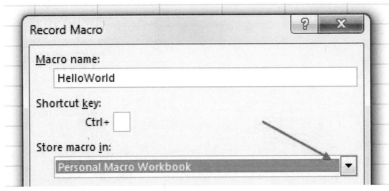

Type Hello in the active cell and press Enter. Then, select View, Macros, Stop Recording. These steps will create a Personal.xlsb on your computer where you can store new macros.

Open the VBA Editor and Find Module1 in Personal.xlsb

From Excel, press Alt+F11. (If you don't have Alt+F11, you can add the Visual Basic command to the QAT and click that.

Your first time in the VBA editor, it might be a vast expanse of grey. From the VBA menu, select View, Project Explorer.

Look for an entry called VBAProject (PERSONAL.XLSB). Click the + icon to expand it.

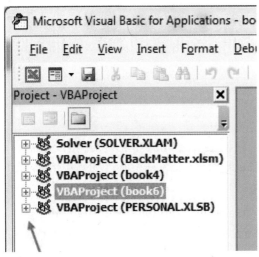

4

Look for and expand Modules. Right-click Module1 and choose View Code.

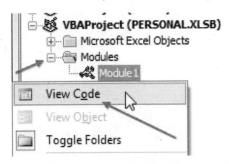

You will see your HelloWorld code. After the End Sub, type any of these procedures.

```
Sub VeryHideActiveSheet()
    ActiveSheet.Visible = xlVeryHidden
End Sub
Sub ShowAllSheets()
    For Each sh In ActiveWorkbook.Worksheets
        sh.Visible = True
    Next sh
End Sub
```

```
Sub UpperSelection()
    For Each cell In Selection.SpecialCells(2, 2)
        ' 2, 2 means xlCellTypeConstants, Text
        cell.Value = UCase(cell.Value)
    Next
End Sub
Sub LowerSelection()
    For Each cell In Selection.SpecialCells(2, 2)
        cell.Value = LCase(cell.Value)
    Next
End Sub
Sub ProperSelection()
    For Each cell In Selection.SpecialCells(2, 2)
        cell.Value = Application.WorksheetFunction.Proper(cell.Value)
    Next
End Sub
```

When you customize the QAT, choose Macros from the top left drop-down menu.

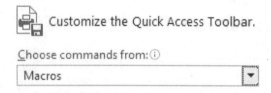

When you choose a macro and click Add>> the icon will default to a flow chart. Click Modify at the bottom right. Choose a new icon. Type a good tooltip.

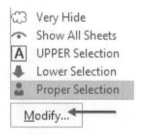

Here is an explanation of how to use these five macros:

- **Very Hide**: Worksheets can be visible, hidden or very hidden. Few people know about Very Hidden sheets because you have to use VBA to create them. A worksheet that is Very Hidden will not show up in Home, Format, Hide and Unhide, Worksheets. (Thanks to -Sagar Malik)

- **Show All Sheets**: It is easy to select 12 sheets and hide them in a single command. But then unhiding the sheets is a one-at-a-time proposition. This macro will unhide all sheets (including very hidden sheets).

- **Upper Selection**: Converts all text in the selection to upper case.

- **Lower Selection**: Converts all text in the selection to lower case.

- **Proper Selection**: Converts all text in the selection to proper case.

Thanks to MF Wong for suggesting some of these macros.

Bonus Tip: Settings in the Excel Options Menu

Consider a few of these settings after you choose File, Options:

General, Start Up Options, Unselect Show The Start Screen When This Application Starts to skip the Home screen. Excel will open directly to a blank workbook. (Thanks to Dave Marriott)

Advanced, Editing Options, Unselect After Pressing Enter, Move Selection. When you type a value in a cell, Excel will stay in the same cell. (Thanks to Ed Hansberry)

Advanced, Editing Options, Automatically Insert a Decimal Point. You type 12345. Excel gets 123.45.

#93 Favorite Keyboard Shortcuts

As I started polling readers about their favorite Excel tips, a large number of them were keyboard short-cuts. Some readers, such as Matt Kellett, Olga Kryuchkova, Mike Dolan Fliss, and @model_citizen, suggested that the book has to include a section on favorite keyboard shortcuts.

These are presented in order of popularity. If a lot of readers suggested a tip, it is at the top. After the first eight or so, they are then sorted by my subjective sequence.

1. Ctrl+1 to Format a Selection

Ctrl+1 (the number one) works to format whatever is selected. Whether it is a cell, SmartArt, a picture, a shape, or the March data point in a column chart, press Ctrl+1.

Ctrl + 1

Thanks to Mitja Bezenšek, Alexa Gardner, Andrej Lapajne, Schmuel Oluwa, Jon Peltier, @ExcelNewss, and @JulianExcelTips.

2. Ctrl[+Shift]+Arrow to Navigate or Select

Your cell pointer is sitting at the top of 50K rows of data, and you need to get to the bottom. If you have a **Ctrl + Shift + ↓** column with no blanks, press Ctrl+Down Arrow to jump to the end of the data set.

In the following figure, Ctrl+Down Arrow will jump to K545. Ctrl+Left Arrow will jump to A1. Ctrl+Right Arrow will jump the gap of empty cells and land on N1.

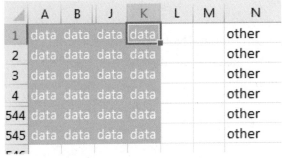

	A	B	J	K	L	M	N
1	data	data	data	data			other
2	data	data	data	data			other
3	data	data	data	data			other
4	data	data	data	data			other
544	data	data	data	data			other
545	data	data	data	data			other

Add the Shift key in order to select from the active cell to the landing cell. Starting from A1 in the above figure, press Ctrl+Shift+Down Arrow to select A1:A545. While still holding down Ctrl+Shift, press the Right Arrow Key to select A1:K545. If it seems awkward at first, try it for a few days until you get the hang of it.

Thanks to Captain Excel, @Cintellis, José de Diego, Mike Girvin, Elchin Khalilov, Crystal Long, Paul Sasur, and @XLStudioWorks.

3. Ctrl+. to Jump to Next Corner

While you have a large range selected, press Ctrl+Period to move to the next corner of the selection. If the selection is rectangular, you move in a clockwise fashion. From the bottom-right corner, press Ctrl+. twice to move to the top left.

Thanks to Crystal Long, and Steve McCready.

4. Ctrl+5 for Strikethrough

This is great for crossing things off your to-do list. Why 5? If you are making hash marks, the fifth hash mark crosses out the first four.

4

5. Ctrl+* to Select Current Region

This one is easier if you have a number keypad so you don't have to press Shift to get to an asterisk. If I could slow down enough to stop pressing Ctrl+Shift+Down Arrow followed by Ctrl+Shift+Right arrow, I would realize that Ctrl+* is much shorter and does not get tripped up by blank cells. It is really superior in every way to keyboard tip #2. But my muscle memory still prefers tip #2. Thanks to @Excelforo.

6. Ctrl+Enter to Copy Formula into Entire Selection

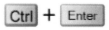

Ken Puls, who is the king of Power Query, says, "You would think my favorite Excel tip would be Unpivot with Power Query, but my favorite all-time is Ctrl+Enter." Say that you want to enter a formula into 400 cells. Select the 400 cells. Type the formula in the first cell. Press Ctrl+Enter, and Excel enters a similar formula in all cells of the selection.

Gavin White points out another use. You enter a formula in G2. You need to copy the formula down but not the formatting. Select G2:G20. Press the F2 key to put the cell in Edit mode. When you press Ctrl+Enter, the formula is copied, but no formatting is copied. Thanks to Crystal Long, Schmuel Oluwa, Ken Puls, Peter Raiff, Sven Simon, and Gavin Whyte.

7. Ctrl(+Shift)+; to Time or Date Stamp

Press Ctrl+Shift+: to enter the current time. Press Ctrl+; for the current date. Note the shortcut enters the *current* time, not a formula. To put both the date and time in one cell, type either keystroke, a space, then the other keystroke. Excel will interpret it as the proper date and time.

Thanks to Olga Kryuchkova, Roger Govier and Tim O'Mara.

8. Ctrl+Backspace to Bring the Active Cell into View

This is a great trick that I never knew. Say that C1 is the active cell. You've used the scrollbars, and now you are looking at ZZ999. To bring the window back to encompass the active cell, press Ctrl+Backspace.

Thanks to Olga Kryuchkova and Schmuel Oluwa.

9. Alt+= for AutoSum

Press Alt+= to invoke the AutoSum function. Thanks to Dawn Bjork Buzbee and Olga Kryuchkova.

10. Ctrl+Page Down and Ctrl+Page Up to Jump to Next Worksheet

If you need to move from Sheet1 to Sheet5, press Ctrl+Page Down four times. If you are at Sheet9 and need to move to Sheet3, press Ctrl+Page Up six times. Thanks to Jeneta Hot.

11. Ctrl+Click to Select Noncontiguous Cells

If you have to select two regions, select the first one, then hold down Ctrl while clicking on other cells or regions. – Thanks toThomas Fries

12. Tab to AutoComplete

This one is maddening. You type =VL to start VLOOKUP. The AutoComplete shows that there is only one function that starts with VL. But if you press Enter, you get a #NAME? error.

The correct way to choose VLOOKUP is to press Tab! Thanks to Ashish Agarwal.

13. Shift+F8 to Add to Selection

Select the first range. Press Shift+F8, and you are in Add to Selection mode. Scroll anywhere. Select the next range. Then select another range. And so on, without ever touching Ctrl. To return to normal, press Esc. Thanks to Neil Charles. A bonus tip from Bill Hazlett: if you select A1, press F8, then click in S20, you will select from A1:S20. Press Esc to exit the Extend Selection mode. Watch for the indicator in the status bar:

14. Ctrl+Spacebar and Shift+Spacebar to Select an Entire Column or Row

Ctrl+Spacebar selects a whole column. Shift+Spacebar selects a whole row. How can you remember which is which? The "C" in Ctrl stands for the "C" in column. Also, the "S" in Shift is adjacent in the alphabet to the "R" in row. Another way to remember which is which: The Shift key is much longer (like a row!) than Ctrl.

Thanks to Michael Byrne, Jeneta Hot, and Bob Umlas.

15. Ctrl+` to See All Formulas

Many folks in the United States think this is Ctrl+~, but it is actually the grave accent to toggle into and out of Show Formulas mode.

16. F3 to Paste a Name into a Formula

I am not a huge fan of this, since you can start typing the name and then choose from AutoComplete. But I know the trick has its fans, including Mike Girvin and Johan van den Brink.

17. Ctrl+Shift+1 to apply Number Formatting

I had never memorized these, but I am going to start using some of them. Ctrl+Shift+1 (also known as Ctrl+!), will apply a number format, 2 decimals, thousands separator, and negatives shown with a minus sign. The other five make some reasonable sense, as described below.

Key	AKA	Formats as	Example
Ctrl+Shift+1	!	Number	-1,234.56
Ctrl+Shift+2	@	Time	2:50 PM
Ctrl+Shift+3	#	Date	29-Jun-15
Ctrl+Shift+4	$	Currency	($1,234.56)
Ctrl+Shift+5	%	Percent	100%
Ctrl+Shift+6	^	Exponential	1.23E+08

Thanks to Matthew Bernath.

18. Ctrl+Shift+2 to Apply Time Formatting

Ctrl+Shift+2 or Ctrl+@ applies a time formatting. Say that you want to meet for dinner @ 5 o'click. Long before it became associated with e-mail addresses, the @ inferred time.

4

19. Ctrl+Shift+3 to Apply Date Formatting

Ctrl+Shift+3 or Ctrl+# applies a date formatting. The # symbol looks a bit like a calendar, if you lived in an alternate universe with three weeks per month and three days per week.

20. Ctrl+Shift+4 to Apply Currency Formatting

Ctrl+Shift+4 or Ctrl+$ applies a currency format with two decimal places.

21. Ctrl+Shift+5 for Percent Format

Ctrl+Shift+5 or Ctrl+% applies a percentage format with 0 decimal places.

22. Ctrl+Shift+6 for Scientific Format

Ctrl+Shift+6 or Ctrl+Shift+^ applies scientific notation. 1.23E+07 infers an exponent. A carat(^) is used to enter exponents in Excel.

23. Alt+Enter to Control Word Wrap

To move to a new row in the current cell, press Alt+Enter. Isn't this the same as turning on Word Wrap? Sort of, but Alt+Enter lets you control where the words wrap. Thanks to Olga Kryuchkova.

24. Ctrl+[to Jump to Linked Cell

You are in a cell that points to Sheet99!Z1000. Press Ctrl+[to jump to that cell. This works if you have links between workbooks, even if the other workbook is closed! Thanks to @Heffa100 and Bob Umlas.

25. Ctrl+F1 to hide or show the Ribbon

To toggle the Ribbon between Pinned and Hidden, use Ctrl+F1.

26. Alt+F1 to Chart the Selected Data

Select some data. Press Alt+F1. You get a chart of the data. You might remember F11 doing the same thing. But F11 creates the chart as a chart sheet. Alt+F1 embeds the chart in the current sheet.

27. Shift+F11 to Insert a Worksheet

I never knew this one, but it makes sense as a corollary to F11. If F11 inserts a chart sheet, then Shift+F11 inserts a new worksheet. You can also use Alt+I, W to insert a worksheet, Alt+I, R to insert a row, or Alt+I, C to insert a column. Thanks to Olga Kryuchkova.

28. Alt+E, S, V to Paste Values

I can do Alt+E, S, V, Enter with my eyes closed. Alt+E opened the Excel 2003 Edit menu. S chose Paste Special. V chose Values. Enter selected OK. Thanks to Matthew Bernath and Laura Lewis.

29. Alt+E, S, T to Paste Formats

Alt+E, S, T, Enter pastes formats. Why t instead of f? Because Alt+E, S, F already was in use to paste formulas.

30. Alt+E, S, F to Paste Formulas

Alt+E, S, F, Enter pastes formulas without copying the cell formatting. This is handy to prevent cell borders from copying along with the formula.

31. Alt+E, S, W to Paste Column Widths

Alt+E, S, W pastes column widths. This is great to use with a block of columns. In the following figure. select A1:H1, copy, then select J1 and Alt+E, S, V, Enter to copy all 8 column widths.

	A	B	C	D	E	F	G	H	I	J
1	Jan		Feb		Mar		Q1			Apr
2	Sales	%	Sales	%	Sales	%	Sales	%		Sales
3	7709	20%	5406	12%	9193	15%	22308	15%		8094

32. Alt+E, S, D, V to Paste Special Add

Alt+E, S, D, V does a Paste Special Add, but does not screw up the formatting.

33. Alt+E, S, E to Turn Data Sideways, I

Alt+E, S, E does a Transpose. To see all the possibilities, press Alt+E, S and then look for the underlined letters.

34. Alt+T, M, S to Change Macro Security.

This shortcut is really useful now that the settings are buried deep in Excel options. Thanks to Ron de Bruin.

35. Alt+T, I to Activate Add-ins

Alt+T, I is faster than File, Options, Add-Ins, Manage Excel Add-ins, Go.

36. Ctrl+Shift+L to Enable the Filter Dropdowns

Toggle the filters on or off with Ctrl+Shift+L. In Excel 2013 and earlier, pressing Ctrl+Shift+L would scroll your screen to the end of the data set. Press Ctrl+Backspace to bring the active cell back in to view. Or, press and release Alt, A, T. Thanks to David Hager and Andrew Walker.

37. Hold Down Alt to Snap to Grid

If you are drawing any shape, Alt will cause that shape to exactly line up with the borders of cells. Thanks to Rickard Wärnelid.

38. Ctrl+W to Close a Workbook but Leave Excel Open

If you have one workbook open and you click the "X" in the top-right corner, you close Excel. Ctrl+W closes that workbook but leaves Excel open. Thanks to Dave Marriott.

39. F5 to Sneak into a Hidden Cell

You've hidden column D, but you need to see what is in D2. Press Ctrl+G or F5 to open the Go To dialog. Type D2 and press Enter. The cell pointer moves to the hidden cell D2, and you can see the value in the formula bar. You can now use the Down Arrow key to move within the hidden column D, and you can always see the value in the formula bar.

40. Alt+D, E, F to Convert Numbers Stored as Text to Numbers

Select a whole column and press Alt+D, E, F. The text numbers are converted to numbers. You are actually doing a default Text to Columns with this shortcut.

41. Alt+O, C, A to AutoFit a Column

Select some cells and press Alt+O, C, A to make the column wide enough for the longest value in the selection.

42. Ctrl+' to Copy the Exact Formula Down (aka Ditto)

You have to sum in D10 and average in D11. Create the AutoSum in D10. When you press Enter, you are in D11. Press Ctrl+' to bring the exact formula down without changing the cell reference. If D10 is =SUM(D2:D9), the formula in D11 will also be =SUM(D2:D9).

From there, you can press F2, Home, Right, AVERAGE, Delete, Delete, Delete, Enter. It sounds crazy, but the engineers at General Electric in Cleveland swear by it.

43. Ctrl+Shift+" to Copy the Cell Value from Above

Use Ctrl+Shift+" to bring the value from above into the current cell, eliminating any formula.

44. Hold down Alt while launching Excel to force it into a second instance

You might want each Excel workbook to have separate Undo stacks. This is one way.

45. Press F2 to toggle EDIT or ENTER while editing a formula in any dialog

Say you are typing =VLOCKUP(in the conditional formatting dialog. You press the left arrow key to go back to fix the typo, but Excel inserts a cell reference. Press F2 to change the lower left corner of the status bar from ENTER to EDIT and you can use the arrow keys to move through the formula.

46. Alt+W, F, F to Freeze Panes

There are hundreds more shortcuts like the ones above which you can easily learn. Press and release Alt in Excel to see key tips for each tab in the Ribbon (plus numbered key tips for the Quick Access Toolbar. Press the letter corresponding to a Ribbon tab to see the key tips for all of the commands on that tab. In this particular case, clicking Alt, W, F reveals a third level of key tips, and Alt, W, F, F completes the command. Thanks to Bradford Myers.

47. Ctrl+C to Copy

48. Ctrl+V to Paste

49. Ctrl+X to Cut

50. Ctrl+B for Bold

51. Ctrl+I for Italics

52. Ctrl+U for Underline

53. Ctrl+N for New Workbook

54. Ctrl+P to Print

55. Ctrl+T (or Ctrl+L) to Format as Table

56. Never Forget to Right-click

Many timesavers that are linked to the right mouse button that are often forgotten. Thanks to Colin Foster. Hey! This is not a keyboard shortcut! But wait…it is. You can open that right-click menu by using the Application key on the bottom-right side of your keyboard or Shift+F10. For more on the Application key, see "For Those Who Prefer Using Keyboard Shortcuts" on page 108. Release the Application key and then press any underlined letter to invoke the command.

#94 Ctrl+Click to Unselect Cells

You've always had the ability to select multiple selections in Excel by Ctrl+Dragging to select cells. In the images below, you might click in B2 and drag to C6. Then Ctrl+Click in C8 and drag to C11. Then Ctrl+Click on F2:and drag to B8. Then Ctrl+Click in F11.

	B	C	D	E	F
2	This	This			
3	This	This			No
4	This	This			data
5	This	This			data
6	This	This			data
7					data
8			is some		data
9			is some		
10			is some		
11			is some		No!

You realize that you did not want to include F3 or F11 in the selection. In the past, there was no way to unselect one cell. You had to start all over with selecting B2:C6 and so on.

If you still have a copy of Excel 2013, try unselecting cells by Ctrl+Clicking them. An odd bug causes the cell to become progressively darker with each Ctrl+Click.

	A	B	C
1	One	One	One
2	One	One	One
3	One	One	One
4	One	One	One
5	Two	Three	
6			

However - that bug was erased and new functionality added to Excel once a posting on Excel.UserVoice.com garnered 327 votes on Excel.UserVoice.com. This is a new feature released in 2018 to Office 365 subscribers. You can now Ctrl+Click on a cell that is in the selection and remove the cell from the selection:

	B	C	D	E	F	G
2	This	This				
3	This	This			No	
4	This	This			data	
5	This	This			data	
6	This	This			data	
7			Ctrl+Click		data	
8			is some		data	
9			is some			
10			is some			
11			is some		No!	
12						

#95 More Excel Tips

More than 200 ideas were sent in for this book. While the following ideas did not get much press here, they are self-explanatory in a 140-character tweet.

- To make Excel open full-screen, right-click the Excel icon and change the Run setting to Full Screen. -David Ringstrom, CPA

- Use a thin light border line to create useful scrollbar maximums when your worksheet contains charts that the scroll bars don't recognize. -Chris Mack

- Highlight duplicate records with Conditional Formatting, Highlight Cells, Duplicate Records. -@Leaf_xl

- Color every other row with this conditional formatting formula: =MOD(ROW(),2)=0. -Pedro Millers

- Have a photo appear after a dropdown list in Excel http://t.co/TjbAtSkJ3t -Michael A. Rempel

- Use pictographs for charts (column and pie): Copy picture: select series, paste. -Olga Kryuchkova

- For a pie chart with too many slices: move small slices to second pie using Pie of Pie chart. -Olga Kryuchkova

- Use X/Y charts for drawing artwork. -Joerg Decker

- INDEX can return an entire row/column and return a cell reference. -Sumit Bansal

- Put an apostrophe in front of an Excel formula to stop it from being evaluated. -@DiffEngineX

- DATEDIF(A2,B2,"Y")&" yrs, "&DATEDIF(A2,B2,"YM")&" mos, "&DATEDIF(A2,B2,"MD")&" days." -Paul Wright

- Insert rows without breaking formulas. Cell above is OFFSET(*thisCell*,-1,0) - Jon Wittwer, Vertex42.com

- Subtract 1 from NPV function to get the Net Present Value of the investment. -Olen L. Greer

- Use EDATE to move the date out one month or year. -Justin Fishman

- Find mystery links in the Name Manager. Ta-da! -Lisa Burkett

- Formulas created in Notepad, saved as CSV, & opened in Excel work. Example: mike,=proper(A1) will give Mike. -@mdhExcel

- Double-click a formula. Excel color codes the cells referenced in the formula. -Cat Parkinson

- Turn off Edit Directly in Cell. Then double-click a formula to show cells used in that formula, even if in external workbook. -Sean Blessitt and David Ringstrom

- Go To Special, Constants helps spot constants within a block of formulas where a formula is overwritten with a number. -@HowToExcel

- Select a random 5% of data using =RAND()<.05. -Olga Kryuchkova

- Mark formulas with Conditional Formatting formula =HASFORMULA(A1). -Justin Fishman

- Double-click a number in a pivot to get the detail behind that number. -@Sheet1

- Array formula to count without COUNT: =SUM(IF(ISNUMBER(MyRange),1,0)). -Meni Porat

- In VBA, use Range("A1").CurrentRegion instead of RANGE(). It is like pressing Ctrl+*. -Arnout Brandt

- You can use hyperlinks to launch VBA macros. Smaller than buttons. -Cecelia Rieb

- Use a macro to color the heading cells that have filters applied. -Peter Edwards

- Use Environ("UserName") in VBA code for restricting workbook access. -Angelina Teneva

- Use a UDF in a hyperlink to change cells mrx.cl/udfhyperlink -Jordan Goldmeier

- There are a variety of games written in Excel (2048, MissileCommand, pleuroku, TowerDefense, Pac-Man, Rubic's Cube, Yahtzee, Tetris). -Olga Kryuchkova

- POINT mode in Excel lets you build a formula using arrow keys to point to cells or ranges. If this stops working, see if you inadvertently pressed ScrLk key. You will see SCROLL LOCK near left side of Status Bar. (ScrLk is near PrtScrn and Break keys). -Vijay Krishnan

#96 Excel Stories

Live – On Stage – In Person: The Power Excel Seminars

That poster from Hatch Show Print on my website sort of started out as a joke. I was flying through

Nashville and saw a display of old country music letterpress posters on the wall. The little sign by the posters said they were produced on a 100-year-old hand-cranked press and that the company was still operating in Nashville. I called them and hired them to produce a "concert" poster for my live Excel seminars. They had to think I was a little nuts. The print shop manager, Jim Sherraden, often did an informative presentation about the history of Hatch, and he cited my poster as the first to list a website URL.

I do my half-day or 1-day seminar for accounting groups across the country. Every large city has a local chapter of the Institute of Managerial Accountants or the Institute of Internal Auditors. The people who belong to these groups usually need 20-30 hours of continuing education (CPE) each year. If you join the organization and go to 12 lunch meetings, half of your CPE is done. The organizations will often sponsor a 1- or 2-day event with speakers so their members can earn the remaining CPE at one time. I often am invited to speak at these events. The poster on the door lets people know that they are not in for the usual tax update. (I don't mean to offend the wonderful people going through the new tax laws…someone's got to do that.)

Excel is used on 750 million devices. I've met a lady in Appalachia who used Excel to design original quilt patterns. I've met people who have designed workbooks in Excel that train people how to fly 737 jets. From quilts to jets, Excel is used everywhere.

When you hand the world's most flexible software to 750 million people, everyone finds interesting things to do or interesting ways to use Excel. I love traveling to do the in-person Excel seminars because I get to meet these people. At every seminar, someone has an interesting story of how they are using Excel. At every seminar, I always learn a few new Excel tricks from the people in the seminar. I joke that my job is collecting the cool and obscure tricks in Excel from people along the road and passing them on to people further on up the road. Many of the amazing tricks in this book came from people in my live Excel seminars.

This is truly a win-win. I have fun doing the seminars. The audience get to take home a cool Excel book. Among the 75 tricks that I show in a day, hopefully everyone will find a few that they can take back to work to start becoming more efficient the next day. Plus, people earn the CPE hours without hearing about any tax updates. Even at the Association for Computers and Taxation, where their annual meeting is all about tax updates, they bring me in to do a 2-hour session to offer a little levity between the tax updates!

The Excel Guru Mission Patch

Do you own a the highly-coveted Excel Guru mission patch?

When I do my live Power Excel seminars, I always encourage the audience to "show me up." Someone in that room is going to have a better way to do something in Excel. I used to offer a small prize to the first person to teach me something during the seminar. I would also predict that the first person to show me up that day walked into the room and sat in row 2.

I have no idea why they often sit in row 2. But I noticed early on that the best Exceller often chooses a seat in row 2. They want to be close. But not front-row close. Almost every time, the first cool idea from the audience comes to row 2. (On the times when the first tip comes from another row, I quip, "Did you arrive late, and row 2 was already full?")

Over the years, the prize varied from a laminated tip card to an Excel Master enamel pin. The current prize is an embroidered Excel Guru patch designed by the same guy who designs mission patches for Cape Canaveral rocket launches.

As Seen in the Wall Street Journal: the Excel Function Clock

It was a Friday afternoon at work and time was dragging. I would look at the clock, do some VLOOKUPs, then look back at the clock and barely a minute had passed.

it struck me that it would be funny if someone made a clock where the 3 was replaced with the Excel function =PI(). This simple function with no arguments returns 3.14. So, =PI() wouldn't be exactly at 3. It would have to be just a bit beyond the 3. The solution would be to use the INT function to return just the integer portion of PI(). =INT(PI()) returns just 3. Perfect! I am sure I pitched both of these ideas to Kevin Adkins, who probably didn't think it was a funny as I did. That never deters me, though.

After writing all 12 functions, I actually found the graphic designer who designed the clocks for the old Signals mail order catalog. The Excel function clock was on Call For Help a few times. Once, Leo Laporte attached it to a lanyard and wore the clock as if he were rapper Flavor Flav. It was funny stuff.

The clock became famous, though, in 2017 when it was featured in a Wall Street Journal article about the CFO of PF Changs saying he was going to dump Excel. People were furious and the WSJ ran a follow-up article with a quote by me and also a picture of my clock. I sold a lot of clocks that week!

Here are the 12 formulas:

1. =MIN(1,10). Min returns the minimum number. Since 1<10, the function returns 1.

2. =MONTH(23790). That is the serial number for my birthday, February 17, 1965. That is month number 2.

3. =INT(PI()). =PI() would've been 1/7 of the way past 3, so =INT returns the integer 3.

4. =LEN("FOUR"). I used LEN daily. =MID(A2,LEN(A2)-7,2) gets the last 2 characters. How long is FOUR? 4.

5. =SQRT(25). The square root of 25 is 5.

6. =FACT(3). Factorials are used to calculate lottery probability. The Factorial of 3 is 3x2x1 or 6.

7. =GCD(77,49). Middle school match is simpler with Excel. The greatest common divisor of 77 and 49 is 7

8. =2^3. The ^ raises 2 to the 3 power. =2*2*2 is 8.

9. =PMT(9%,9,-53.96). If you borrowed $53.96 from the bank to buy some MrExcel books and had to pay it back over 9 years with a 9% interest rate, each yearly payment would be $9.

10. =LCM(2,5). Another one for the 7th graders. The Lowest Common Multiple of 2 and 5 is 10.

11. =ROMAN(2). Hmm. My fascination with =ROMAN() began before my 40th book. The =ROMAN(2) is II, which looks sort of like 11. Just like XL sounds sort of like Excel.

12. =COLUMN(L1). tells you the column number of a cell. L is column number 12.

If you are thinking you need to get one of these for yourself, head over to mrx.cl/excelclock.

The MrExcel Message Board Community Answered 1 Million Excel Questions

When I launched MrExcel.com in November 1998, I would get up every morning and answers yesterday's e-mailed questions before heading in to work. Initially, it was a question or two each weekday. But, by May 1999, I was getting more questions than I could answer in an hour. I was answering questions from 5 AM to 6 AM and then heading in to work. I either had to start getting up at 4 AM or find another way.

I downloaded WWWBoard from Matt's Script Archive. I asked people to post their question at the message board. And I asked that, after posting, they look at the last few questions to see if they could help someone else out. It was like the take-a-penny, leave-a-penny tray at a cash register. If you need help, post a question. If you can help someone else out, help them out. It worked. People started posting and answering questions.

In the early days, I noticed a few people would stop by almost every day and answer a question or two. Ivan F. Moala. Cecilia. The late Dave Hawley.

One day, at work. I was stumped. I went out to my own message board, and described my problem. An hour later, Ivan F. Moala from New Zealand had posted an amazing answer. I knew I had something.

The board transformed over the years, morphing into bigger platforms. I was on a $10-a-month hosting plan at Pair Networks in Pittsburgh. One day, I get a call from them wondering what I was doing. "You are on a $10-a-month plan, but you are using as much traffic as our $1,000-a-month plan!" Apparently, the MrExcel Message Board had taken on a life of its own.

Today, the amazing people at the MrExcel Message Board have answered 900,000 questions about Excel. We've attempted to keep every question live on the site. There are some massive competitors (I won't name them, but their anagram is "is Comfort" or "of Mr Stoic") who have competing forums, but they have no problem wiping out their history. I run into people all the time who say they use my forum. I ask what their UserID is. "Oh – I've never had to post – I just search. Every answer is already there."

The MrExcel community is staffed by volunteers. Over the years, various experts have worked tirelessly as moderators and administrators. My sincere thanks to Andrew Poulsom, barry houdini, Colo, fairwinds, Ivan F Moala, Joe4, Jon von der Heyden, Juan Pablo Gonzalez, NateO, PaddyD, Peter_SSs, Richard Schollar, RoryA, Scott Huish, Smitty, Starl, SydneyGeek, VoG, Von Pookie, zenou, and Zack Barresse. Suat Ozgur and Scott Pierson handled the tech issues with the board.

As far as the people answering questions, 45 people have answered more than 10,000 questions at the board. This is a staggering contribution to the Excel community. Thanks to Aladin Akyurek with 84,000 posts. Andrew Poulsom and Norie have over 70,000 posts each. VoG has over 60,000 posts. Others with over 10K posts: Joe4, Jonmo1, Peter SSs, Rick Rothstein, RoryA, Smitty, Richard Schollar, mikerickson, shg, barry houdini, Scott Huish, pgc01, Domenic, erik.van.geit, hiker95, Fluff, jindon, T. Valko, Michael M, xenou, AlphaFrog, JoeMo, Marcelo Branco, My Aswer Is This, MickG, PaddyD, lenze, Von Pookie, SydneyGeek, Juan Pablo Gonzalez, Mark W., Yogi Anand, Tom Urtis, GlennUK, tusharm, oldbrewer, Zack Barresse, Jon von der Heyden, just jon, JLGWhiz, MARK858, and Greg Truby.Many of the experts at MrExcel.com are awarded the MVP Award in Excel from Microsoft.

If you ask Google any Excel question, the odds are pretty good that one of the top answers will be from MrExcel. If you can't find your answer on Google, it is free to post a new question. Make sure to give the post a title that describes what you are trying to do. Even in the middle of the night, someone will likely have an answer.

#97 Index

EXCEL
DYNAMIC
ARRAYS

RANDARRAY FILTER SORTBY DynamicArrays SORT SEQUENCE UNIQUE

STRAIGHT TO THE
point

BILL JELEN

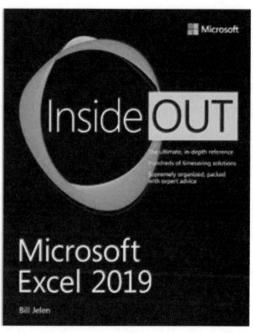

Microsoft

Inside OUT

The ultimate, in-depth reference
Hundreds of timesaving solutions
Supremely organized, packed
with expert advice

Microsoft
Excel 2019

Bill Jelen

EXCEL
JAVASCRIPT
UDFs

STRAIGHT TO THE
point

SUAT M. OZGUR

Connect with Bill Jelen on Twitter, LinkedIn and YouTube

Follow @MrExcel on Twitter for Excel Tips in 280 characters plus retweets of cool Excel tips from my friends.

Search for Bill Jelen on LinkedIn and click Connect. Optionally, mention "I was in your seminar" or "I read your book". However - I accept all connection requests on LinkedIn.

Search for MrExcel.com on YouTube for a collection of 2200 Excel videos. Click Subscribe to help me get to the magic 100K subscribers and the coveted YouTube 100K award.